# INDUSTRIAL GERMANY

# INDUSTRIAL GERMANY

## A STUDY OF
## ITS MONOPOLY ORGANISATIONS AND
## THEIR CONTROL BY THE STATE

by

## HERMANN LEVY

CAMBRIDGE
AT THE UNIVERSITY PRESS
1935

CAMBRIDGE UNIVERSITY PRESS
Cambridge, New York, Melbourne, Madrid, Cape Town,
Singapore, São Paulo, Delhi, Mexico City

Cambridge University Press
The Edinburgh Building, Cambridge CB2 8RU, UK

Published in the United States of America by Cambridge University Press, New York

www.cambridge.org
Information on this title: www.cambridge.org/9781107623321

First published 1935
First paperback edition 2013

A catalogue record for this publication is available from the British Library

ISBN 978-1-107-62323-1 Paperback

TO

J. H. CLAPHAM

# CONTENTS

## PART III

# THE ORGANISATION OF INDUSTRIAL COMBINATION

## PART IV

# EFFECTS OF INDUSTRIAL COMBINATION

# PREFACE

When in January and February 1934 I was lecturing in the University of Cambridge about industrial combination in Germany I became impressed with the idea of dealing more fully with what is at present one of the foremost English industrial problems. As I was one of the first to write on English monopoly organisations and have some knowledge of the special features of the problem in England I felt myself qualified to write a book with the express purpose of comparing the German and English conditions of quasi-monopoly. Whether I have succeeded in doing this the reader must decide. It may seem audacious to choose so comprehensive a title as Industrial Germany for a book which mainly describes and analyses certain aspects of industrial organisation. But in fact the problem of industrial combination is so intimately connected with the most prominent economic, organisational, administrative, legal, technical, financial and even sociological conditions of German industry that I am anxious to show by the title that the aim of the book is to draw a picture of cartels, concerns and trusts against a background of the general structural development of German industry.

HERMANN LEVY

# PART I

# VIEWS AND FIGURES

### CHAPTER I

## A COMPARISON OF THE GERMAN AND ENGLISH ATTITUDE TOWARDS INDUSTRIAL COMBINATION

THE problems of industrial monopoly, if not studied from a merely theoretical and abstract viewpoint, may afford a welcome opportunity of improving our insight into the differences in the economic structure and organisation of the nations. In fact the development of "Kartells" and trusts or monopolist associations of any kind or type has been in every country influenced by the specific attitude of its producers, by the structure of law and legal principles, by a different attitude of the State towards monopoly, not to mention the different material conditions favouring or checking the growth of combines. A theory of monopolies based upon marginal utility reflections and mathematical formulas will never lead to the necessary understanding of their actual conditions, effects and deficiencies, however interesting such deductions may be from the point of view of the theorist, while on the other hand a theory of modern industrial combination based exclusively upon the experiences of a single country would be of little general value, unless the specific structure and organisation of that country's industry was taken into account. The study of industrial combination must necessarily be "comparative" and the truth evolved out of the study of the conditions of a single country may have to be regarded as essentially "relative". In failing to apply this presumption to its investigations of cartels and trusts economic science has frequently been led into generalisations and conclusions which are not borne out by the international aspect of the problem.

In the United States as well as in Germany the organisation of industrial monopoly has developed along pretty clear lines. One may say that the structure of the American "trust" seems less complicated than the far more differentiated monopoly form of German cartelisation. In England the evolution from free competition to associative organisation has been obscured in many respects. Although at an early date books like that of Mr Macrosty or myself had called the attention of the public to the monopolist development in British industry, the Report on Trusts of 1919 (and 1924) with its statement that there were ninety-three quasi-monopolist associations in England, regulating prices and production, came as a surprise to the general public. Yet it was expressly stated by Mr Percy Ashley in that Report that by far the greater part of these trade associations and combinations restricting competition and controlling prices "had come into existence since the end of the century".

The belief that British industry would ever be characterised by a system of monopolist organisation such as was known to exist and to be on the increase in the rival German industry was shaken by many circumstances and considerations. In the first place, the development of industrial monopoly organisation in England came certainly much later than in Germany. Here as early as in 1883 the first cartels were "discovered" and described by Prof. Kleinwächter. The first official investigation into the cartel problem in 1905 revealed the fact that there were no less than 353 associations of that kind. In the chemical industries alone forty-six associations were reported, while a good many more were said to be in existence. In England, on the other hand, there was very much less publicity given to industrial combination. Associations and even amalgamated companies were led to hide anything in their business management which could be interpreted as a monopolistic control of prices or output, for fear of being prosecuted as infringing the law against restraint of trade. Certainly German industrial monopolists had to be careful not to arouse political anger with regard to their price

policy. But there was no law penalising or forbidding monopolies as such. On the contrary in many cases the formation of
cartels seems to have had official support from an early date; the
State, as in the case of coal and potash, becoming a partner in
private syndicates. Since, by the end of the 'nineties, the
wave of German economic liberalism, never a very strong factor
in political life, had almost spent itself, there was never a real
popular opposition to cartels from any individualistic or liberal
standpoint. If there had been any strong antipathy to the
growing power of combines it would have been dictated by
anti-capitalistic feeling rather than by the desire to uphold the
principles of free competition. In view of the very weak position of the German Liberals of that time, any powerful opposition
in parliament to industrial monopolies had to come from the
social-democratic benches, which alone were free from the influence of industrial capitalists. Socialists, however, were not
likely to oppose too strongly these forms of organisation, which
in their eyes did not differ in principle from any other giant form
of capitalist organisation, such as big banks or department stores,
but which could be regarded as the forerunners of a future state
socialism.

A third reason why cartelisation in England was much less
conspicuous than in Germany was the fact that English monopoly associations were not to be found in those industries which
are most likely to attract general interest. In Germany the playground of cartels and amalgamations was from the beginning of
the movement to be found in the great extractive and heavy
industries, such as coal, potash, iron ore, iron and steel, and the
heavy chemical productions. These industries enjoy a sort of
general popularity. Important events happening or developing
in such industries can hardly be silenced by the press or hidden
from public knowledge. They will be a topic of general economic
discussion. The price of coal or iron to-day is almost as important
as that of bread or butter. In England amalgamations and
associations were at first mainly formed in industries, which were
of a special type or character, as for instance in textile specialities
or in certain finished goods (Coats, Fine Cotton Spinners and
doublers, calico printing, wallpaper, rails as contrasted with pig

iron or raw steel, etc.). A coal trust or a steel combine would probably have aroused public interest and political discussion in England as much as in other countries and the "cartel" problem would have swiftly become a topic of general public importance. It was, however, the most important English industries such as coal, iron, steel, shipbuilding, cotton spinning and weaving which, generally speaking, all seemed to be left outside that sphere in which English amalgamations developed. It was only with the foundation of the Chemical Trust that the existence of a really powerful and dominant monopolistic organisation was brought to the knowledge of the English public. All these circumstances may explain the fact that up to the present the trust and cartel movement in British industry has been far less conspicuous than in Germany. This being the case it is only natural that a specific explanation had to be found for the supposed absence of monopolies. It was pretended over and over again that the English producer by his individualistic attitude towards business management was unwilling to form or join combinations. In popular language this meant that English entrepreneurs did not like to have other people poking their noses into their affairs; while expressed in terms of traditional economic theory it was the belief in free competition, in the survival of the fittest and the greatest possible efficiency of the individual subject which effectively checked the movement towards cartelisation. It may be conceded that English psychology was not very favourable to the formation of industrial monopolies. The German producer was certainly not hampered in his decisions by any doctrine of *laisser-faire* or economic liberalism. Very early on a writer like Prof. Lujo Brentano—one of the foremost pioneers of German liberalism—pointed out that the principle of coalition might just as well suit the egoistic instincts of capitalist producers as that of individual competition, if in the long run the competitive system proved harmful to each individual manufacturer. There was certainly very little resistance to combination from that point of view among German producers. But has this individualistic attitude in England *de facto* prevented the formation of combination where it was possible and profitable? We do not believe it. It is well known that, between the end of the eighteenth and the middle of the nineteenth century, there existed a most powerful combination among northern coal owners—the Newcastle Vend—a cartel which was the first of its kind. This combination should not be confounded with many of the loose or unconventional associations frequently styled as "cartels". We possess an agreement dated 1835 which with its thirty-three paragraphs differs in no way from the much later statutes of the Rhenish-Westphalian Coal Syndicate. In fact the first genuine cartel in the coal industry is to be found not in German, but in English economic history. Moreover, this combination seems to have been just as complex in its regulations as many of the most modern German "cartels", combining with the regulation of prices and output at the collieries regulations regarding the shipping of coal and common agreements with the London coal trade and its distributive organisation. The cause of the collapse, in the 'forties, of this powerful combine was not the awakening of individualistic feeling among colliery owners, but merely the rapid progress of railway communication throughout England, as a result of which the London market became open to competition from almost every English mining area, thereby freeing itself from the monopoly of sea-borne coal. Thus the theory of the individualistic attitude preventing effective combination has always been refuted by events, wherever material conditions were genuinely in favour of combined action on the part of the producers.

On the other hand it cannot be denied that German manufacturers, with their complete freedom from any prejudice against concerted action, may have found it much easier than their English colleagues to form monopolist organisations wherever the opportunity arose. While in England the fierce battle against monopolies during the reign of Charles I had left an almost inextinguishable mark on English economic sentiment, the freeing of German industries from the rules of crafts and guilds and from the domination of privileged companies (corresponding to the English "patents of monopoly" in the seventeenth century) was effected in 1810 and 1811 (Gewerbefreiheit) as a timely concession to the rise of modern methods in industry and as a result of the development of the factory system.[1] The organisation of early industrial monopoly in Germany had never been exploited by German petty princes in their own interest, at any rate not to the extent that it was done by the Tudors and Stuarts who recklessly bestowed their economic privileges upon capitalist entrepreneurs, patentees and projectors in order to diminish the financial straits of the Crown. Monopoly organisation in eighteenth-century Germany was far more guided by the aims of paternal government. The abolition of monopolist organisation came much more as a bureaucratic reform, necessitated by new economic and technical developments, than as a measure of revolution following a popular outburst against monopolist exploitation. This difference explains why it is that the word "monopoly" has never acquired any popular meaning in German economic terminology, that no "anti-monopolistic" spirit or reasoning can be found among the German masses and that it would have been quite incomprehensible to the German mind, if for instance protective tariffs had been attacked along the lines of the popular English argument that protection was in itself a kind of monopolising of the home market. All such considerations are quite unfamiliar to the German economic mind. In Germany there was no definite outcry against monopolies

---

[1] In a book published in 1933 by Allen and Unwin Dr Piotrowsky tries to refute my views regarding the period of English and German early monopolist organisation, cp. my book on *Monopolies, Cartels and Trusts in British Industry*, 2nd ed., pp. 90 ff. While in my opinion the formation of early industrial monopolies in Germany came much later than in England and developed under rather different, i.e. less damaging, conditions than under James I and Charles I, the author, following the research work of Strieder, is concerned to point out that German monopolies existed about 100 years before the English development of monopolies. The facts to which Dr Piotrowsky alludes are certainly correct, but they are not to the point. Owing to the nature and object of my studies, I purposely dwelt on industries which belong to the early period of modern "industrial" capitalism. A monopolist organisation of such groups of industry must be carefully distinguished from monopolies of a commercial character, which existed at any time in mediaeval history, as also from certain mining organisations and from the monopolist domination of handicrafts by capitalist or commercial entrepreneurs. There can be no doubt that the manufactures which were most prominent in the monopoly organisation in England and Germany during the seventeenth and eighteenth centuries, and which represent the first stages of modern industrial capitalism and mark the beginning of the factory system, had never developed or at any rate not developed on the lines of modern "industrial" capitalism in the days to which Dr Piotrowsky alludes.

intimately connected with the most important political and democratic reforms, and as a result the word "monopoly" never had that importance in economic terminology that it attained in England where it passed from the mouths of the excited people into the classic writings of men like Adam Smith and David Ricardo. One may say that in Germany there has never existed what might be called the "sociological" aspect of monopoly, that is a deep and almost immovable psychological distrust of everything which might lead to the restriction of unlimited competition. Mr Patrick Fitzgerald could argue rightly in his book on industrial combination in England in 1927, that "not many years ago" it was the custom in England to regard the trust movement as "purely alien". We have been trying to explain the manifold reasons for that attitude, which were to be found in the relatively late development of industrial associations and amalgamations in England, in their lack of publicity, in the existence of an anti-monopolist spirit leading to a fanatical belief not only in the benefits of free competition but also in its un-impaired position in English economic development.

In Germany—in sharp contrast to the English attitude to-wards combination—economic science tried at an early date to reconcile the new monopolist movement with the still existing academic "respect" for a system of individualism and free competition. Economic historians, like Gustav v. Schmoller, whose followers had for a long time the first claim to chairs of political economy all over Germany, did not dislike the revival of a system of organisation which certainly bore more resemblance to their own favourite field of study, i.e. paternal and govern-mental industrial organisation in the time of mercantilism, than that of the "Manchestertum" and *laisser-faire* of the nineteenth century. He expressed the view (in 1905) that cartels meant the beginning "of quite a new order of public life", with more resemblance to mediaeval ideals than to the nineteenth-century worship of freedom of trade, and Arnold Wolfers quite properly remarks that this attitude was characteristic of the whole German theory of industrial combination of that period.

From the beginning, the development of industrial combina-tion was regarded in Germany as a change in organisation rather than as monopolistic profiteering. Economists like Kleinwächter, Schaeffle and others had for some time been arguing that the much admired system of free competition was most likely to end in "anarchy". The development of producers' associations to control output and price came to them as a verification of their views. "The cartels have suddenly struck down like a flash of lightning from the unclouded sky of faith into the free play of forces and the harmony of competition", wrote Schaeffle in 1898. To economic writers of the socialist type or those with an inclination to socialist ideas cartelisation was from the very beginning a most welcome proof that even private enterprise was trying to get away from uncontrolled competition and favouring some sort of planned organisation. While radical-socialists adhered to the thesis that the movement towards combination was merely a preliminary to general socialisation—the first of these was Schönlank, who called the cartels a "Durchgangsstufe zum Sozialismus"—the later school of reform or moderate social-democrats (revisionists) like Calver or Hilferding were eager to point out that industrial combination might have a stabilising and harmonising effect within the framework of capitalism. Sombart regarded the "replacement of free competition by a principle of mutual agreement" as one of the facts which signalised the beginning of the decay of the epoch of "Hochkapitalismus" system, which in his opinion had reached its climax and was gradually showing symptoms of senility.

It seems rather strange that support of cartelisation and even trustification should have arisen from the ranks of the very hottest opponents of the capitalist system, while in fact private industrial monopolies had to be regarded as the most powerful exponents of the capitalist order. The reason is that socialism has been for a long time the expression of the German liking for organised control. We may again quote Wolfers, who, writing of the most recent attitude of German socialism to industrial combination, says that the latter was regarded as "eine höhere Wirtschaftsstufe", a higher stage of economic evolution. This stage, if once reached, is formulated as "organised capitalism". Economic policy must take it into account. Cartelised capitalism is welcomed, because it is preparing the way for state-controlled economic organisation. It is not so much the cartels themselves which are considered to be the pioneers of socialism as the newly created power of the State to control and even to exercise an influence upon these associations. The private monopoly, controlled by the State, is regarded as the last step towards that condition of economic organisation, in which the State incorporates industrial combinations as self-governing administrative bodies in its scheme for the socialisation of certain groups of industry.

This being the socialist attitude, any serious attack on industrial combination from that quarter would be based only on the actual price policy, which might in some cases appear hurtful to the public, and not on general economic principles. The bureaucratic tendencies inherent in socialism found their counterpart in the "organic" administration promised by cartels and trusts, reconciling, at least in this sphere, the bitter antagonism between the leaders of industry and the representatives of the working classes, so conspicuous in other fields of political life. The "monopoly" argument against industrial combination was of no value to socialist thought. The only political party which was by its principles prepared to fight monopoly organisations as destroying the order of free competition and individual efficiency, the liberal party, was on the down grade at the moment when cartelisation became a much discussed topic. Its voice was practically unheard and frequently enough ridiculed as being in conflict with the present trend of events, which in many fields of German economic and administrative life—for instance in the growing number of state and communal enterprises—showed a much greater tendency towards collective and corporate organisation than ever before.

What may be called the "organic" or organisational significance of industrial combination seemed to gain a new justification, when after 1924 the movement towards rationalisation set in. It seemed evident that the tremendous financial and technical task involved in the programmes of rationalisation could be solved on much safer and more efficient lines by a concerted action of producers or by the big amalgamated firms than by smaller manufacturers acting on their own individual lines and having in most cases insufficient capital. In fact industrial combination seemed at one time the very condition necessary for the effective execution of the programmes of rationalisation. When, after 1929, the rationalisation fever was slackening and the high hopes of social benefits from the rationalisation movement had ended in disappointment, the big firms were frequently criticised for not having had due regard for the practical limits of technical expansion. The argument was developed that the big concerns had done much too much in the way of technical "improvements" which may have appeared very tempting to a body of zealous directors, but proved in fact to be quite out of proportion to the real demand of the markets for increased production. The enthusiasm for rationalisation was followed by sharp criticism of what was now called "over-rationalisation". Now again, after a long interval, certain doubts were voiced as to the organising ability of cartel and trust directorates, and some writers at least were found to praise individual efficiency and to point out the dangers of over-organised bodies of directors not always in touch with the actual life of the industries in question. These criticisms came mainly from representatives of commercial science (Betriebswirtschaftslehre). Thus Prof. W. Hasenack, of the Technische Hochschule, Berlin, declared in a very able study published in 1933 that the organisation of cartels had always been in his opinion the most dangerous "bazillus" threatening commercial versatility in the management of industrial units. He sharply criticised those results of industrial combination which were leading to a rigidity excluding free mobility in the exchange of goods and thereby preventing in many cases a possible short-term compensation of supply and demand on the one side, while planning on the other hand was decided in many cases on a long-term basis not perhaps in accordance with the genuine demand of the future. This was indeed the first time that objections were raised which could have come from the ranks of the old liberal school of economic thought.

A review of the psychological attitude to the problem of industrial combination in Germany and England, as it has here been attempted, shows a very remarkable contrast between two countries which are industrially not so very different. While in

England a number of circumstances has certainly caused the importance of associations and amalgamations in the organisation of modern large scale industry to be underrated, in Germany the forces of economic and political thought were actively supporting this "new form of organisation" or at any rate not obstructing its progress. It is interesting to note, with this contrast in mind, that of late a decisive change has taken place in England. From being an organisation at first regarded with the gravest suspicion and later on as a sort of "alien" import, un-English in itself, and hardly defensible on the lines of traditional English economics, the movement towards industrial combination has in recent years become a much discussed topic in English public life. Things have changed so drastically that the lack of industrial combination and co-operation among producers suddenly came to be considered as a defect in English industrial organisation; the coal mining industry and the iron and steel industry were sharply criticised for not entering into an effective agreement to regulate output and control prices, shutting down inefficient works and setting up common rules for the working of the most efficient plant. How much opinion as regards "monopolistic" organisations had changed was to be gathered from the fact that the maintenance of protection to the steel industry was made dependent on the inauguration of some sort of combined action, i.e. the formation of a national cartel, by the iron and steel manufacturers.

As an instance of this change of attitude one may take the speech delivered by Sir Ernest Gowers, Chairman of the Coal Mines Organisation Commission, to the Cardiff Business Club on 24 February 1933. Discussing the question of amalgamations Sir Ernest said: "I believe amalgamations to be vitally necessary to the industry, but that is because I do not see how it can be set right without them...they are not the final goal, but they are a means to an end". The scheme drafted and approved by the National Committee to consider plans of reorganisation of the steel trade followed the same line of thought. The incorporation of the Iron and Steel Corporation of Great Britain was proposed, a body intended to supervise approved associations in the iron and steel industry in all matters of general policy in order to secure the orderly progress of the industry, to promote desirable amalgamations, etc. "Compulsory amalgamation" has for some time now been a favourite term in many official circles, the State instead of being called upon to act against monopolist associations being rather invited to bring them into existence. A good number of new expressions has been invented to make the monopolistic structure, which is necessarily inherent in any kind of effective association to regulate output and prices, more palatable to the public mind, such as "reorganisation", "orderly production", "reconstruction", "planning", but all of them lead to the same end. As Sir Ernest Gowers put it in the speech already referred to:

I believe myself that what we really want ultimately is not only amalgamations but also a looser form of cooperation over an area wider than the industry is willing to take as its unit of production. I do not think this can be done except by building a ground floor of amalgamations first and adding this looser form of wider cooperation as an upper storey. In other words, it would mean grouping the units of production into much bigger associations—call them cartels or what you will—with two main purposes. One purpose would be to cooperate in selling and distribution. The other would be to exercise a general control over the development of the area and share the expense of buying and closing mines which no single unit might think it worth while to acquire because it could not be sure enough of getting their trade.

One recognises in these utterances that the question of combination in England had indeed undergone a remarkable change, since any hint as to the possibly monopolistic effects was deliberately avoided. One may confront this argument with the drastic refusal only a few years ago of any sort of industrial combination by high authorities on English economics. Thus Prof. Gregory in 1926 declared emphatically: "All industrial combinations begin with a heavy financial charge which they get back from the community in the form of higher prices or from shareholders in the form of watered capital. The trust movement hinders the development of industry". Seven years later, in 1933, Mr Harold Macmillan, M.P., in his study on "Reconstruction"—a plea for "national policy"—was certainly in agreement with the majority of his readers and with a good many English politicians and economists, when he wrote: "We are faced then with this choice: either to allow haphazard and unco-ordinated competition to go on producing its wild lurches from normality to depression, or to face the problem of finding a method by which the interest of monopoly-producing organisations can be brought into harmony with the interest of the nation as a whole".

From being considered an instrument unsuited, on the whole, to English conditions and needs, monopolist organisation, if properly and harmoniously managed, came suddenly to be regarded as a "device" to save a critical economic situation. In recommending the formation of industrial combinations as one of the few means of escaping the continuance of severe economic depression in the big industries, the point was hardly considered that organisations of that kind are not merely dependent on the determination of manufacturers to abandon free competition for a sort of combined action. Though much may depend on the willingness of manufacturers or traders to enter into agreements, if conditions are favourable to combination, little can be effected by this willingness alone, if material conditions making for successful monopolist organisation are wanting. Those who to-day support the formation of industrial combination in England have hardly grasped that there is a very decided difference between forming, say a co-operative society among farmers, which can be done by persuasion and propaganda, and forming an efficient amalgamation or cartel. In the latter case the mere belief in concerted action, the theoretical knowledge of the advantages to be gained by a policy of associated planning, are of very little practical use, if the material conditions are unfavourable to the final realisation of possibly very attractive proposals. The history of the English coal trade in the last forty years is full of examples of well-defined plans to form national or local associations of collieries, but the far too great number of units in the local as well as the national area of English coal mining has been over and over again the primary obstacle to all these schemes. We certainly do not underrate the influence of psychological and even sociological factors on the development of industrial associations, factors which we have been trying to reveal in comparing the history of the German and English attitude to monopoly. But it would be most erroneous to overestimate the influence of that attitude, either by pretending that individualistic feelings were in the long run capable of checking the movement towards combination, or on the contrary by arguing that it merely needed economic insight or associative education and persuasion to induce manufacturers to modernise the organisation of industrial economy.

The history and the latest developments of monopoly organisation in Germany can show better than any other evidence that the road to industrial combination is a very steep one, cumbered with difficulties and complications of many kinds. The formation of large amalgamations has seldom been the outcome of a scheme invented by some public-spirited leaders or of advice by well-meaning Government representatives: it has generally been the outcome of bitter fighting between industrial units of different size and structure, and the result of revolutionising company organisation by forms, whose success at first seemed doubtful, and which do not even to-day seem to be the final stage of the movement. The trust movement in the United States, owing to the entirely different nature of American industrial conditions, resembles European forms of industrial organisation only in its broadest aspects; but industrial combination in Germany may be considered as in many ways typical of European development. A study of its characteristics and peculiarities may prove not only useful in itself, but also of comparative value with regard to developments outside Germany.

### CHAPTER II

# A STATISTICAL REVIEW OF CARTELISATION

THE industrial organisation represented by cartels and trusts can hardly be elucidated by statistics. On the contrary, one may say that there is no field of economic organisation in which figures prove or even explain so little.

Amalgamations and fusions, resulting in the formation of dominant combines or trusts, have never been statistically enumerated. If it were done, they would have to be separated from cartels, as being associations of producers, while from the point of view of monopoly organisation they ought to be grouped together. Thus a general and comprehensive survey of all genuine monopoly organisation seems a statistical impossibility. Moreover, efficient statistical review of industrial monopoly or quasi-monopoly organisation ought to lay stress on the fact of dominant control, either by associations or trusts or even by big concerns, while the form of such monopolies would be a matter of secondary consideration. The figures showing what percentage of production is actually controlled by trusts and associations or both, should be the essential and primary object of a statistical survey of modern monopoly organisation. In the U.S.A. the predominance of the trust type of monopoly facilitates such a task. In Germany, where the monopolist organisation of industry is partly represented by cartels, partly by trusts, and partly by a combination of both forms, this method of surveying the total field of action of the monopolies in contrast to the remaining sphere of free competition has never been attempted.

The number of cartels, which as already mentioned was stated as being 353 by the Kartell-Commission of 1905, had enormously increased when, about twenty years later, the Reichsverband der Deutschen Industrie (Federation of Industries) gave a survey of industrial combination. They were then estimated to be 1500. The German Government stated in 1925 that the whole number of German cartels amounted to 3000, of which 2500 belonged to the sphere of industry, while the rest was distributed among wholesale and retail trade.

It is, however, important to note that such enumerations do not give anything like a true picture of German cartelisation. Liefmann declares quite rightly that they probably comprise such organisations as "Konditionen-Kartelle", which in fact are merely agreements concerning certain trade usages which do not regulate output or fix prices, and thus correspond to "trade associations" in the U.S.A. One may be entitled to range an agreement between a number of hotels in the Black Forest, fixing the prices of their rooms and certain general conditions of catering, as a "cartel", but with regard to the general and important problems of industrial combination such agreements bear an entirely different character. On the other hand Liefmann quite rightly explains that the goods which are affected by combination in Germany show a very great diversity, ranging from the economically most important goods to those of a rather specialised or secondary importance. For more than 1000 different kinds of goods there have been cartels in existence. Again in the different groups of industry there is a great multiplicity of cartels to be found. We may quote the most important of these groups and the number of cartels which were in existence in each group when the Reichsverband der Deutschen Industrie made its enquiry in 1923. The iron- and steel-finishing industry together with the iron-producing industry (blast furnaces) took the lead with 307 cartels; then followed the textile and clothing industries with 201 and 71, engineering with 147, the paper industry with 107, brewing, milling and malt industries with 97, the chemical trades with 91, the metal industry with 78, mining with 51, boiler-making and engineering (not enumerated in the foregoing group) with 48, food industries with 49, and leather and leather manufactures with 46, wood-working industries with 46, stone and earth with 30, oils and fats with 36, sugar and allied industries with 24, glass industries with 20, metal furnaces and semi-finished metal manufactures with 17, motor cars and motor cycles with 8, shipping and carrying with 4, ceramic industries with 10 cartels, and the railway waggon manufactures with one cartel.

This list, while showing how widely industrial combination has been scattered over the whole of the German industrial area, can hardly elucidate the really important features of the condition of industrial combination in Germany. The student who is not conversant with the facts might be led to deduce, for instance, the importance of cartels in the textile and clothing group of German industry, whereas in this very group, as we shall explain in a later chapter, the number of really important monopolist combines is insignificant. On the other hand the existence of only a single cartel in the railway waggon industry is easily explained by the fact of the paucity of firms in that group. A multitude of cartels in a certain group of industry may be simply explained by the fact that there may be many specialised trades in that line of manufacture (Liefmann tells us that there is not only a cartel specially organised for the manufacture and sale of toilet paper, but also one for the making and distributing of crêpe toilet paper). On the other hand an industry possessing only a few cartels, but those in its leading lines, may in fact be much more cartelised than a group of industry having cartels in many, but only secondary, branches of production. Important as the number of cartels may appear as revealing the general tendency towards industrial associative organisation, it counts little as regards the actual significance and weight of the cartel in the framework either of a single group of industry or of national industry as a whole. This latter could only be brought to light by a detailed and elaborate survey of the percentage of production actually controlled by cartels or trusts. We possess some examples of such statistics, but they do not cover anything like the whole field of associative activity in German industry; on the contrary they are only found in some prominent cases of monopolist organisation such as coal, iron or steel.

Again, in observing the multiplicity of industrial associations, one has to remember that a great deal of interlocking may take place among the cartels themselves. Manufacturers may, owing to their line of production, become members of more than one cartel. In 1923 not less than 137 associations were affiliated to the Verein Deutscher Maschinenbauanstalten, one of the big combines in the finishing lines of the iron industry. In the iron and steel industries themselves vertically combined works are, according to the different stages of their production, necessarily members of a good many cartels or syndicates. If, as in the case mentioned before, the members of such cartels are affiliated to a central cartel or association—regulating certain phases of the manufacture or its distribution—this "Rahmen- or Grund-kartell", as Liefmann has rightly called it in the case of the Deutsche Rohstahlgemeinschaft of 1924, may possess a much more far-reaching influence than any of the single associations, a fact demonstrating again the unimportance of "numbers". Moreover, it is to be borne in mind that the strength of any cartel may depend on a very few of its members, especially in cases where amalgamation has been going on. Some few members of a cartel may indeed have a dominant influence and control the whole industry. This is the case in the Mühlenbauindustrie (works for the construction of milling plants); here a few big firms only, concentrated in the "Miag"-Concern (Miag Mühlenbau-Industrie A.G.), are the dominant factor in the cartel as well as in the industry, although there are still in existence about thirty smaller works affiliated by price agreements to the "concern"-group, but in fact of very little influence in the cartel.

An insight into the strength of cartels in German industry cannot be gained by the figures relating to their numbers in certain groups of industry. Yet it can be taken as a fact that an essential part of the power of monopolist organisation and the principal forces in its historic development are to be found in the extractive industries and those industries dependent on mineral production. This is so evident that at one time it was generally assumed that industrial monopolies of our days were the outcome of a monopolisation of such instruments of production as could not be increased indefinitely or at any rate at equal or decreasing cost. This view was largely supported by the consideration that most American trusts were connected directly or indirectly with the "monopolisation" of land, as explained by Theodor Vogelstein and others. Like all explanations attempting a "wholesale" interpretation of the causes of monopolist organisation by alluding to certain "special" conditions, such as the existence of tariffs or the pressure of depressions, etc., this theory may be useful in part, but can never give a satisfactory solution of the general causes underlying the formation of industrial monopolies. We know to-day that there may be monopolies of producers in free-trade industries as well as in protected ones and there are examples to prove that protective tariffs by no means necessitate the formation of cartels and trusts, as may be shown by the paucity of effective combines in the highly protected German cotton spinning and weaving industries. We have experienced an increase of industrial combination in a time of depression, as a means to save manufacturers from a depreciation of their fixed capital investment (Brentano was the first to allude to this tendency), but one has also noticed that times of prosperity have given a new impulse to industrial combination, the manufacturers being led by the desire to make the most out of the boom by concerted action. Again, there have been a good many failures of agreements in times of depression, as some people are inclined at such times to break away from their obligations, in order to catch business by individual methods, a tendency which has been dangerous to a good many "Interessengemeinschaften" since 1929.

The same remark may apply to the argument that monopolies predominate wherever there is mineral wealth to be exploited. In English coal mining, which after so many attempts at cartelisation, has up to the present not succeeded in getting an effective central organisation of its producers, we have a very striking example showing that the mere existence of extractive industries will not infallibly encourage monopolisation. One might even argue that a good many cartels or trusts in the field of mineral production, as for instance in the case of the German potash industry, would not have had a very long life, if the State had not stepped in and forced newcomers into the combination by means of compulsory cartelisation. Certainly the existence of mineral resources, which can easily be monopolised, will be in many instances an effective condition for the making of cartels or trusts. But however much weight one may attach to this condition, it would be erroneous to generalise from it.

No doubt the large prevalence of mineral resources has greatly favoured the formation of German cartels and amalgamations, not only directly but also by demonstrating to other industries the advantages of industrial combination. In that respect coal and, before 1918, iron ore have to be mentioned in the first place; after the war the development and use of brown coal, as will be described later on, made enormous strides, potash, the mineral production of which was before 1918 entirely a German domain, rock salt, and some metallic ores, chalk, cement have to be added to the list of important German industries connected with the possession of land. The importance of the mining industry in Germany may be gathered from the fact that out of a total production value, in all except the food industries, of about 61 milliard R.M. in 1927–28, according to Dr Wagenführ, 4·230 milliards were represented by mining, 2·775 milliards by the industries connected with stones and quarries, 6·9 milliards by the iron and steel industry, 3·75 milliards by the iron, steel and metal finishing industries, and 5·7 milliards by engineering, manufacture of apparatus and metal wares, while textiles as a whole represented not more than 8 milliards, the chemical industries (which in some lines were also connected with extractive German industries) only 3·6, the wood and wooden material industries 3·4, the paper industries 3·5 milliard R.M., so that in fact the leading rôle, which cartelisation played from the beginning in the German coal, iron and steel trade and allied industries, may be contrasted with the much later and on the whole far less important industrial combinations in many other, though not all, groups of industry, which—for example textiles, paper, leather or wood—had to import the bulk of their raw materials. If "net" figures of the value of production are taken into account the figures concerning mining and iron and steel become still more significant, as of course in the "brutto" figures the finished and semi-finished goods show a relatively enhanced value, including the value of the goods entering the preliminary stages of production. If the "net" value of production at the date mentioned is taken as being 33–34 milliard marks, the value of the mining produce, of stones and quarries and of the iron and steel producing and finishing industries alone would amount to 8·5 milliards, that is, to about 25 % of the whole, even if the food industries are included.

A great number of German industrial combinations will therefore come under the heading of monopolies connected with mineral resources. On the other hand, another group of combinations must be taken into account, the structure of which has little or nothing to do with the foregoing conditions. This is the case where monopolist combination is mainly the result of a concentration of plant or of units of business. Such concentration may be the result of a long and painful process of absorption of smaller firms by bigger ones, a process accompanied by hard fighting on the one side and frequent reorganisation on the other. It may be the outcome of fierce competition in long existing industries and among firms proudly fighting for what they consider to be their "independence". It may have been in recent times the final stage of a process of rationalisation or planning to safeguard industries from utter ruin. Moreover, there are industries of a modern type which from their very beginning have shown a tendency towards big units, thereby facilitating the conclusion of agreements. This has been the case in the making of rails from the very beginning of that industry, in contrast to other lines of the heavy iron and steel industry. The railmakers have been among the first to conclude agreements leading very soon to an international cartel, of which even English steelmakers were early members. But the chief example of combinations of that kind, resulting from an inherent tendency towards concentration, is furnished by the so-called "new industries", which started their type of unit on a basis of technical expansion and financial outlay unknown in the 'eighties or 'nineties of the last century. Dr Wagenführ mentions, as examples of such "young" industries in Germany, the making of briquettes, the motor car industry, the radio industry, the manufacture of nitrogenous fertilisers, the making of artificial silk, the electrical industries, the rubber industry and others. These industries may be contrasted with the "old" industries, such as the manufacture of porcelain, leather goods, musical instruments, linen yarn, ships, gas mantles, gloves, etc. Dr Wagenführ, in a very able study published by the Institut für

Konjunkturforschung in 1933, has grouped together some of the more prominent of the "old" and "young" industries and constructed an index of their comparative progress. According to these figures, which represent of course a segment only of both groups, the young industries have stood the strain of the times much better than the "old" ones. If the 1913 figure is taken as being 100, the production index of the "new" industries had risen to 405 in the peak year 1929, dropping to 262 in 1932, while the production index of the old industries selected by Dr Wagenführ shows a decline to 53 in 1928 and to 19 in 1932. Inasmuch as the new industries are generally characterised by a much greater concentration from their start than the traditional, much differentiated older industries, with their generally much smaller capital and technical outfit, one may in reading these figures come to the conclusion that it has been cartelised and trustificated industry which has stood the downward movement of productivity best. There may be exceptions here and there, but even in the rayon industry, which in Germany, England, Holland and Italy, in spite of being a highly-concentrated new industry, has not shown permanent prosperity, this would probably have held true, if a very reckless international over-production had not counteracted the normal tendency.

## PART II

# INDUSTRIAL COMBINATION IN GROUPS OF INDUSTRY

### CHAPTER III

## MINING

I N trying to give a review, however condensed, of industrial combination in the main groups of German industry, the foregoing remarks will be of some use. They certainly tend to suggest that an analysis of monopoly organisation grouped by industries should begin with the extractive industries and those manufactures directly or indirectly connected with mineral production. Here, as in the following chapters of this book, in so far as they deal with monographical descriptions of cartels or amalgamations, it will not be our task to give anything like a full list or a full statistical "tableau" of German cartels and trusts. Readers anxious to get some detailed information about almost all really important industrial combination existing at that time in German industry and trade may safely apply to the "Verhandlunge und Berichte" of the so-called "Enqueteausschuss", reports published between 1929 and 1930, and quoted in the appended list of the main publications used in this book. It will be necessary, however, to remember that many statements and developments treated at length in these exhaustive and elaborate reports have no longer the actual importance which they might be supposed to have by the unbiassed student. In the first place the work of these commissions and subcommittees was spread over a rather long period, and many facts had become obsolete, when the reports were at last published, and secondly, the three or four years which have elapsed since these publications have brought about many decisive changes and reorganisations in industry. It is not the intention of this book to accumulate facts, which, however weighty at the present time, might very soon become out of date, and it is a consolation to the economic chronicler of the problems of industrial monopoly, that generally such facts seem rather more important to the *ad hoc* writer or the "day by day" politician than to those who are interested in the principal and more permanent aspects of the problem. It is therefore far more our task to select those examples of industrial combination out of the great number existing, the description and study of which promises some results in establishing the characteristic features of certain industrial monopolies and their structural differences. We do therefore lay stress on the fact of selection. And in starting this review of monopolies with some prominent examples from the extractive group we wish to underline the very contrast between these examples and those in the following chapters.

The German coal mining industry has, from the beginning of its modern development, had definite advantages to offer to a movement towards combination, since the coal mining properties of the empire are locally or territorially concentrated. The main districts of German coal mining have always been the Rhine and Ruhr basin on the one side, and the Upper-Silesian coal fields on the other. Both districts had always and have still, besides exporting, their competitive and non-competitive trade, but the mere fact that by transport charges the dominant German coal districts had a sort of "protection" in the Empire itself gave a very strong stimulus to do away with competition. Since the end of the War this territorial concentration of the German coal properties has been further increased, as by the peace treaties the German Empire was deprived of its coal mines in Ost-Oberschlesien. We may illustrate this by two sets of figures, first by those of the available resources (reserves) of coal of proved coal fields to a depth of 1000 m. According to official statistical estimates this reserve amounts to 55,100 million tons in the Ruhrgebiet, to 7100 million tons in the Nord-Krefelder Gebiet, to only 4000 million tons in West Upper-Silesia, while other districts like Niederschlesien, Aachen, Brüggen-Erkelenz, Saxony and Hanover represent less than 2000 millions each. The Saar territory figure amounts to 12,200 millions of tons. The concentration of actual mining at the present time may be illustrated by the following figures, to which we add those of the production of coke. In March 1933 the production of coal and coke amounted to:

| District | Tons | |
| --- | --- | --- |
| | Coal | Coke |
| Ruhrbezirk | 6,378,144 | 1,358,360 |
| Aachen | 664,406 | 118,333 |
| West-Oberschlesien | 1,366,688 | 77,612 |
| Niederschlesien | 374,816 | 67,505 |
| Freistaat Sachsen | 277,780 | 18,052 |

In January 1934 the Ruhrbezirk produced 7,639,806 tons of coal, while all other districts produced 2,794,476 tons, the corresponding figures with regard to coke being 1,622,110 and 284,073. Of course it must not be overlooked that the German "Steinkohlen" industry has, since 1918 and the occupation of the Ruhrgebiet, experienced the rise of a new competitor in the form of the briquette-making industry and the much enlarged use of brown coal (lignite). The necessity of economising hard coal, forced upon the Reich in the first years after the War, led to a greatly increased efficiency in the use of coal, so that in 1925 it was stated that Germany had been enabled to get 10 % more out of a given unit of fuel than before the War, simply through a rationalisation of fuel economy. The lignite industry, on the other hand, became the supplier of many branches of industry hitherto not accustomed to this kind of fuel, which in the U.S.A. had not been considered as fit for industrial purposes at all, such as glass-making and electrical industries and the manufacture of ammoniac fertilisers. The lignite production, which in 1913 had amounted to not more than 87 million tons, compared with 190 millions of coal, had risen in 1933 to 122 million tons, while that of coal had dropped to 104 millions; in fact in the "boom" year of 1929 the lignite figure had reached the peak of 174 million tons. Between 1913 the production of lignite briquettes had almost doubled; in 1933 the figure was still 30 million tons as compared with 21·5 millions in 1913, in spite of the very heavy depression. The production of briquettes, like that of "raw" lignite (Roh-Braunkohle) is centred in two districts, in the so-called "Middle-German" District and the Rhineland. In January 1934 the production in tons was as follows:

|  | Production of raw lignite | Production of briquettes |
|---|---|---|
| Mitteldeutschland | 8,141,745 | 1,979,949 |
| Rheinland | 3,680,578 | 803,982 |

There is no production reported from other districts, so that the territorial concentration becomes evident.

The German coal mining industry has for a long time shown a tendency towards increasing technical units. According to the reports mentioned above, the collieries producing up to 500,000 tons a year amounted to as much as 72·77 % of all the collieries in 1900. In the year 1928 this figure had come down to 23·75 %! The percentage of collieries producing from 500,000 tons to one million tons rose in the same period from 27·23 to 60·29. The number of working collieries had been reduced from 350 in 1913 to 294 in 1928. The same experience applies to the production of coke, one of the most important by-products of coal besides gas, tar, benzole, ammonia, etc. By the so-called "Zentralkokereien", central coking plants, the production of coke has been concentrated and improved. From 1913 to 1928 the production of coke ovens increases from 1·4 million tons to about 2 million tons per oven. Again, there has been a rapid expansion of coal-cutting machinery in the German mines. It may be recalled that the use of coal-cutting machinery is of recent date. In America at the beginning of the century 25 % of all bituminous coal was cut by machinery and the proportion in 1924 was nearly 70 %. In England in 1901 only 1½ % of the total output of coal was cut by machinery and by 1924 the proportion had grown to 19 %. In Germany coal-cutting by machinery made great progress after the War. The percentage of machine-cut coal in Germany and England was:

|  | German Empire | Great Britain |
|---|---|---|
| 1925 | 59·4 % | 20·8 % |
| 1928 | 77·7 | 26·0 |

It will readily be understood that the improvement in the "technique" of coal mining either by the employment of more machinery and other technical progress or by a more economic utilisation of the fuel through by-product manufacture led necessarily to larger industrial units. This was all the more so as all these improvements necessitated a larger and rather risky outlay of capital not available to smaller undertakings.

The rôle which cartels and syndicates have played in this process is a double one. On the one hand the increasing units and the increasing size of the undertakings facilitated the formation of industrial combination by reducing the number of competitors and preparing the road to agreement. On the other hand, the cartel, once formed and established, accelerated the process of unification, as it lay in the interest of the big collieries to acquire quotas of weak competitors, to shut down their pits and add the quota to their own more economically working plant. As we shall have to describe later on, the movement towards vertical combination in the iron and steel industries, which was partly the outcome of the movements towards a monopolising of the coal-fields, greatly accelerated this process, strengthening the desire to acquire more coal mines by the big combined works. So one may say that the cartel movement in the German coal industry was partly facilitated by the movement of concentration of units and undertakings, and partly, on the contrary, a means of accelerating this tendency.

Important fusions in the German coal mining industry date as far back as the 'thirties of the last century, for instance the formation of the "Vereinigungsgesellschaft für den Steinkohlenbergbau" of 1836. But the real movement towards combination started in the 'seventies and 'eighties. As far back as 1878 there existed combinations of certain of the more important groups of German mines for the purpose of combating overproduction and controlling prices. Following some earlier associations dating back to 1882, the Westphalian Coke Syndicate was formed in 1890, and in 1893 the Rhenish-Westphalian Coal Syndicate, which eventually absorbed the Coke Syndicate and the Briquette Selling Association. By the beginning of the World War the Rhenish-Westphalian Coal Syndicate had become one of the most powerful industrial combinations in the world. It was a cartel of the most highly organised type, with a system of quotas, called Beteiligungsziffern, for its members, price fixing and pooling arrangements, a definite policy of coal exports, joint selling agencies, etc. During the first years of its régime it had been generally feared—in accordance with the general view of the restrictive policy of cartel production—that the syndicate would lead to a reduction of output to keep prices up. But the reverse happened. The production of coal by members of the syndicate almost doubled between 1893 and 1904 and was again increased by the same amount up to 1914. And even this increase of output was not sufficient to comply with the demand, so that in some years there was, in spite of heavily increased output, a sort of "coal famine", compelling the cartel to import coal from England in 1906 in order to comply with its obligations. As, curiously enough, in other years the reverse happened and dearth was followed by overproduction and large supplies, this period, according to Liefmann, has demonstrated that important changes in business conditions (Konjunktur) cannot decisively be influenced even by mighty combinations, although their effects might be mitigated to some extent. The period following, i.e. immediately before the War and after its outbreak, witnessed some rather critical times for the coal syndicate. The concentration movement, by which the coal mining industry had become linked up with the iron and steel industries, had far outstripped the original movement towards larger units in the coal industry itself. The giant firms now controlling coal mines as well as furnaces and steel works had ceased to be genuinely interested in the coal syndicate, which at one time had been regarded by them as an instrument to fight competition. In fact they had succeeded in acquiring coal fields and in concentrating their coal production in the most efficient mines. The agreement of the coal syndicate was to end in 1915, and the discussions for new arrangements were started as early as 1911, as from the beginning the difficulties of coming to terms with the big "mixed" works and the increasing number of outsiders were clearly realised. In the year 1912 the syndicate had succeeded in getting the Prussian State, as the principal outsider, into the syndicate. But in the same year the Prussian Secretary of Commerce gave notice to quit, as he did not consent to the rise in prices decided by the syndicate. In February 1914 the *pourparlers* concerning the renewal of the syndicate came to an end, as there was no possibility of reconciling the interest of the so-called "reinen Kohlenzechen", that is, the collieries solely engaged in coal mining, with those of the "Hüttenzechen", that is, those mines which were integrated with the iron and steel works. It was the War which saved this critical and almost hopeless situation. A breaking up of the syndicate could not be allowed during the War from reasons of economic emergency and the agreement was renewed under pressure from the Government. On 12 July 1915 the Government made a decree to establish compulsory cartelisation, if the syndicate was not reconstituted by 15 September. Under this pressure a transitional syndicate (Übergangssyndikat) was formed, of which the state mines of the Ruhr district became members. This agreement was to end by 31 March 1917, but as early as October 1916 a new and definite cartel agreement was reached of which all mines of the Ruhr district, including those of the State, were members. This syndicate was composed of 93 mining undertakings, 19 of which were "Hüttenzechen", that is members who were making use of their coal in their own iron and steel or other works (Verbrauchsbeteiligung). This agreement was to last up to 1 April 1922. The termination of the War and the outbreak of the Revolution encouraged the idea of socialisation and brought about some new changes; among these the Kohlenwirtschaftsgesetz of 1919 (March), by which the coal cartel became a compulsory syndicate. The number of individual undertakings has since diminished again, being now 56. The independent action of the coal syndicate has been limited by important bodies such as the Reichskohlenverband, a national coal committee, and the Reichskohlenrat, a Coal Council of the Reich, whose powers and tasks we shall discuss in a later chapter. The Secretary of Commerce to the Reich is entitled to protest against any decisions of the syndicate. The seat of the Rhenish-Westphalian Coal Syndicate has always been at Essen. The name of the syndicate has been changed to that of Ruhrkohle A.G. In recent times co-ordination in the German coal trade has made further progress. Since 1 April 1934 the big mining companies of the Aachen District, such as the Eschweiler Bergwerksverein and others have joined the Rhenish-Westphalian Coal Syndicate. Although of course coal mining in the Aachen district cannot be compared in magnitude with the industry on the Ruhr, this consolidation of district interests has been welcomed as a step forward towards a "national" coal organisation of the Reich. At any rate the considerable overlapping between the two districts in their sale in South-German markets will now disappear. As in fact the Rhenish-Westphalian Coal Syndicate is by far the most important cartel in the whole coal mining industry of Germany it does not seem necessary to give a description of combinations of minor importance. It may be mentioned, however, that the Upper Silesian Coal Syndicate represents the same kind of organisation in the mines of that district. This syndicate has, in 1933, been prolonged until March 1938. The three largest coal mining concerns of that district formed at the same time a selling organisation of their own for their products under the name of "Interessengemeinschaft Oberschlesischer Steinkohlengruben (Kohlen I.G.), G.m.b.H., Berlin".

The factors then which have essentially influenced the formation and duration of monopolist organisation in the German coal industry are the following:

1. The territorial concentration of coal mining.
2. The early concentration in the technical and financial units of collieries and the concentration of mining undertakings.
3. The compulsory action of the State.

It is worth while to make comparison with the conditions of the English coal mining industry, which form a regular counterpart to those existing in Germany. It is well known that the United Kingdom abounds in coal almost everywhere. Coal districts of almost equal commercial importance are spread over the whole economic territory of Great Britain, whether we look to Northumberland or Durham, Scotland or Wales, Yorkshire or Lancashire, the eastern counties or the midlands. Since the development of railway traffic it has not been possible for any district to rely for the formation of a cartel on a condition of "local" monopoly. It must not of course be forgotten that the above mentioned districts do not all produce the same quality

of coal, and in so far as some districts have for this reason a preference in the market they are not always in competition with
each other. But if any one district were to attempt to put up
prices to any marked extent, consumers could obtain coal supplies
from other districts, though possibly of different quality, the
only exception being the anthracite district in the extreme west
of South Wales. The relatively small size of Great Britain
coupled with an industry scattered over the whole country makes
the position with regard to competition very different from what
it is in Germany, where the natural concentration of coal fields
in two main districts and the protective influence of long distances on markets was favourable to industrial combination.

As regards the concentration of units and undertakings the
German figures given above may be compared with English
data published by the Report on the Coal Industry of 1925.
This Report stated that there were at that time 2481 mines
producing coal as the principal mineral, a figure which may be
contrasted with the German figure of 295 coal mining units in
1928, or the 312 units in the lignite industry. Under these
conditions a most astonishing diversity was disclosed in English
coal mining. Many mines employed less than 50 men, others
more than 3000. Some produced coal at 12s. a ton, some at a
cost of 30s. The Commission visited a mine in Lanarkshire,
which employed 24 men and had a capital of £350. It was also
engaged in extracting some good coal, accessible by an adit, that
had been left unworked many years ago. The coal was sold in the
neighbourhood, a small motor lorry conveying it. This was the
structure of a coal mining industry, which had not experienced
the closing down of uneconomic or technically backward pits by
any central association or any quota arrangements between
members of a combination. We have quoted a figure showing
that in Germany in 1928 mines producing up to 500,000 tons of
coal a year were reduced to 23·75 % of the whole number of
collieries. In Great Britain, however, in 1925 out of 613 undertakings (not even mining units!) 443 had an output disposable
commercially of from 5000 to 400,000 tons! The Report was well
aware of this contrast between German and English sizes of
unit. It was expressly stated that the Westphalian coal field was

very differently organised in that respect from English mining. "The output of that field in normal years is in the neighbourhood of a hundred million tons, but the number of separate undertakings responsible for this large output is only seventy." The figure of 653 undertakings given in the Report on the Coal Industry represented an output of 239 million tons of coal in England. Not less than 43·6 % of this output was produced by undertakings producing from 500,000 to 600,000 tons a year. Of course things have changed a good deal since then in the English coal mining industry. The figures of to-day, if available, would probably show a far more concentrative picture, although the last Report of the Coal Mines Reorganisation Committee (1933) has not been very optimistic with regard to effected rationalisation. But the German figures prove at any rate that the movement towards associative concentration of units and undertakings had long begun when little of it was heard of in England and that it had reached a very high level between 1924 and 1928, when a keener interest in the desirability of such developments was just awakening in England. There can be no doubt that it has been the lack of concentration which has been the main impediment to effective associative organisation in the English coal industry. As, however, we could see from the history of German coal organisation that even strong cartelisation would in all probability not have held its own, if the State had not come to the help of the shattered Ruhr-Kartell before and during the War, so we are led to the conclusion that in England too a mere facultative and voluntary arrangement between coal owners would probably not have been of a permanent character. The reluctance of any English government, up to recent times, to enforce amalgamation or to enact compulsory combination, if voluntary action should fail, has certainly kept back the movement towards combination in the coal trade. It has, however, lately become evident, especially as regards the English steel industry, that voluntary agreements, as Sir William Firth has put it in a speech before the London Iron and Steel Exchange in January 1934, would only be consented to by the parties interested, if the prices agreed to were showing a profit to the "least efficient" plant. The same reason has in all probability reacted against the frequently discussed arrangements in the English coal mining industry and will probably lead to further failures of well-meant schemes, just as in Germany the coal cartel would have broken up without the interference of government legislation.

The second important group of German extractive industries presenting a notable example of combination is the potash group. Here an unique advantage was bestowed on German producers. In contrast to the coal industry, which is open to international competition, the potash mines were, up to the end of the World War, a natural monopoly of the German Empire. There was in fact no competition to be feared from any quarter of the world, when the costly process of producing potash from wood ashes or sea salines was superseded by potash mining. The potash reserves of the world, up to the last ten years, when the Spanish potash mining industry began to be developed and Russian prospects for potash mining became brighter, were in fact centralised in German territory by Nature, and there was no reason for the German potash industry to be afraid of any international competition. Before the War Germany possessed two distinct districts of potash properties, those situated in Middle Germany, mainly near Stassfurt, Magdeburg, Halle, Mansfeld, Hanover and the Südharz mountains, and the Alsace-Lorraine potash mines, which Germany lost to France after the War. It was then that for the first time the German potash mines had to face a competitor, but terms of mutual understanding were soon arranged between the two parties. In 1932 Germany produced 6·4 million tons of raw potash salts (against 11·9 millions in 1913), while France produced in those regions formerly belonging to the Reich 1·9 million tons. Russian potash production, which was frequently said to be becoming a serious competitor in world markets, has not yet practically developed to that stage, while in the last few years the potash production of Spain has made remarkable strides and the U.S.A. were producing 129,000 tons in 1932. These developments, however, have as yet hardly touched the monopolist position of the German-French potash industry.

It was certainly this monopolist condition of the industry

within the world market, which gave the first impulse to combination. Of course, there were even here, in a production so exclusively confined to a definite area, certain limitations as regards the exploitation of monopoly. In many cases, both with regard to inland consumption and to the big consumers in the newly developed agricultural areas overseas, especially in the U.S.A., the increasing use of the new fertiliser, however cheapened by the development of the potash supply from mines, was largely dependent on its price. An attempt to overstrain the power of monopoly by putting prices very much up would certainly have reacted promptly on the demand, especially where the use of potash would not have seemed a stringent necessity to farmers. It was among others this reason, which led the Government of the Reich to refrain from the attempt to take a share of the prosperous development of the industry in the form of an export duty, however tempting from the mere treasury's viewpoint such a measure seemed to be. It was frequently discussed, but never carried through.

Yet there was ample room for an effective association among producers to exploit the monopolist position of the industry. The first "Kalisyndikat" was founded as early as 1879. There were not more than four firms existing at that time, two being privately owned and two owned by the State. Even twenty years later there were no more than ten undertakings. This shows the very striking difference between the opportunities for association in the potash industry and those in the older extractive industries such as coal. The formation of a cartel was really a matter of little difficulty. But another epoch soon followed. The mining of potash had become recognised as a most profitable business. There was a general rush into the industry, a "Kalifieber", as it was called. Undertakings increased rapidly, as on the one side the syndicate seemed to offer a good protection against unprofitable prices and on the other it was not possible to forbid newcomers to join it. At the beginning of the century a great number of new reserves were discovered, in Middle-Germany as well as in Alsace, and the number of undertakings increased still faster than before. By 1908 the undertakings had increased to 50, by 1910 to 68! As the existing works now showed great differences as regards the cost of production, a good number of the newly opened mines being less efficient than the older ones and there having been considerable overcapitalisation since the "Kali-rush", very grave conflicts arose within the syndicate. In fact, the most efficient works would have approved of the restoration of free competition, in order to fight their weaker competitors and to be able to make full use of their productive capacity instead of seeing their output limited by the quota. Thus a breakdown of the cartel and the beginning of cutthroat competition would have been an unavoidable stage of their development, if the Prussian State had not stepped in with compulsory measures. The compulsory syndicate (Zwangssyndikat) was formed by the Kali-law of 1910.

Economists conversant with the problems of industry, such as Prof. Liefmann of Freiburg, had predicted that this step would hardly lessen the evil in question, that is overcompetition. Looking back now to the experiences of those days one may come to the conclusion that overproduction in the potash industry would in fact have been abated with greater success by leaving competition alone, as this in the long run would have led to a "survival of the fittest". The participation of the State in the cartel and the policy inherent in such half-governmental organisation, to protect the weak elements in industry against their more efficient competitors, has increased overproduction instead of diminishing it, much to the "detriment of the German economic development", as Liefmann remarks. The increase of undertakings and pits was so much accelerated after the compulsory cartelisation, that in 1913 the number of undertakings had risen to 167 and to 207 in 1916. A catastrophic amount of overcapitalisation accompanied this development; while Liefmann asserts that "about a dozen efficient works with about 100 Million Mark of capital investment could supply the whole demand", already before the War 2000 millions of marks were invested in the potash industry. Yet in the long run the movement towards concentration could not be checked by these conditions; on the contrary it became far more urgent. The concentration movement in the German potash industry has been partly fostered by legal enactment as, for instance, through the Stilllegungsverordnung of 1921 (an act to enforce the closing down of inefficient plant); it has partly been effected through amalgamations financed and promoted by capitalists and bankers specialising in that line of industrial activity. The Enqueteausschuss (the committee on German industrial conditions already mentioned) was able to state that, while the sale of pure potash had been reduced from 100,000 dz. (100 kilo) per unit of mine in 1912 to not more than 59,000 dz. in 1921, it was again increased to 237,000 dz. in 1928. The same development has been going on in the potash factories, producing the chemical product $K_2O$. This has been achieved through an entire reorganisation of the units of production and a very complete rationalisation. As to the technical side of the latter, it may be mentioned that the costs alone resulting from the use of power and fuel had been reduced by about 50 % per 100 kilo of potash between 1924 and 1930. The German potash industry, which in spite of compulsory cartelisation and state interference, has been going through very harassing times for a long period, has of late been endeavouring to increase the chemical side of its business, called Kalichemie. While the French potash producers were desirous of expanding and increasing the mining productivity of the newly acquired industry, German producers were increasingly devoting their attention to the manufacturing processes and the chemical utilisation of potash, thereby making up for the losses resulting from the Treaty of Versailles.

All these conditions have led to a movement of concentration of undertakings within the German potash cartel. What neither the syndicate nor governmental action had been able to effect, the dire necessity of economic development has accomplished during the last few years. It is perhaps too early to speak of trustification in the German potash industry, but a movement towards it can certainly be discerned. The leading concern has been for a long time the "Wintershall-Deutsche Kali-industrie" group, its quota in the syndicate being 41 % in 1933. Two other dominant groups are Burbach and the Salzdethfurt concern, the latter's share in the syndicate's production being almost 25 %. It comprises the three very important and efficient undertakings: Salzdethfurt, Kaliwerke Aschersleben and Westeregeln.

The works of the Prussian "fiskus" and that of Anhalt have become of secondary importance, and so has the production of some private works. The Salzdethfurt concern is prominent through its combination of important manufacturing works with its mining activity. The Westeregeln company for instance owns besides mines two factories producing chloride of potassium, one factory producing sulphate of potash and sulphate potash-magnesia, and one electro-chemical works. Salzdethfurt possesses a power station of its own, representing 4000 kilowatt. Over-capitalisation in the potash industry, as can be studied from detailed reports of the Enqueteausschuss, has recently been drastically dealt with by reducing the share capital; the last transaction of that kind was the withdrawal and cancelling of shares of the value of 16·65 million marks by the Wintershall concern in the spring of 1933. The process of concentration and reorganisation, however, does not yet seem to have reached its final stage. At any rate the historical development of the potash mining industry presents an interesting example of the many different facts which may finally be decisive in the formation of industrial combination. The condition of monopoly of land, here so definitely present, has not prevented the industry from passing through very critical periods, which have even occurred lately, leading to drastic reductions in the dividends of the great concerns. The German potash industry has been far from prosperous in recent years. Its case shows that the formation of industrial combination in the form of cartelisation is not an all-round remedy against depression, resulting from overproduction and too many producers. Probably if the industry was starting to-day, the lessons of its fifty years' development would find expression in measures counteracting the reckless multiplication of mines, by giving the cartel some definite powers to regulate the number of new mines; an attempt which was in fact made for some years in the 'nineties by the so-called "Schutzbohrgemein-schaft" (an association to regulate the number of new potash enterprises). It is interesting to note, that the same circumstances, which have led to a weakening of the potash syndicates in Germany, had once operated to undermine the position of the Limitation of the Vend in the northern English coal fields, the number of new participants in the combine reducing the allocations of all mines concerned to the detriment of the most efficient undertakings. It will be seen in the future how far the movement of amalgamation in the potash industry will correct the mistakes made by a prominent cartel and by the former cartel policy of the State.

Another group of German salt mining is that of the saline salt industry, the organisation of which is largely connected with the potash industry. Germany produced as much as 2·1 million tons of rock-salt in 1933, being the second largest producer of salt in the world after the U.S.A. The North-German Salt Syndicate was renewed in December 1932 until the end of 1937 and the name changed to the "Norddeutsche Salinenvereinigung G.m.b.H." About 60 % of the German salines are owned by the potash industry, who also control the Rock-Salt Syndicate. Of the 22 works concerned, 8 with a quota of 15 % have been closed down and received compensation at the rate of 10 R.M. per ton of output quota.

A very important rôle in the cartelisation and trustification of many countries has been for a long time played by the cement industry. Cement belongs to those not very numerous industries which have shown an upward trend of production since the beginning of the World War, up to about 1928–29. Germany has been able to increase its production of cement from 6·8 million tons in 1913 in the former territory of the Reich to 7·5 millions in its reduced area in 1928, the U.S.A. from 15·8 millions to as much as over 30 millions, Great Britain from 2·9 million tons in 1913 to 5·9 millions in 1931, and there has been the same tendency in Japan, France, Belgium, Spain, and even Russia. After 1929 a severe setback was experienced. Production in Germany dropped to as little as 2·7 million tons in 1932. The position of cement—by which we mean Portland cement, as it represents more than 75 % of the world's output—is the very reverse of that in the potash industry. While potash had to be regarded right up to recent times as being the natural geographical monopoly of a single restricted national area, cement is in fact produced in almost every industrial country. As the raw material for the making of cement can be supplied in almost any part of the world, it is in general the demand which dictates the location of the industry and the principal consumer countries have become the principal sources of supply. Yet this industry based upon a product of such ubiquity has been a field of great activity as regards industrial combination. In Great Britain from 70 to 90 % of the production has been controlled by the Associated Portland Cement Manufacturers, which indeed is one of the oldest English industrial combinations, having been founded in 1900. In the U.S.A. four firms control about 35 % of the output, in Norway and France the same number 100 % and 60 %, in Germany five undertakings control about 60 % of the industry. The conditions in general do not seem to favour combination. As Fitzgerald rightly states: "There are in the cement industry practically unlimited sources of raw material; the process of manufacturing is relatively simple". But, on the other hand, in England as in Germany: "The existence of a comprehensive federation naturally enables the cement makers to exploit the large measure of national and local protection conferred by the heavy cost of transport". In fact like the potash industry the German cement trade—although local cartels were in existence—has been at times a field of great overcompetition. During the War this led to a restriction of new production by State action. The erection of new works was forbidden in 1916 and a strict regulation in other, though minor, respects enacted, which lasted up to 1923. A central body, called the Reichzementstelle, was created to make these orders effective. The endeavour to bring about a national cement cartel, comprising all producers and uniting local cartels, failed; an association of a loose type called the "Zementbund" was the only outcome. On the other hand, within the local districts a strong tendency towards concentration has been going on. In fact the industry of to-day is dominated by four leading concerns:

1. The Wicking Cement-works at Münster (comprising fifteen undertakings of the Wesphalian district).
2. The Heidelberger works (comprising fourteen works in the State of Baden).
3. The Dyckerhoff concern (with works in the Rhineland and Southern Germany).

4. The Upper-Silesian works (Schlesische Portlandzement-industrie).

All these groups are characterised by a very strong tendency towards concentration. The Upper-Silesian works are with one exception concentrated in the Schlesische Portlandzement-industrie A.G. Before the War there were eleven independent works outside the cartel. Since then the process of amalgamation went on, resulting in the formation of big concerns, which after some time tried to come to a common basis of management by forming Interessengemeinschaften, i.e. a community of interests. It is only natural that such development had to lead one day to the national cartel, which, in spite of many efforts, would not have been realised as long as local interests were not completely unified. In March 1933 the four cement groups in Germany came to an agreement for the next three years, which enabled them to cancel their special competitive quotations. An arrangement was also reached with various outside firms with a view to curtailing output. This new arrangement facilitated agreements with one of the foreign competitors. The Dutch cement interests under-took not to deliver further quantities of cement to Germany and quotas and minimum prices were fixed for the Dutch market.

The history and structure of monopolist organisation in the cement trade is certainly of marked importance. The example of this industry shows that a theory of monopoly cannot be con-structed upon the increasing costs characterising the production of the soil or extractive industries. It would never have been possible to "monopolise" cement by monopolising land, as had been the case with coal or iron ore, even if we do not take into consideration the fact that there was always potential competition from Roman cement and cement derived from iron-furnaces (Eisenportland- und Hochofenzement, Hüttenzement). The condition of monopoly was rather the "protection" afforded to local procedure by the incidence of the freight. But it is again interesting to note that this monopolist advantage could never have been exploited unless a strong movement of amalgamation and even State action to suppress new competition had led to a thorough concentration of works within the districts and from that to the wider combination among the districts themselves through their respective monopolist organisations. So in fact it is again the increasing size of the industrial and commercial unit which has been of dominating influence.

One of the leading pre-War domains of German extractive industry, which since 1918 has very much diminished in importance, is that of iron-ore mining. In 1913 the Reich produced as much as 40 million tons of iron ore, while in England mines were producing 16·2 million tons and in the U.S.A. about 63 million tons. By 1929 the German figure had dropped to 6·3 million tons and the increasing economic pressure since then has brought about another diminution of iron-ore mining results to 2·6 millions in 1931 and even 1·339 millions in 1932. This enormous decrease to an almost insignificant figure has mainly to be attributed to the fact that Germany lost by the Treaty of Versailles the most important of its iron-ore mines, i.e. those of the Alsace and Lorraine area, called minette ores, on the utilisation of which the German iron and steel industry was mainly dependent. To-day the Ilsede district, the Lahn and Dill district, and the Siegerland are the main sources of German inland supply of iron ores. Certainly it must be borne in mind that the loss of the "iron-ore" provinces will not alone account for the shrinking of production, for France produced in 1932 only about 6 million tons more than in 1913, although the whole of the Alsace-Lorraine ore territory has passed into her hands. But the principal cause of the enormous drop of German production has certainly been the territorial changes since the end of the War.

The German iron-ore problem and its history have been a very prominent factor in the building up of the monopolist structure of the iron and steel industry, while in England the iron-ore supply has never played any rôle in the framing of industrial combination. Indeed, there is a fundamental difference in the organisation of the iron and steel industry of both countries resulting from the very different aspect of the ore problems. English iron and steel producers have for a very long time used more foreign than national ores, a fact partly due to the easy access and the highly developed shipping facilities which this country offered to the imports of ore from Spain and Sweden, partly to the necessity of importing high grade (haematite) ores to be used by the Bessemer and Siemens-Martin acid processes. Under these circumstances the acquisition of iron-ore mines by furnaces or steel mills was never considered as a necessary move to evade a monopoly of raw material. If Mr Fitzgerald points out in his valuable book on *Industrial Combination in England* that "the change in England has come about much later" and if the Survey of Metal Trades of 1928 points to the fact, that it is estimated that pig-iron manufacturers in England control their ore supply in this country or abroad to the extent of about 72%, it must not be forgotten that combination of that kind was certainly more due to purely economic considerations than to any idea of acquiring ore properties with the intention of ousting others from the cheapest sources of supply and of forming a monopoly. There is a marked difference between an iron industry producing about 50 % of its pig iron from foreign ores and furnaces relying for their main supply on home-mined ores from certain geographically concentrated inland districts, as was the case with the German supply from Alsace, Lorraine and Luxemburg. This situation, almost like that in the coal industry, produced quite different results as regards industrial combination and monopolist tendencies than would have been the case, if German iron and steel manufacturers had relied for a large percentage of their ores on imports from distant countries.

The German iron and steel manufacturers, by adopting the Thomas process at an early stage, in contrast to their English colleagues who adhered to the making of acid steel, have raised the neglected high-phosphoric iron-ore reserves of the Western European districts to a great importance. The greatest concentration of the iron and steel industry in the Ruhr district was based before the War upon the smelting with local coal of the so-called "minette", the situation resembling to some extent the geographical situation of Lake Superior ores in the U.S.A. shipped to the furnaces of the Pittsburg iron district. But besides the Rhine and Ruhr the big iron and steel works in the Saar territory, in Lorraine and Luxemburg, owe their existence to the developing of these iron ores. In Lorraine and Luxemburg the production of pig iron rose, the 1880 figure giving 100, to 1267 and 977 in 1913, the production of raw steel to 1339 and

5751, while in the whole Customs Union of the Reich the figures were only 707 and 966. But the special significance of this rise of the West and South German production of iron and steel with regard to the question of ore supplies lies in still another fact. A very pronounced division of labour had been developing between the then German western and south-western steel works and others existing in Reich territory. The western works were concentrating their activity on the production of "Massen-material", that is the cheap qualities most in use, produced by the Thomas process. For this purpose the Lorraine-Luxem-burg iron ores were the most suitable basis. Therefore the manufacture of semi-finished products on a large scale suited these concerns, especially as their location was well adapted to the shipping of iron and steel abroad. The highly finished kinds of goods in the German iron and steel industries were mostly produced in the Ruhr district. This was due partly to technical considerations, partly to the existence of traditionally trained workmanship, while the generally higher costs of freight in bringing the ore to the coal or coke were compensated by the fact that the highly finished products required relatively more fuel, while the ores transported to the Ruhr from the western districts represented the return freight of the coke needed by the Lorraine-Luxemburg iron and steel works. Moreover, most of the western and south-western works erected by German or foreign firms had by that time, for reasons of finance as well as through personal circumstances, become the property of the great Rhenish undertakings, and the works in the different localities had since then been more or less linked up by common interests in organisation and in the disposal of their produce. The natural geographical connection between the western iron-ore districts on the one side, and the coal fields and traditional iron and steel manufactures of the Ruhr-Rhine district on the other, had led to an organic interdependency of both interests, which was characterised by a growing and finally almost com-plete vertical combination of all important works. After the War and by the territorial enactments of Versailles these organic relations were suddenly interrupted. By the loss of their iron-ore properties, which had formed the basis of their profitable

management, the organisation of big iron and steel works under-
went considerable changes. Besides, the first years after the
peace brought severe political repercussions, the inflation period
was most detrimental to the import of foreign ores and the
temporary scarcity of coal and coke meant an increasing necessity of relying on high grade ores. These circumstances were
partly mitigated by the Franco-German trade agreement of 1924,
but the conditions of the 1919–1924 period left their mark on the
structural organisation of the ore supply. The proportional use
of inland mined ores doubled itself in comparison with pre-War
times and only by 1928 receded to its former level. From the
time of the restoration of normal commercial conditions and
relations the imports of foreign ores increased heavily. The
imports of iron ores from Sweden had risen from 4·6 millions in
1913 to 7·4 millions in 1929, but the new economic depression
since that year brought the whole imports of foreign ores down
to 3·4 million tons in 1932, of which Sweden supplied 1·6
million tons. The German iron and steel industry being to-day
largely dependent on the import of foreign ores there has been a
growing tendency for the iron works to move from the original
"Ruhr" district to the border of the Rhine in order to get an
easier access to the river and the canals, and to profit by the
facilities for cheaper water transport. This tendency also applies
to other districts. The Dortmunder Union, the Hoesch steel
works and the Hörder Verein are linked up with water transport
by the Dortmund-Ems Canal, the Rhine-Herne Canal is doing
the same for the Schalker Verein, and Krupp and Mannesmann
have sought for their new works locations situated near rivers or
canals. This movement is all the more important since the
minette ores, formerly conveyed by rail, are now shipped by
water, making use of the newly developed Rhine port at Strass-
burg. In general, however, the French interests are much more
directed towards an increasing export of pig iron than that of the
raw material, although it will be hardly possible for France to
renounce the profitable shipping of iron ore to Germany.
Although the Rhine route has been a means of cheapening
the supply of iron ores to the German iron and steel industries,
there is no doubt that the Rhenish-Westphalian works compare

disadvantageously in the matter of freight with their foreign competitors, especially in England. Even where the English iron works draw their ore supplies from inland sources the freight charge from mine to furnace is very low. The Cleveland iron ores have to be transported about 40 kilometres to reach their destination; the relatively few ores which the Rhineland may derive from near mining districts, the Siegerland and the Lahn-Dill district, have to be carried about 150 to 250 kilometres to the furnaces. For the same reason the iron and steel industries of Lorraine, of Belgium and Luxemburg, are to-day enjoying considerable advantages over their German competitors.

From all that has been said about the German iron-ore supply in the past and at the present time, it will be understood that post-War developments have had a decisive influence on monopolist organisation in that group of industry. The monopolisation of iron-ore mines by the big concerns had been going on on exactly the same lines as in the coal trade, as in fact the concentration of the minette ores in Lorraine and Luxemburg (which before the Treaty of Versailles belonged to the German Customs Union) offered the same facilities to monopolisation as that of the coal fields in the Ruhr district. Yet, as iron ore was solely used in German industry, and owing to its special qualities, neither having an outlet abroad, nor being used, like coal, for other than smelting purposes, syndicates, though they existed, have never played anything like such a distinctive rôle as they did in the coal mining or the coke industry. It is a vertical combination with the steel industry, the big undertakings acquiring iron-ore mines sufficient to meet their demand, which has led to a strong concentrative movement in the iron-ore mining industry. While the Treaty of Versailles, as we have explained, has interrupted this combination as regards the iron-ore mines which lie to-day in non-German territories, the mines in the remaining iron-ore districts of Germany belong exclusively to the big iron and steel undertakings. The economic condition of these iron-ore districts has been for a long time in a very depressed state. "Without the big iron works on the Ruhr and the Rhein", so writes Dr Hans J. Schneider in his elaborate description of the reconstruction of the German iron and steel industry, "these districts of iron-ore mining would long since have ceased to exist...they are in a true sense emergency districts." The big iron and steel concerns have sunk a fair amount of capital in these mining properties, being led not only by the desire for economic combination of works, but also by a regard for the preservation of these mining resources as the last remaining to the Reich after the War. On the other hand the Reich has been assisting the management of these mines by according temporary subventions (Erzförderungssubvention) and by granting special reduced freight to the Siegerland and other districts.

The important part which the iron-ore problem has played in the framework of German industrial organisation belongs to history. The necessity of acquiring ore mines to avoid mono-polisation and to derive the benefit of combination has not led here to an antagonism between cartels and giant firms, as in the coal mining industry. Yet the concentration movement in the iron-ore mining industry of the former German territories has been a very important factor in the development of industrial combination in the German iron and steel industries, as it has been largely responsible for the early rise of huge combined undertakings.

CHAPTER IV

# THE IRON AND STEEL INDUSTRY

ALTHOUGH seriously affected by loss of territory and post-War political events, the development of the iron and steel industries of the Reich has not been discouraging. This can be proved by a comparison of the output of iron and steel with that of other countries:

|  | In millions of tons Pig iron | | | Steel | | |
|---|---|---|---|---|---|---|
|  | 1913 | 1929 | 1933[1] | 1913 | 1929 | 1933[1] |
| United Kingdom | 10·26 | 7·59 | 4·12 | 7·66 | 9·64 | 7·00 |
| Germany[2] | 10·73 | 13·19 | 5·18 | 11·99 | 15·99 | 7·44 |
| France[2] | 8·93 | 10·20 | 6·21 | 6·86 | 9·55 | 6·40 |
| U.S.A. | 30·97 | 42·61 | 31·75 | 31·30 | 56·43 | 23·57 |

The circumstances which led to the remarkable development of German iron and steel figures up to 1929 are due to the effort to regain the advantages lost by the circumstances mentioned in the foregoing chapter. The very disastrous loss of iron-ore properties in the minette district was partly met by the importation of foreign ores and by an increased use of scrap (up to 1924), partly by the cheapening of transport facilities through a transference of works to the most economic shipping points, partly by a movement of combination on a much larger scale than before resulting in a reduction of general costs, partly by the introduction of elaborate systems of research and the introduction of a good many technical improvements, better fuel economy and rationalised production. Indeed the period in question might be described as one of "compulsory reconstruction" of the whole German iron and steel industry. A rather decisive change came about in January 1925, when the "free import" quotas, to which the Reich had been forced by the Treaty of Versailles, came to an end, and the import duties were fully restored, while quota arrangements were entered into between the Governments of Germany, France and Luxemburg regarding

[1] Estimate.　　　　[2] Present territory.

the importation of iron and steel from Lorraine, the Saar district (which was included in the French Customs Union area as from 10 January 1925) and Luxemburg. Moreover the conclusion of the Dawes agreement had attracted foreign capital to German industries, of which the iron and steel industries did not have the least share. Other capital to be invested in iron and steel works came from the money compensations accorded to undertakings for their losses of property in the former German provinces, as such funds had to be reinvested in works within the Reich territory. Those iron and steel companies too, which before had no works outside the lost territory, were getting compensation on condition that all such capital had to be invested in the building up of new iron and steel works within the remaining borders of the Reich. All these circumstances led to the result that in spite of her very heavy losses the German iron and steel industry was able to regain her pre-War position almost within ten years, a development which, as regards the actual output of iron and steel (not the productive capacity), was only interrupted by the new pressure of general economic conditions since 1929.

A large amount of this remarkable success in the reconstruction of an industry, which had suffered more than others by the post-War rupture of its traditional and organic economic connections, was certainly due to the concentrative organisation, which had been developing long before the War and its fatal consequences to the German iron and steel works. The same kind of natural territorial concentration, which we have been describing in the coal mining industry and its concentrative organisation, was characteristic of the iron and steel industry of the Empire. In fact the two main and dominant centres lay here also in the Rhenish-Westphalian district on the one hand and the Upper-Silesian on the other. This concentration has increased even more since the end of the War, under the territorial decisions of the peace treaties.

According to the Census of Occupation of 1925 not less than 62 % of all persons employed in the heavy iron industry belonged to the Rhenish-Westphalian district. In 1927 the pig iron furnaces of that district produced not less than 79 % of the whole German pig-iron production, the figure being even 82 % in 1929. The respective figures for the production of steel in that district were 79·5 and 81·1 % of the whole German production. The remaining percentage is split up among many secondary districts, so as to give a still larger predominance to the Rhenish-Westphalian iron and steel works, which in fact are to-day the whole domain of the German iron and steel trade. While Rheinland-Westphalen produced in 1929 more than 13 million tons of raw steel, the North, East and Middle German districts together produced not more than 1,300,000, the output of the Silesian works having dwindled down to only 536,000.

We have pointed out in the foregoing chapter one of the main causes of this concentration. It was due to the favourable location of the industry as regards coal and, formerly, iron ore, and to the excellent shipping and freight facilities. In fact, the Rhenish-Westphalian iron industry, compared with that of other districts, was for a long time characterised by the domination of the "combined" works in contrast to the so-called "reine" Werke, "pure" works. This applies to the making of pig iron as well as to the steel-rolling mills. It has been estimated that 90 % of the pig iron produced in that territory comes from furnaces belonging to undertakings which possess steel-rolling mills of their own; in that district only 10 % of the production consists of foundry or haematite pig iron. In the other mining districts—much less important ones, as was shown above—things are different. In the Siegerland, the Lahn-Dill-Revier, in Silesia and other districts, the production of these kinds of iron amounts to 30–40 % of the whole production of pig iron, although of course as regards absolute figures the Rhein-Ruhr production leads in these kinds of pig iron too. But the Rhenish-Westphalian furnaces producing pig iron of the general sort supply a good deal of this to the steel mills of the other districts.

The importance of such territorial or "local" concentration of industry cannot be overrated. It is quite evident that it has led to a community and thereby to the unification of interests. Here again things are different in British industry. In England the production of pig iron according to official statements in 1927 was distributed among a great number of districts, the North-east Coast district having the lead with 2·2 million tons out of 7·2 millions, but "Lincolnshire and Leicestershire", the "Yorkshire, Derbyshire and Nottinghamshire" district, "South Wales and Monmouthshire", "Scotland", the "Lancashire and North-Wales" district each sharing the whole production with only 500,000 to 900,000 tons each. The same applies to the production of English steel works producing ingots and castings, and to the British iron and steel industry in general. The similarity of conditions in the great centre of the German iron and steel industry was a very important cause of an early development of combination and amalgamation in industry. As the most favourable location for iron and steel making was to be found in a few districts, the works in these districts—in Rheinland-Westphalen as well as in Upper Silesia, which owing to its remoteness had market conditions of its own, and later in Lorraine-Luxemburg—had a very pronounced interest in securing and safeguarding for themselves the conditions and opportunities on which the successful working of the iron and steel making in these locations depended. This led very early on to the desire on the part of these works to make themselves secure from the dangers of monopolies latent in the supply of coal, iron ore and chalk-stone, by combining their undertakings with a supply of raw material of their own. One may argue that the economies to be effected by such combination, especially the cheapening of the supply of raw material by freeing the furnaces from market buying, might have been a sufficient inducement to get into vertical combination even without the menace of the monopolisation of coal and iron ore. The recent English example would justify such an argument. But it must be remembered that at the beginning of the movement—besides some rather unlucky experiments in moving the industry to the coast in order to enjoy the opportunity of buying imported non-monopolised raw material (Hochofenwerk Lübeck)—one urgent reason for the acquisition of coal mines and ore properties by iron and steel works was the growing power of cartels and syndicates in the extractive branches, on which furnaces and steel works depended. This certainly does not preclude the fact that aims mainly directed towards greater economy and more rational collaboration of the interdependent technical units were an important factor in the considerations leading to the vertical combination of works. As the Enqueteausschuss on the German iron and steel industry (1930) pointed out with great emphasis, the improvement of fuel economy has been largely brought about by such combination; for instance an iron furnace combined with a coking plant enjoys the advantage of cheaper as well as a better handled quality of coke, while the coking gases may be replaced by the less valuable waste gases of the iron furnaces and thereby may become free for use in other directions (this "exchange" of gases plays an important part in modern fuel economy).[1] All these circumstances will have to be carefully borne in mind in enumerating the considerations which led to vertical combination but it must be remembered that technical and organisational advantages of this kind—as also the combination of iron and steel works with the production of electric energy[2]—are of a much

---

[1] The importance of these results of fuel economy on the organisation of the iron and steel industry is fully recognised by the English Survey on Metal Trades (Committee on Industry and Trade), 1928. The Report says on page 8: "The new methods of fuel economy meant that, in order to carry on production with the lowest consumption of fuel and with the greatest efficiency, it was as a rule desirable to concentrate coking ovens, blast furnaces, steel works and rolling mills all on one site, so that waste gases from the former might be available for use in connection with the two latter, and the hot metal from the blast furnace could be converted into steel and then rolled without being allowed to get cold". The Report stated on the other hand on page 25 that "in the efficiency of its coking plant and in the organisation of the coking industry Great Britain still undoubtedly lags behind the United States and the Continent of Europe". The Report gives a very careful explanation of this difference, noting for instance the influence of currency inflation in Germany as stimulating capital outlay and the replacement after the War of destroyed coke ovens in France and Belgium by those of the most modern type. But there should be no doubt that the early recognition of vertical combination in Germany has greatly favoured the improvement and the organisation of the coking industry in that country.

[2] The improvement in fuel economy has been greatly assisted by an institution called the "Wärmestelle", which was established in 1919 by the Verein Deutscher Hütteneisenleute. The Wärmestelle does not itself undertake research to any great extent, but acts as a centre for co-ordination and propaganda in the interests of fuel economy. Recording and measuring apparatus is installed at all important points in the works, with a view to keeping close check on fuel consumption in each process, and to detecting the cause of any wastage. Fuel control on these lines is now practically universal in the German iron and steel industries. An interesting description was given by the Enqueteausschuss on the German Iron Industry, 1930, pp. 151 ff., pp. 25–27 and passim.

later date than vertical combination in Germany. The movement towards vertical combination and the formation of "mixed" undertakings for the reasons mentioned may rightly be taken as a very important factor in the post-War development of the iron and steel industry, but the beginning of this tendency has to be traced to a period when other considerations were at work. It was certainly the apprehensions with regard to the monopolisation of raw materials by cartels and syndicates which at first led to the policy of combining in one undertaking the preliminary stages of production with the finishing industries.

It was between 1895 and 1899 that the first period of this development set in. It was fully described at an early date by Hans Gideon Heymann in his study on the *Gemischten Werke in der deutschen Grosseisen Industrie* (1904). In those days the "pure" works in the finishing lines began to suffer heavily under the then existing difficulty of securing an adequate and economic supply of raw materials and eagerly sought to acquire works of the preliminary processes. In those days, industries which had never had any connection with coal were getting hold of collieries, in order to free themselves from the "open" market and its cartelisation. This was the case in the chemical and sugar industries. As regards the iron and steel industry the process of vertical combination was penetrating into the highly finished stages of production. Engineering firms, wire works, etc., were acquiring collieries and furnaces. Even the biggest German locomotive works of Henschel in Cassel got possession of a coal mine and a furnace. An early example of vertical combination in the finishing and high-class production was that of the Friedrich Krupp A.G., in Essen. In 1913–14 this firm was producing 833,970 tons of rolled products; it had its own steel works, producing 1,593,608 tons, pig iron produced by its own furnaces to an extent of 1,285,172 tons, coke plants producing 1,307,366 tons and iron ore and coal mines with a production of 1,064,055 and 7,599,234 tons.

The movement towards vertical combination which started in the firms interested in the finishing lines reacted promptly on the big "pure" mining concerns. These undertakings were losing to a certain extent their best and largest customers. It was only natural that the remedy they sought was to get into vertical combination by acquiring iron and steel works or at any rate by seeking to combine themselves with existing mixed undertakings. These tendencies bore a very striking likeness to the changes and struggles preceding the formation of the United States' Steel Corporation. In the early days of monopoly formation in the steel industry of the United States the tendency for vertical combination started from the acquisition, by the iron furnaces and rolling mills, of control over iron and coal mines, and then reacted on the producers of raw material, who became afraid of losing their best customers by this very development and became anxious to counteract this new condition by combining extractive industries with finishing works. Thus from the one movement towards vertical combination another one was developing. While the furnaces and steel works which had acquired ore and coal properties had been described as Hüttenzechen (colliery-furnaces), the mines which combined their business with that of furnaces were soon called Zechenhütten (furnace-collieries). To-day only the Harpener Bergbaugesellschaft can be cited as a really "pure" colliery concern. This great undertaking situated in Dortmund and representing a share capital of as much as 90 million marks ordinary and 300,000 marks preferred shares, with a quota of 6·63 % in the coal syndicate, is in fact the only dominant pure mining undertaking of the Ruhr district. It produced over 8 million tons of coal in 1929 and 4·6 million in 1932, besides about 2 million tons of coke in 1929 and 944,000 tons in 1932. It represents one of the most up-to-date coal-mining enterprises of the Reich, being equipped with the latest technical appliances, possessing very modern works for the production of by-products and being financially affiliated by partnerships to undertakings like the Ruhrchemie A.G. and the Ruhrgas A.G. of Essen. It is said that the satisfactory working of this company even in the recent unfavourable times was due to the very effective rationalisation carried out in its works.

However, the Harpener type of "pure" colliery is quite exceptional to-day and stands in direct contrast to the general structure of the industry dependent on coal and iron ore, or of collieries dependent on the sale of their produce to iron and steel companies. By far the most important prototype of the big "mixed" undertaking, indeed the beginning of the trust type within the German steel industry, is represented by the "Vereinigte Stahlwerke A.G." of Düsseldorf. This giant undertaking was founded in 1926 under the pressure of a very heavy crisis in the iron and steel trade; by the end of 1933 its organisation had been subjected to very important changes, which will be sketched in a later chapter, as in fact these changes, though of great importance to the structural shape of the concern, do not affect the aims of its primary and initial development, which found expression in the desire to form a vertical combination of giant dimension.

The "Stahlverein", as the Ver. Stahlwerke are generally called, represents a fusion of the following very important German mining, iron and steel companies:

Deutsch-Luxemburgische Bergwerksgesellschaft A.G.
Gelsenkirchner Bergwerks A.G.
Bochumer Verein für Bergbau und Gussstahl-Fabrikation.
Phoenix A.G. für Bergbau und Hüttenbetrieb.
Rheinische Stahlwerke A.G.
Thyssen Hüttenwerke in Hamborn.

To these were added at a later date the most valuable parts of the Stumm and Rombacher concerns, also the Charlottenhütte in Lower Silesia and a number of smaller works. All these undertakings had of course their own history of horizontal or vertical combination, which can be followed up in many of the earlier descriptions of the cartel movement in Germany. The position of the new concern can best be judged by the different participations of the Stahlverein in cartels and syndicates shortly after the before-mentioned additions to its original status had been effected. The production of the Stahlverein ranged from 35 to 55 % of the syndicated German output. The Stahlverein's part in the pig-iron syndicate was as high as 48.47 % of its production, in semis it ran up to 56·44 %, in structural steel (Oberbaumaterial) to 55·77 %, in hoop iron to 48·59 %, in thick plates to 47·13 %, in bar iron to 41·94 %, in coal to 35·84 %, in tubes to about 50 % according to the prospectus, in wire rods to

38·75 %, all these figures relating to the percentage of the Stahlverein in the production of the different cartels or associations. On the other hand the Stahlverein's policy has been to concentrate on the iron and steel production and to part with the further finishing lines as for instance engineering. A new concern, the Deutsche Maschinenfabrik A.G. (Demag), was formed with a capital of 30 million marks, the Stahlverein merging its Thyssen engineering works into the new company, which was based upon a reconstruction of a big existing undertaking.

According to the latest available figures, the position of the Stahlverein as regards its productive powers is remarkable. It owns 13,400 ha. of land (one ha. equal to 0·45 acre), of which 2900 ha. consist of industrial sites, and 58,314 dwellings connected with the works (Werkswohnungen). Its coal fields represent a reserve of approximately 5300 million tons, its ore fields a reserve of about 560 million tons. Its yearly capacity of coal production amounts to 36 million tons. It owns 19 cokery plants with 2790 coke ovens and a productive capacity of 10 million tons a year. In the blast furnace group it embraces nine blast furnace works with 52 furnaces and a productive capacity of 9·7 million tons a year. It owns 27 steel works with a productivity of 9·25 million tons a year. The Stahlverein also possesses the most up-to-date plants in the finishing branches of the steel industry, among them bridge-building factories, ship-building works, wire works and others. The railway tracks owned by the Stahlverein amount to 1300 kilometres, the waggon park to about 11,500 and 421 locomotives. The company has besides at its disposal 14 ports, partly owned and partly rented, with 78 cranes. It further possesses 209 power stations (Kraftzentralen) with an efficiency of about 481,000 kw. As regards the steel producing capacity of the Stahlverein of about 10 million tons it may be useful to compare this with an English figure; the Report on Metal Industries stated that in 1926 the twelve largest groups of companies (enumerated in the Appendix of that Report) representing the principal English producers of heavy iron and steel were capable of producing 7·2 million tons of steel yearly. The much larger concentration of the iron and steel industry in Germany thus becomes evident.

The status of this organisational concentration cannot, however, be fully appreciated unless due regard is paid to the network of financial connections linking up the Stahlverein—and similarly giant German concerns in other groups of German industry— with important industrial undertakings of all kinds. The Enqueteausschuss laid great stress on this point. We read in this Report: "A statistical description of company concentration ought not to overlook the fact that amalgamation is reinforced by the linking up of several independent undertakings through a rather tight network of financial relations; such combination, while leaving formal independence to the single undertakings, brings them into the field of bigger groups of interest. The following example may be cited: the biggest iron-producing undertaking of Germany, the Vereinigte Stahlwerke A.G. is the greatest shareholder in the Mitteldeutsche Stahlwerke A.G., which controls by far the greatest number of steel works and rolling plant in Middle Germany. At the same time the Mitteldeutsche Stahlwerke owns on its part the majority of the shares of the Vereinigte Oberschlesische Hütten A.G., i.e. of the company in which the main works of another great centre of production have been concentrated. While statistically the three great undertakings, which were themselves the result of former amalgamations, are more or less independent of each other, they are grouped *de facto* by personal relations and organisational connections into one compact whole, allowing a division of labour". Besides the before-mentioned steel works in Middle Germany the most important participations of the Stahlverein relate to the Essener Steinkohlenbergwerke A.G. in Essen (it is intended to get rid of this participation in the near future), the Demag (engineering), the Ruhrgas A.G., the Ruhrchemie A.G., the Gesellschaft für Teerverwertung (a company dealing with the utilisation of tar) and the Austrian Alpine Montan Gesellschaft. The organisational structure of the German iron and steel industry under the influence of industrial combination and in regard to its nascent trustification will have to be discussed in a later chapter. The development as described here has sufficiently demonstrated the important rôle which vertical combination, started first under the pressure of monopolistic apprehensions and completed later on by economic, technical and organisational considerations, has played in the history of industrial combination in the iron and steel industry of the Reich.

But horizontal combination of units and cartelisation was also an early characteristic of the German iron and steel industry. It can easily be understood that in the German iron industry, which started so much later than the British, the technical unit was never so much split up as in the English iron and steel manufacture with its much longer tradition. It is much more convenient to start a factory on "modern" lines, that is in our days on a "big" scale, than to adapt old-fashioned and smaller works to the growing size of the technical or commercial unit. At the end of 1913 there were in the Reich 313 pig-iron furnaces in blast, the production of pig iron being then 16·7 million tons; in 1930 the production of pig iron amounted to only 9·6 million tons, but there were not more than 107 furnaces working and the number of existing furnaces had been reduced from 330 in 1913 to 158. In England the pig iron produced in 1927 amounted to $7\frac{1}{2}$ million tons, but the number of furnaces amounted to not less than 437! "A number of new blast furnaces of large capacity have been built", so stated the Report on Metal Industries in 1928, "but there are still many small furnaces in existence with a capacity far below that which is found most efficient from the point of view of quantity of output in modern practice...." In 1925 the output of pig iron per furnace in blast was on the average 138,000 tons a year in the U.S.A., 96,900 in Germany and not more than 41,354 in England.[1]

The relatively small number of furnaces and commercial units in the German iron industry prepared the way towards cartelisation in quite a different way from that in the English iron industry and the same held true for the steel manufacture. Here also technical progress on the one side and the diminution of undertakings by vertical combination on the other had led to

[1] According to the Enqueteausschuss, *Die deutsche Eisenerzeugende Industrie*, 1930, pp. 36–37, the English steel furnaces were producing in 1927 about 15,000 tons per furnace in the year, in contrast to 27,000 tons in Germany.

a gradual but drastic reduction of commercial units; as regards the latter point it is evident that the desire to combine vertically on a large scale was leading by itself to the buying up of a good many smaller works in order to get the supply of raw material or semi-finished products on a sufficiently large scale to comply with the demand of huge finishing works. While on the one hand cartelisation, largely assisted by horizontal combination, had been an important though indirect impetus to vertical combination, vertical combination on the other hand developed the tendency to enlarge the sphere of horizontally combined undertakings.

At any rate the rapidly growing size of the unit and the constant diminution of single undertakings was the dominant factor responsible for the formation of cartels and syndicates in the iron and steel industry. But another factor must not be forgotten. The German iron industry has enjoyed tariff protection uninterruptedly from 1879 to the present time. The tariff first granted in the 'seventies, after a short period of free trade tendencies, as a measure to protect an "infant industry" (as in fact the introduction of the Thomas process and the development of the utilisation of "minette" seemed at first to be a rather risky experiment), has become an unshakable element of German tariffs. The duties on iron and steel would have been ineffective if competition among the producing companies within the Reich had brought prices down below the level of "world market prices plus duty and freight". The only way to avoid this was to fix prices through the medium of cartels, syndicates or conventions. Thus the desire to make the utmost out of the protection afforded by the State, instead of losing its "benefit" by over-competition, became a very strong stimulus to the formation of industrial combination. It will be understood that industrial associations have by no means been able to maintain permanently the highest possible level of prices, i.e. the world market price plus duty and freight. But this fact does not dispose of the argument that prices would certainly have developed at times in a very different way if the policy of effective syndicates had not prevented their "free" play. Schneider gives the following figures concerning the level of bar-iron prices in the last few years:

| Year | German price R.M. per ton | Belgian price R.M. per ton | German duty R.M. per ton | German price (+) higher (−) lower than Belgian price + duty |
|------|------|------|------|------|
| 1924 | 128·08 | 122·92 | 25 | − 19·84 |
| 1925 | 129·33 | 113·47 | 25 | −  9·14 |
| 1926 | 129·80 | 104·78 | 25 | +  0·02 |
| 1927 | 131·00 |  98·88 | 25 | +  7·12 |
| 1928 | 135·46 | 112·15 | 25 | −  1·69 |
| 1929 | 138·00 | 120·59 | 25 | −  7·59 |
| 1930 | 137·33 | 111·17 | 25 | +  1·16 |

The figures, which will not be scrutinised here from the point of view of cartelistic price "policy", evidently show that the German price, though subject to considerable fluctuation, has been oscillating around the level accorded by tariff protection, sometimes even advancing above the world market price plus German duty. The same has been the case in other branches of the iron and steel industry. As regards pig iron the price of haematite pig iron from the Rhenish-Westphalian district has been since 1925 considerably higher than the English price for East Coast haematite (Middlesbrough) plus German duty; in March 1930 the price was 91 R.M. per ton in Oberhausen, while it was 77·16 R.M. in England. The duty being 10 R.M. per ton the larger difference is accounted for by the freight charge to be added to the price of the syndicate (Verbandspreis). According to the Enqueteausschuss and under the assumption that the transport radius would amount to 100 km. on the average the freight to be added to the "Verbandspreis" would run to about 5·30 R.M. per ton.

There can be no doubt that cartels and syndicates, however their price policy may be judged or criticised, have been the means of raising prices to the level conceded by the grant of tariff protection and that it has been one of the avowed objects of cartelisation and syndicates to bring this about. Neither can there be any doubt that in this sense the tariff has been a stimulus to cartelisation, although this must by no means be considered as one of its chief causes. The most important cartels in the German iron and steel industry are to-day: the pig-iron association, the Roheisenverband; the syndicate regulating the output of unmanufactured steel, the Rohstahlgemeinschaft; the so-called "A"-Produktenverband, a cartel regulating the sales in the semi-finished and heavy groups, including semi-finished steel such as ingots, slabs, blooms and billets; railway materials such as rails, ties, fish-plates, bolts, spikes, bed-plates and structural steel, together with $T$, $U$, and $I$ beams more than 80 mm. face. Both steel syndicates are annexed to the Stahl-werksverband A.G. in Düsseldorf, an association, which also represents the commercial management of the Stabeisenverband (bar-iron syndicate), the thick plate, the Grobblechverband (syndicate) and the Bandeisenvereinigung (hoop iron association). Besides there are cartels in parts of the so-called "B"-product groups, which include rods, steel bands, barrel hoops, rolled wire, sheet metal, tubes, cast-steel railway axles, steel forgings, steel rollers, etc. Although in these groups there have been fairly efficient syndicates, such as the Tube Association and others, the cartelisation in the iron and steel trade is undoubtedly chiefly to be found in the stages of production from the raw material to the half-finished produce and the heavy material.

The Stahlwerksverband has for a long time been by far the most interesting and also the most important of all monopolist associations existing in the German iron and steel trade. The history of this combine also shows how far the formation of giant concerns within the cartel may lead to a serious conflict of interests between its members. Before the War the heavy branches of the industry had since 1904 been federated in the Stahlwerksverband, a union of steel producers, which con-trolled output and prices of the simpler kind of products, while within the Verband a strong tendency towards concentration of undertakings had manifested itself, marked, as we have seen, by special integration of businesses at successive stages of produc-tion. The conflicts within the cartel led to its lapse in 1919. For several years the industry was unregulated, at any rate in so far as steel and steel products were concerned. The factors we have mentioned above, as regards the increase of productive capacity on the one side and vertical combination on the other, resulted eventually in the absence of any pooling of interests, in an increase of production beyond the capacity of the market to absorb it and a consequent price war. After long discussions the

Rohstahlgemeinschaft was formed on 1 November 1924. It was agreed that this combination was to regulate output. Each firm belonging to the syndicate is registered as having a certain capacity of output. From time to time the syndicate as a whole agrees to restrict output by a given percentage, and every member has then to reduce his production in a similar proportion below its agreed capacity. The syndicate, however, does not regulate prices, nor is it in any sense a joint sales organisation; but all orders given to individual members have to be reported to the syndicate, which allocates them to a particular works, whether that of the firm which has received the order or another. The syndicate represents therefore, as Liefmann has put it, "eine blosse Angebotskontingentierung", an allocation of supplies federated with a "production cartel". Price fixing does not belong to the sphere of the syndicate. It is left to the special associations formed for various groups of the iron and steel industry, as for instance semis, wire products, wire rods, bar iron, plates, rails, tubes, etc. The Deutsche Rohstahlgemein-schaft, therefore, can be defined as a "frame" or "base" cartel. It may be mentioned that in the group of wire and wire products there were in 1930 alone 17 different syndicates. The general structure of industrial combination in the German iron and steel industry therefore presents the following picture:

(a) The Stahlwerksverband, being the managing roof organisa-tion for the sale of the various products subject to syndicated organisation.
(b) The Rohstahlgemeinschaft, being (to-day) an organisation production for controlling and allocating the $A$ as well as the $B$ products, in so far as they are cartelised.
(c) The various cartels federated to the Stahlwerksverband fixing the prices of their products, but restricted in their functions of production and distribution by (a) and (b).

By the end of 1929 the Rohstahlgemeinschaft was renewed and enlarged by the formation of new associations in certain branches. The various associations have been affiliated or federated to that main organisation by agreements lasting over a period of ten years, that is, up to the end of 1940. A very important and novel function has been added in the renewing of the Rohstahl-gemeinschaft in the form of the so-called "Gruppenschutz" (group protection). During the agreement mentioned above the manufacture of new products by the cartel-partners will not be allowed without the consent of a newly formed "Vertrauens-stelle", a sort of "trustee-board". This does not only apply for products syndicated or to be syndicated, but also for the manufacture of such products as might be allocated to one or to several firms for reasons of division of labour. This measure is intended to help in the direction of a further stabilisation of iron and steel production and to lessen the danger of overproduction.

Modern industrial combination in the German iron and steel trade is certainly very complex. If one had expected that the beginning of trustification in the industry by the formation and growing strength of the Stahlverein would have lessened the organisational task and aims of cartelisation and syndicates, this view will certainly be promptly refuted by the description we have given of the development of the latter. There is not yet an alternative between "trustification" and "cartelisation". Although within the sphere of industrial combination represented by both cartelisation and trustification the huge amalgamations of the last years may have attracted the greatest attention and interest, they have by no means lessened the importance of cartels and syndicates. Without doubt the formation of so big a merger as that of the Stahlverein has in some ways facilitated the task of cartels. In that respect it was very interesting to hear the evidence given by Herr Nothmann of the Tube Association before the Enqueteausschuss with regard to the effects of the Stahlverein on the cartel organisation of his branch. He declared: "The amalgamation of the Vereinigten Stahlwerke has greatly facilitated management within the tube syndicate. The manufacturing programme of four big works has been put together and the association was relieved of the necessity of deciding in each particular case, whether an order was better suited to the working of this or that works, which may have been expecting it. The Vereinigten Stahlwerke now undertake to distribute the orders among the amalgamated works, a task formerly belonging to the association. The concentration of the sales departments and warehouses of the four concerns has also greatly facilitated the distributive task of the association, as to-day not four separate firms in each district of the industry—that is a total of 16 of such firms—send in their orders, but only four in all. These orders being very large are much better adapted to the necessity of large and uniform specifications, which are wanted by the Association with regard to a more rational way of work, and therefore such orders may be passed on without going into an examination of the manufacturing programme".

It becomes evident from what the witness explained to the committee that the formation of the Stahlverein has not weakened the position of the tube cartel and may not weaken the position of others, as in fact the concentration of organisational power within the syndicates may be in line with cartelistic aims and even facilitate their realisation. No doubt, there may be cases and questions in regard to which the interests of syndicates and those of trustificated concerns within their membership may show considerable disagreement. But as regards the question of greater rationalisation and standardisation and other problems of economic and technical unification the interests of the cartels are certainly deriving advantage from the trust movement within their borders. The question how far trustification fits in with the aims and necessities of cartels and other associations will certainly depend very much on the number and diversity of the firms associated. If, as formerly in the coal and potash industries, a great number of rather small and weak undertakings belong to the combination, the interest of the big concerns in the cartel will greatly differ from that of such firms. This will sooner or later result in a very sharp and in the long run fatal struggle within the association. A strong movement towards concentration, as has been witnessed in the German steel industry in the last twelve years, will eventually not dispose of the necessity of mutual understanding by associations but rather strengthen their power.

### CHAPTER V

## THE CHEMICAL AND ALLIED INDUSTRIES

THE development of industrial combination in the chemical trade of Germany may be rightly considered as being in direct contrast to that of the groups of industry discussed in the former chapters. While coal and potash mining and other extractive industries as well as the manufacture of iron and steel were developing from a great number of very small commercial units, in comparison with those of our days, to gradually increasing undertakings and finally into huge concentrated concerns, modern chemical works were characterised from the beginning by relatively large-sized undertakings. This is not characteristic of Germany alone. A comparison, say, of English coal mining and textile or iron manufactures with the foremost chemical products, would give the same result, though of course the most important branches of the modern English chemical industries have developed much later than in Germany.

As early as in the 'nineties a very strong concentration of the leading manufacturing firms, especially in the branches of chemical dyes and pharmaceutical products, was to be found in the German chemical industries, mostly due to the fact that the manufacture was to a considerable extent based upon patents and that a great outlay of capital was needed for the manufacturing processes and continuous and costly research.

The nucleus of the most important undertakings in the industry were the:

Badische Anilin and Soda Fabrik in Ludwigshafen-Mannheim.
Elberfelder Farbenfabriken vorm. Bayer and Co.
Höchster Farbwerke verm. Meister, Lucius and Brüning.
Aktiengesellschaft für Anilinfabrikation (Berlin).

The form of combination characteristic of even the early development of the industry was that of "Interessengemeinschaften", communities of interest. The first of these was concluded between the Höchster works and Leopold Casella and Co. in October 1904, and only a month later there followed the much more important, but similar agreement between the Badische Anilin and the Elberfelder works, which was joined a few weeks later by the Aktiengesellschaft für Anilinfabrikation. This community of interests—agreed to for a period of 50 years —was based upon the principle of pooling profits, of declaring the same dividends and partly upon an exchange of shares. While up to 1916 the two groups "Badische Elberfelder, Aktiengesellschaft für Anilinfabrikation" and "Höchster Farben-Casella" were working independently of each other, in that year a new Interessengemeinschaft of the two dominant groups together with two outside companies was formed, also for a period of 50 years. In 1925, however, it was decided to substitute for this form of organisation a closer union. Retaining the old name, a trust was formed, "Interessengemeinschaft Farbenindustrie Aktiengesellschaft", which is usually called I.G. Farben. The capital in ordinary and preference shares was 646 million R.M. It amounts to-day to about 1000 million R.M. The process of formation was that one of the companies—the Badische Anilin and Sodafabrik A.G.—increased its capital and exchanges shares with the other companies.

The combination thus formed represents in fact not only the most important trustification in German industry, but indeed one of the most important trusts in the international economic sphere. German chemical industries still lead the international dye markets. Although since the War many traditional markets have been lost to the German dye industry by national programmes of production, yet in 1928 Germany produced 43·6 % of the total world output of coal-tar dyes, the U.S.A. 22·5 %, Great Britain 11·7 %, while the percentage of production in other countries, including Japan, was much less. Of the European production of dyes of 142,000 tons in that year, the German industry produced 85,000. Moreover, it must be taken into account that the German produce is on the average, and with the exception of Swiss makes, far more valuable than that of its foreign competitors, especially of those who have not been very long in the business. In 1928 the average value per kilo of coal-tar dyes exported amounted in R.M. to 4·86 as regards German exports, but only to 1·78 in England, 2·71 in France, 1·83 in the U.S.A. and 0·96 in Japan. Switzerland, however, was able to show a figure as high as 6·5 %, but her whole production amounted to only 11,000 tons or 5·6 % of the world's production. There are unfortunately very few figures showing the dominant position of the German chemical trust in German industry. According to a quotation of the Dresdner Bank, in the German synthetic dyestuff industry in 1927–28 about 100 % of the actual national production was controlled by the I.G. Farben, Imperial Chemical Industries, Ltd., controlled about 40 %, in France the Établissement Kuhlmann about 80 % of the national output. Of the production of synthetic nitrogen the German trust was responsible for about 85 % of the national output, while Imperial Chemical Industries controlled about 100 %, Établissement Kuhlmann about 30 %, the Montecatini trust in Italy about 60 %, and the E. J. Du Pont de Nemours concern in the U.S.A. a certainly dominant percentage of national production.

The name of I.G. Farben certainly no longer expresses the enormous field of activities covered by the huge German chemical combine. Indeed to-day the colour business does not even represent the most lucrative side of the concern. Here are some of the leading manufactures besides dyestuffs in which the trust is interested: nitrogen fertilisers, various acids, including oxalic and formic, pharmaceutical and photographic chemicals, films, film and tracing papers, artificial silk (viscose, acetate, cuprammonium), motor spirits (methyl alcohol, butyl alcohol and motalin), lubricating oils, volatile oils, and perfumes, aluminium, copper and electron ferro-alloys (molybdenum, wolfram), gypsum, zinc-white, artificial horn, synthetic resins, varnishes, artificial precious stones, tanning materials. The firms connected with these products are firstly those which have been associated to form the trust, i.e. the five above-mentioned concerns which were joined by a number of other rather important companies such as Kalle and Co. in Biebrich, Weiler ter Mer, the Griesheim chemical works, etc. The trust is also associated with a great many subsidiary concerns, which again show such a diversity of production that they may be divided into a number of separate groups according to their programme of manufacture. There are the following groups of subsidiary concerns:

1. Fertilisers and Agriculture.
2. Chemicals.
3. Electro-chemical and Metallurgical.
4. Coal, Brown Coal, Oil.
5. Artificial Silk and Textiles.
6. Special Gases.
7. Sundry products (chalk and enamelling works, wood-working factories, etc.).
8. Finance and Credit Institutions.

Considering this variety of products one is led to the conclusion that I.G. Farben represents in fact an industrial combination of not one, but of a number of products, although, of course, the combine has not in every one of the above-mentioned groups anything like a monopolistic position. But the fact remains, that in contrast for instance to the Stahlverein and other giant industrial combinations in German industries, the I.G. Farben is surrounded with a network of interests leading into branches, which at first may seem quite heterogeneous with respect to the nucleus of its primary production, such as rayon or liquid fuel or photography. In order to manage these diffused interests the trust has divided its products into five distinct groups: (1) dye-stuffs, (2) nitrogen and nitrogen products, (3) pharmaceutical and allied manufactures, (4) photographical production and rayon, (5) inorganic products and intermediate products. The many working plants of the trust have been geographically divided into four groups: those of the Oberrhein, those of the Mittelrhein, of Niederrhein and Middle Germany.

The development and basic conditions of the chemical trust give a very good illustration of the great diversity of factors which may ultimately lead to industrial combination. The structure of the chemical combine, which differs by its many and various outlets from the rather clear-cut construction of the Stahlverein, bears resemblance to other combinations only in having ultimately become a giant unit in the trade. But the circumstances which have led to this final position must be distinguished from those dominant in other groups of industry and must be investigated separately.

The strong position of the chemical combines, in their early days as in their latest development, is certainly due to a great extent to the importance of patents and special processes. This applies to the original aniline dyestuff industry as well as to the later developments of the pharmaceutical and photographical branches and the many chemical manufactures connected with the industry. The most important patents, however, and the developing of new processes, which were sometimes considered for many years as of merely "theoretical" interests, necessitated from the beginning of the industry two conditions which could hardly be found among smaller and financially weaker undertakings. The one was the building up of costly institutions of research, the other the disposal of great funds, necessary to support scientific work in laboratories and elsewhere, to finance the costly beginning and the sometimes slow progress of new processes and inventions and to compensate for the risk and the possible losses which might be incurred. It may be mentioned that the Leuna Werke, the great nitrogen plant near Merseburg, which in fact represents the largest unit of the trust and which forms the nucleus plant for the utilisation of the nitrogen fixation process (Haber-Bosch) and the manufacture of nitrogenous fertilisers (Leunaphos, Nitrophoska, etc.), is constituted as a limited company, of not less than 135 million R.M. of which the I.G. owns 101·25 millions and the Leopold Casella the remnant. No smaller firm would ever have been able to enter into the gigantic scheme of building up this new industry, which has resulted in the erection not only of new plants of a huge size in Leuna and Oppau (Baden) but in the creation of whole settlements and towns for the working population and the staff necessary for the development of the new branches of industry. Another factor connected with the financial requirements of the industry is to be found in the large outlay required for purposes of propaganda. This applies to a large degree particularly to the introduction of fertilisers which, though of the greatest possible efficiency, might be rejected or only slowly accepted by the farming communities, if not propagated by a very arduous and certainly costly work of enlightenment.

The outlay of capital, which has been and still is devoted to research work first by the former independent concerns and to-day by the trust, may be called generous. We may quote the words of praise of an English commercial secretary in Berlin, Mr C. J. Kavanagh: "This large chemical group has not been content to rest on its laurels in dyes alone, and has advanced rapidly to fresh conquests, for which, principally, they have to thank their foresight in encouraging the enlistment to their ranks of large numbers of technically trained chemists, and minutely directing their efforts to definite ends. In experimental work they have shown extraordinary patience and perseverance and have ever been ready to finance a line of investigation which, although holding no immediate prospect of results, was, nevertheless, sufficiently promising to return its due reward". Inasmuch as in recent years the chief interest has tended to move from the field of dyestuffs to that of nitrogen and fertilisers on the one hand and to that of the production of oils and fuels from coal and coke by the methods of liquefaction and synthesis on the other, one may say that the outlay of capital for the purpose of research and experimental work has reached still greater dimensions. The futility of competing with the big concerns in that respect has been further increased by the formation of the trust, as the I.G. Farben has considered it as one of its chief tasks to increase the efficiency of the many different branches of research federated with the originally separated undertakings, by a much closer degree of collaboration through central control and supervision. Needless to say that by the participation of the trust in coal, lignite and oil undertakings increasing benefits have been accruing to the scientific investigations in the sphere of synthetic fuels from coal and other research. As regards nitrogen fertilisers, large experimental grounds have been established with a view to investigating crop yields and the conditions most favourable to an intensification of harvests. The great outlay of capital required for the whole field of research would never have been found by small or even medium-sized undertakings. It was this financial condition which gave to the large undertakings a sort of immunity from smaller competitors and a monopolistic position wherever the costly experiments were crowned by success. On the other hand, the big chemical concerns of former days and the trust of to-day became, by this very circumstance of financial superiority, the first to be informed of all new inventions or discoveries outside their own laboratories, as inventors and discoverers regarded these companies as the most capable from a technical as well as a commercial point of view of exploiting new processes on a large scale. This "protection" from smaller competitors, however important as regards the foundations of its monopolist place in industry, has by no means saved the chemical combines from all competition. Actually in the last few years important competition has arisen as regards fertilisers from the increasing large-scale supply of synthetic nitrogen from coal mining companies. Big coal mining firms, partly in collaboration with potash works, have invaded the German nitrogen markets. But as competition among the "great" has generally been settled after some fight by common understanding, one may expect that arrangements will be made here as well, as regards the regulation of output, a nitrogen syndicate having been in existence for some time, fixing prices according to market requirements. Patents, however, and the heavy outlay of capital per technical unit, due to the special circumstances of the manufacture, are not the only causes responsible for the strong position of chemical concerns in the past and of the trust of to-day. The size of the commercial undertaking, as it is to-day represented by the I.G. Farben and its subsidiary concerns, is largely the result of combinations which cannot be called exactly "vertical", but yet represent a particular linking up of the primary and initial productions of the industry with other branches. The increasing demand on a large scale for certain raw materials, through the increasing size of chemical concerns, has led to the tendency to secure some private supply of such materials, as for instance coal. Certainly coal does not play the same rôle in the vertical structure of the chemical industry as it does in iron and steel. Yet it has become of increasing importance to the huge concerns and later to the trust. The result was the linking up of the trust with coal mining through getting a partnership of 44·9 % in the Rheinische Stahlwerke of Essen, which has a quota of about 4 million tons in the coal syndicate, and of 2½ million tons in the coke syndicate, and further, by getting into a close union with the Riebeck Montanwerke (lignite) in Halle (capital 50 million R.M.) and by acquiring a partnership of 91 % in the Gewerkschaft Auguste Victoria. Besides this, the I.G. Farben own a great number of collieries, producing coal and lignite, near Bitterfeld and also in the West of Germany. In 1933 the lignite production of I.G. Farben amounted to 16·4 million tons! But still more important seems the fact that another kind of combination in many different branches has been the direct outcome of new processes started by chemical industries and the research work connected with them. In fact, many new processes of manufacture have led to new industries, and it is only natural that the trust, being to a great extent responsible for their origin, has retained a dominant position in their present organisation. This is particularly the case with the nitrogen fertiliser industry, but it holds true as well of the connection of chemical concerns like the Agfa (Aktiengesellschaft für Anilinfabrikation) with the photographic groups of industry or the financial connection of the trust with the two leading German rayon concerns, that of the Vereinigte Glanzstoff in Elberfeld and of the I.P. Bemberg works. It is the particular development of the chemical research, of discoveries and inventions resulting from the work of chemistry and its personal leaders, such as Dr Bergius, Prof. Fischer, Prof. Bosch, Prof. Haber and many others, which has led to the result that the "dyestuff" trust has become a dominant concern in groups of industry, which may seem as heterogeneous as rayon textiles, photographical apparatus, petrol, fertilisers, or artificial precious stones. The amalgamation of the dominant English firms producing dyestuffs, explosives and alkali through the merger of the Dyestuffs Corporation, United Alkali, Brunner, Mond and Co. and Nobel Industries into Imperial Chemical Industries may suggest that a similar tendency prevails in the great chemical industries of other countries. But though doubtless a tendency to expansion of combines into many heterogeneous or distantly related branches of manufacture may be inherent in the structure of the chemical industries, the diversity of fields of activity presented by the German chemical trust has hardly a parallel in the world. As we shall see in a later chapter the outcome of so many technical conditions concentrated in one giant undertaking has led to a great many international connections of the I.G. Farben. In fact, the trust can be considered in many directions, technically and commercially, as representing a combine of an international character.

The existence of the chemical trust has not made cartelisation entirely unnecessary. The quasi-monopolist position of I.G. Farben finds its most important expression in making new competition more difficult and in rendering small-scale competition impossible, but this does not mean that other competition is non-existent in a good many branches. We have already mentioned the position of the trust in the synthetic nitrogen industry and the existence of "Stickstoffsyndikate". Another very important syndicate is the Verkaufsvereinigung für Teererzeugnisse in Essen. This very strong syndicate controls all the tar products of coke ovens and gas works and also the sales and exports of these products, e.g. tar, including prepared tar for road-making purposes, naphthalene (pure), anthracene (40 % pure), creosote for impregnating wood, etc., pitch, etc. All purchasers must obtain their supplies through the syndicate and not from individual members.

Essential as has been the formation of the I.G. Farben to the whole organisation of German chemical industry and trade— the importance of trustification with regard to rationalisation, etc., will be discussed in a later chapter—the commercial well-being of the industry cannot be expected to depend on that factor alone. The German chemical industry, in almost all its branches and especially in the field of synthetic dyestuffs, is largely dependent on the sales to foreign markets. New international developments after the War, the creation of the dye industry of Great Britain, the drastic reduction of dye imports by China, which had been one of the biggest overseas customers of the European producers, has not reacted favourably on the German export trade. Yet in 1928, which may be considered as the last "normal" year before the beginning of the period of aggravated international depression between 1929 and 1933, the Reich's share in the quantity of coal-tar colours exported by all nations was 52·7 %, which was equal to 63·8 % of the value of these exports.

### CHAPTER VI

# ELECTRICAL ENGINEERING AND ELECTRICITY

THE electrical industry, which may be divided into the two distinct groups of "electrical engineering" or "electrical manufacturing" (Elektrotechnische Industrie) comprising the manufacture of generators, motors and transformers, of electro-technical material, lamps, apparatus of all kinds, installation of electrical plant, production of accumulators, batteries, scientific instruments, etc., and "electricity" (Elektrizität) power works and electrification (electricity supply), presents in its organisation a picture very much like that of the chemical industry. It is a "new" industry like that of dyestuffs or other "modern" chemicals, it has been based and continuously expanded on the utilisation of patents, as for instance in the manufacture of lamps or later on in the development of the speaking film or the radio; it has been subjected from the beginning to the necessity of a great outlay of capital, especially as regards the installation of electric plant, electrification, and the carrying through of big public contracts; here as in the chemical industries new industries were evolving out of electro-technical progress and most naturally linked up with the initial and pioneering concerns of the industry. In particular the participation in the supply of electrical power, where private firms in many cases had to compete with public works, was bound to need a large outlay of capital. There was no room for small private enterprises; indeed, there is hardly one modern industry so dependent on large capital investment and financing on a large scale as the electric industries are. As to the supply of electric power, about half the costs are due to the writing off and the interest on capital and the same feature of "rigid" costs applies to the cost of labour and staff, while the outlay necessary for the supplies of fuel and material are relatively secondary. This also explains the necessity of big units in this industry, as it is well known that the increase in the size of the industrial unit has in general been largely dependent on the increase of fixed capital as compared with other less rigid items in the cost of production scale.

The German electrical industries have been the pioneers among their European competitors, and the progress of electricity and of electro-technical trade has been most pronounced in that country. It is estimated by the Dresdner Bank that in 1913 about 50 % of the world's trade in electro-technical products was represented by Germany, a percentage which fell to about 25 % by 1925 and rose again to about 29 % by 1928. Here as in the chemical trade the War and post-War events had led to the progress of electric industries in many other European countries, especially in England, France, Russia, Holland and Sweden. As to electricity, the production per head of population in kilowatt-hours in 1931 was 399 in Germany, 1100 in the Saar territory, 375 in Great Britain and 329 in France, while in Switzerland, Belgium and Sweden, owing to special circumstances, this figure was higher, though the absolute electric production was very much higher in the three first-named countries. Vast production, coupled with the circumstances already mentioned as favouring from its very beginning the large technical unit of industry, had led to an early concentration of the most important electrical undertakings. It is not our task here to give a detailed chronicle of this development which has been associated with the achievements of two names, that of the Siemens family, whose head had won the reputation of a scientific pioneer in electricity, and that of the Rathenaus, who became financially the most important exploiters of the new inventions. These names represent the two leading concerns still existing in electric engineering: the Siemens-Schuckert group on the one hand and the Allgemeine Elektricitäts Gesellschaft (founded by the Rathenaus), the A.E.G., on the other. A third concern, the Bergmann Elektrizitäts-Werke A.G. in Berlin, is controlled by both groups. It is said that the two groups controlled about 80 % of the whole industry before the War. The A.E.G. controls, besides its electrical plants, undertakings which owe their existence to the latest inventions such as the Klangfilm Gesellschaft in the sphere of

the talking film and Telefunken in that of radio, and in addition
both groups are federated with locomotive works, the A.E.G.
with the Borsig Locomotive works, the Siemens group with
Maffei-Schwartkopf. It has been frequently rumoured that a
fusion between the two groups was imminent, and this would
really mean an electro-trust of dominant proportions. But such
final fusion has not yet been effected, and as Liefmann suggests,
would never take the form of genuine amalgamation. He writes:

Even if the fusion were effected, which is not to be expected, the
relationship of the parent company to the factories in the finishing
lines or the suppliers of raw materials or to the manufacturers of
specialities such as lamps, motors, wire, telephone work, accumulators, as well as those to local electricity companies and lastly to
holding and financing companies would certainly retain the form of
a concern-company; it is just this diversity and the special features
of the electro-technical undertaking which have had the result that
the two big firms, though no longer the biggest (Liefmann is probably
alluding to the giant concerns in the "electricity" group of industry,
which, however, ought not to be mixed up with those of electrical
engineering and allied lines), are producing the most different kinds
of goods.

Moreover, some years back, the A.E.G. entered into a closer
alliance with the American General Electric, which is said to own
a third of its share capital. This has again reacted unfavourably
on the fusion of the two groups. But there are many cartel
agreements, partnerships and commonly controlled interests
existing between them, which prevent any competition which
would be hurtful to one of the big companies.

A field of electrical manufactures which deserves a special
interest and survey is that of electric lamps (Glühlampen). This
group of electrical manufacturing seems to be one of the few
industrial branches which are developing even under the manifold economic repercussions of the last 20 years on steadily
progressive lines. If the world production of lamps is taken as
having been 100 in 1913, it had advanced to 256 in 1929![1] It
is not surprising to find that an industry promising so successful
a progress has been the field of very hot struggles among those
who wanted to capture the market. This was all the more the

[1] Exclusive of the U.S.A. and Canada.

case, as from its very start the manufacture of electric lamps was decidedly influenced by the existence of patents of the most important kind. The first German factory manufacturing electric lamps was the Siemens and Halske Company, which started as early as 1881 under the direct influence of Werner v. Siemens. The lamps produced were of the carbon filament kind, greatly improved during the next 25 years, through new inventions such as the tantalum filament lamps and Nernst lamps, while the invention of the drawn tungsten wire filament lamp (first produced by the American General Electric in 1909) brought about a new line of production, to which in 1913 the gas-filled lamp was to be added. In the meantime Emil Rathenau had secured for the A.E.G. the utilisation of the American Edison-coal-filament lamp patents for the German supply. The Deutsche Edisongesellschaft was transformed in 1887 into the A.E.G., and in fact the production of electrical lamps was the backbone of the Rathenau business in its earlier days. Early agreements were entered into between the two groups with regard to their respective spheres of manufacture and the fixing of prices. When the drawn tungsten wire filament lamp invention was introduced from America by the A.E.G., a patent fight of unknown dimensions broke out and endangered the position that company possessed with regard to the most important patents in Europe; not less than thirty parties contested the patent rights of the A.E.G., indeed there followed one of the greatest patent struggles in the history of the German patent law, which at last led to the securing of the patent by the A.E.G., which had found the support of Siemens and Halske, the General Electric and the third big undertaking in the lamp branch: the Auergesellschaft. This company, which from its beginning had devoted its manufacture to the metal filament system, became the first to exploit the Osram lamp patent (inventors: F. Blau and H. Remané) and expanded its activity into many foreign countries, in which subsidiary factories were erected, as for instance in 1908 the Osram Lamp Works in Hammersmith in collaboration with the G.E.C. of New York. The three dominant concerns, Siemens, A.E.G. and Auer, were not exactly fighting each other on strictly competitive lines. There were understandings from the beginning, and in March 1911 these understandings were stabilised by a Patent-Interessen-Gemeinschaftsvertrag, an agreement concerning the mutual utilisation of patent rights and the granting of licenses, which in fact was a preparatory step towards the union of the three lamp-producing concerns into the Osram Gesellschaft m.b.H. This company, which to-day dominates the German market of electric lamps, was founded on 1 July 1919. An interesting vertical combination of this company, due to the initiative, in early days, of the A.E.G., is the control of the Vereinigten Lausitzer Glashütten, which has been acquired to secure an independent glass supply to the lamp works. Two other important undertakings, which have merged their interests in those of the Osram Company, are those of the Bergmann Elektrizitätswerke A.G. and of the Julius Pintsch A.G., both in Berlin. So in fact the domination of the electrical lamp business by the Osram Company must be considered complete. The German development in the electric lamp business is not without parallel. In England as well the bulk of the lamp business is concentrated in a few large firms, the English General Electric (Osram-G.E.C.-Lamp Works) controlling about 50 % of the whole English demand. Besides this the British Thomson Houston Co., the Edison Swan Electric Co., Ltd., the Metropolitan Vickers Electrical Co. Ltd., and the Siemens Electric Lamp and Supplies Ltd. have a strong position in the manufacture of lamps. The first three companies are financially controlled by one corporation, the Associated Electrical Industries, Ltd., which has existed since 1928. As in Germany, where the first cartel in the lamp trade was founded in 1903, the English electrical lamp manufacture has been strongly cartelised. The impetus came from the same reasons that we have mentioned with regard to the German development: in order to avoid the costly litigation which appeared likely to ensue (and had really ensued in Germany), owing to the overlapping of the patents, each of the firms concerned agreed to recognise the other's patents, to license the other for its patents and to interchange factory and laboratory experiences. That was exactly what had led to early understandings between Siemens-Halske, A.E.G., Auer and the American G.E.C. A selling arrangement was also effected by the English cartel. The firms holding the principal patents and others thus came to form in 1913 the Tungsten Lamp Association, followed by the Electric Lamp Manufacturers' Association of Great Britain, Ltd. (E.L.M.A.) which was incorporated in 1919. As in Germany, there has been a good deal of vertical combination in the English lamp manufacture too, the large lamp manufacturers producing semi-raw material such as tungsten filament, glass bulbs, lamp caps, argon, hydrogen and liquid air. But this sort of vertical combination has not endangered the economic position of smaller makers, as by the above-mentioned cartel agreement they enjoy the advantage of being supplied with these materials from the big firms which guarantee that the materials are of the same quality as those used in their own lamp manufacture. The English cartel is said to control 85–90 % of the trade in lamps. It is in all directions, with regard to the fixing of prices, terms of delivery, rebates to traders, etc., a most thoroughly organised monopolist association. Yet in a very able study of the lamp manufacture, William Meinhardt, former director of Osram and a recognised German authority on the subject of electrical industry, expressly alludes to the fact that "the English undertakings do not concentrate on electric lamps, but also manufacture along other lines, the consequence being that in England no such huge concerns have been formed in the manufacture of electrical lamps as in the U.S.A., Germany, Holland or Hungary, where such firms deal exclusively with the manufacture of electric lamps". This may be true. But the differentiation of units of manufacture has not been great enough to prevent the formation of a strong English cartel. As to the German cartel development in the lamp industry we shall have to describe its international significance in the next chapter.

All branches of the electrical industries have been of late overshadowed in their financial and, one may say, organising importance by the astounding development of the supply of electric power. This development has by no means yet reached its final stage. If the average capital investment is taken as being 1000 R.M. per kilowatt—a figure to be considered as too low rather than too high—the capital invested in all plant in the world installed for electrical supply purposes was estimated to reach the figure of 90–95 milliards of R.M. by 1929. Coal and water power being the principal sources from which electricity supply is to be derived, the importance of the utilisation of coal has remained of dominant importance in the countries rich in coal, even though the utilisation of water power has also made progress. Thus in Germany the percentage of electricity supply derived from coal was 75 in 1928, while that derived from water power was estimated to be approximately 13. In Germany as well as in England electrification has not progressed at the same pace as in the U.S.A. and other countries possessing rather "young" industries equipped from their start with the most modern appliances. Of the total of existing generating and allied machinery (Kraftmaschinen) in industry about 75 % in in the U.S.A., 70 % in Germany and 50 % in England were in 1928 driven by electricity. This percentage is very much higher in countries like Norway, Sweden or Canada, which were able to build up their industrial development on the utilisation of their vast water power resources, but it must be borne in mind that all figures on this subject are rather approximate. As to one field of the progressing use of electric power, that of railroad communication, it may be mentioned that in Germany 2·4 % of the whole mileage had been electrified by 1928, representing 1290 kilometres, while the figures in England were 1·6 % and 640 kilometres. In Switzerland the figures came up to 62·3 % and 3346 kilometres. As regards the electricity supply the Reich in 1931 was producing 14,408 millions of kilowatt-hours in public works and 11,380 in private works, while the respective figures were 12,813 and 4000 millions in Great Britain (including all undertakings allowed to supply electricity, also railway and tramway companies). It must be remembered that the production of electricity supply on the one hand and the production of electric engineering or manufactures on the other hand are closely linked together and that the progress of the one means the progress of the other. The development of electricity supply carries with it a demand for the products of most branches of the electrical manufacturing industry, e.g. dynamos, motors, switch gear, cables and other heavy apparatus as well as domestic appliances.

Although much of the basic scientific work underlying the electric manufacturing industry was carried out by British scientists, prior to the War Great Britain lagged greatly behind other important countries, such as Germany, in the growth of consumption of electricity for power purposes. A high level of steam engineering, based upon cheap and plentiful supply of coal, had been attained in Great Britain, and the British manufacturer doubtless hesitated to discard a system with which he was closely familiar in favour of electric power. While the development of the manufacturing side of the British electrical industry was thus directly retarded, in addition progress was greatly impeded by the lack of satisfactory provision, both legislative and technical, for the public supply of electrical energy. The Report of the Electrical Trade Committee presented in 1917 laid great emphasis on the defective character of the legislation then governing the administration of the electricity supply industry, which had encouraged development on a local instead of upon a national basis. This structure of the industry has greatly changed since, especially through the Act of 1926, which aimed among other things at the eventual concentration of generation in a limited number of inter-connected stations to be operated by the owners on account of the Central Electricity Board, and termed Selected Stations. In Germany the process of concentration was characterised by a number of decisive factors. The importance of electricity power supply to the engineering and manufacturing side of the industry, especially as regards the industrial penetration of "newly" industrialised overseas countries, was early recognised by the leading German electrical concerns. The electro-technical industry, as already mentioned, is greatly interested in the quick progression of electrical energy for the sale of its products. It was therefore at an early date the aim of the big German manufacturing companies to enter the field of electricity supply either by getting control over power works or by financing new power schemes or by erecting private power stations to supply the requirements of particular firms or groups of firms, sometimes disposing of excess energy to public electricity-supply boards. However, two other movements have recently limited this activity of the large manufacturing firms

6

in the electric industry. Firstly, large power-supply plants have been created which have their own financial affiliations. Secondly, the purely private undertakings have had increasingly to meet the competition of works owned and managed by the State or municipalities or by firms controlled by public as well as private interests, so-called "gemischt-wirtschaftliche Unternehmungen" (mixed undertakings). This was also the tendency during the years of aggravated economic crisis. While in 1928 the number of public works, producing electricity supply, were responsible for the supply of 14,146 millions of kilowatt-hours, the figure had reached 14,408 millions in 1931. The figures relating to private works were 13,724 and 11,380 millions. It is interesting to note that the degree of utilisation (Ausnützungsfaktor) of existing plant is by no means the same in public and private works. The best utilisation of plant is shown in the private works affiliated to certain groups of industry such as chemical or metal manufactures, to mining or the iron and steel industries, as also to the paper and printing trade. As the Enqueteausschuss stated, the "Ausnützungsfaktor" of the public works lagged far behind the figures for the private ones, as these works handle only part of the electricity supply to the big industrial concerns and are mostly suppliers to small and domestic consumers of electricity. The difference is astounding. While for instance in 1928 the average of consumption of electricity by chemical and metal industries ran up to 4164 hours in the privately owned plant, the figure amounted to only 392 hours as regards the small agricultural customers getting electricity from public supply bodies. The figures relating to domestic consumption are said to be still lower.[1] The tendency of recent years, beginning with 1926, has been towards a diminution of newly created privately owned industrial power plants, so-called "Eigeninstallationen", in favour of an increasing supply of electricity from plants not belonging to the industrial users of electricity, that is by so-called "Fremdstrombezug". The industrial undertakings have

[1] The "Ausnützungsfaktor" represents the average time during which the plant supplying electricity is actually used. The full utilisation of the efficiency of installed plant would represent 8760 hours a year, equivalent to 8760 kilowatt-hours (kw.-h.). In English terminology this is expressed by million "units" (kilowatt-hours) generated per annum.

been working their own power plant to its utmost capacity, but to obtain additional supplies they have not enlarged their electricity plant but have relied on an increasing supply by "outside" power plant, especially by the large works in the branch. This has been partly effected by electricity-supply contracts (Lieferungsverträge) between manufacturing companies and large electricity concerns. The Rhenish-Westphalian Elektrizitätswerk for instance has since the spring of 1929 entered into such contracts with the Vereinigte Stahlwerke, the I.G. Farben, the Mannesmann works, the Gutehoffnungshütte and with a number of other firms in the Düsseldorf district. There is no doubt that for the industries using electric energy this arrangement seems more profitable than the further erection of their own generating plant, while the public supply works have in their turn greatly profited by such arrangements, as they have been able better to balance their efficiency with the actual demand, being now able to rely on the more regular and much more intensive demand of large industrial customers. With regard to the former structure of electricity distribution by the public works, this means a considerable diminution of fixed costs.

The development alluded to has certainly increased the concentration movement in electricity. It has laid the necessary basis for unification of production and distribution according to geographical districts. While in fact the private power plant affiliated to a certain manufacturing company meant necessarily a decentralisation of electricity supply (though from the viewpoint of vertical combination it might be considered as being in line with the development of larger units in industry), the separation of electricity supply from the industrial undertaking making use of it offered an opportunity of concentrating generation in a comparatively small number of power stations, possibly inter-connected by high tension main transmission lines. The big power-producing works have since continued to acquire participations in other producing and distributing concerns in order that the consumer may be brought closer to the source of supply, and this linking up of the various electrical concerns has the support of the new Government of the Reich.

This process of co-ordination has already been of the greatest advantage as regards the reserve electricity "store", which the public supply works are obliged to keep. These reserves, which are necessarily a heavy charge on general costs, could be greatly diminished by the interlocking of power works and the placing of mutual reserves at common disposal for additional demands.[1]

The most important industrial combination, which has so far resulted from this concentration movement in the electricity trade, is represented by the Rheinisch-Westphälische Elektrizitätswerk A.G. of Essen (R.W.E.). It would lead too far to chronicle the process of amalgamation and co-ordination, by which this concern has reached during the last ten years its powerful position. To-day it represents the biggest "gemischt-wirtschaftliches Werk" (see above) of the whole continent of Europe. The territory, which comes into the sphere of its supply, measures about 45,400 square kilometres (one kilometre equal to 0·386 square miles), including the greater part of the West-German industrial area. The high-tension system of the area of supply is connected with the water-power supply of Southern Germany and the Alps and the sources of electric energy of Middle Germany. The yearly production of the concern is about 20 % of the German electricity production. The efficiency of the power plants of the R.W.E. amounts to about 1,060,000 kilowatts. The network of its plants represents a co-ordination of interconnecting supply mains. Besides this the concern has been able to secure long-term contracts with the most important single industrial users of electric power in Germany. It has also concluded long-term contracts for the supply of electricity with neighbouring distributing firms which have been interconnected with its mains. The R.W.E. is, besides, a typical example of vertical combination, as the company has been intruding with great vigour into the coal mining business. The latest step in this direction was the acquisition of 21 million R.M. shares of the A.G. für Braunkohlenbergbau and Brikettfabrikation in Cologne, generally called "Rheinbraun", from the Charlottenhütte in Düsseldorf, and an additional 8 million R.M. from Fritz

---

[1] It is statistically proved that the larger the power works the greater has been the actual utilisation of its generating efficiency.

Thyssen. The rich lignite deposits, the large power works and the considerable liquid assets together with the high earning capacity of "Rheinbraun" made this transaction attractive for the R.W.E. A community of interests was agreed upon for a period of 50 years. The agreement provided among other clauses for a participation of shareholders of "Rheinbraun" in the liquidation of reserves belonging to the latter concern, which among other valuable assets owns 40 % of the Harpener Bergbau A.G., the best coal mining concern of the Ruhr district. The participation of the R.W.E. and its federated concerns in the Rhenish Lignite Syndicate now amounts to not less than 57 %. The share capital of the R.W.E. was 246 million R.M. in 1933. Reserve: 77 million R.M. The partnerships of the giant concern are besides considerable. It owns about 75 % of the well-known Lahmeyer Company of Frankfurt, it controls the Roddergrube and Brikettwerke Roddergrube A.G. in Brühl near Cologne by a direct partnership as well as by the control of "Rheinbraun" and other mining or power-work undertakings. The development of the R.W.E. presents a typical example of concentration and industrial combination in the German electricity supply. Others are: the Thüringer Gas and Elektrizitäts Gesellschaft, the Prussian Elektrizitätswerke A.G. and the Sächsische Werke, which by concerted action have co-ordinated the electricity interests of Middle Germany, especially those of Thüringen and Saxony, in a similar manner to that described with regard to the Rhine and Ruhr district, and the same movement is going on in Silesia. Undoubtedly the chance for any smaller competitors, either in electric manufacturing or engineering or in the supply of electricity, has passed. It must be left to the future how far the development of concentration will be accompanied by a further increase of State and communal interests in the industry, and how far the "gemischt-wirtschaftlichen" undertakings will be considered a satisfactory medium between purely private and public corporations. The very elaborate system of international relations of the German electric industry already alluded to in parts of this chapter will be discussed in the next.

### CHAPTER VII

# GERMAN INDUSTRIAL COMBINATION IN THE INTERNATIONAL SPHERE

THE network of economic, technical and financial relations linking up German industrial combinations with international industrialism is a very elaborate one. It may be said that it is relatively much more comprehensive than that in other highly developed industrial countries; besides it matters little whether—as generally happened—German industrial combination is or has been the active force in bringing about such developments, or whether, as in branches of the industry just mentioned, foreign corporations have sought a closer co-operative alliance or even combination with giant German industrial concerns. Certainly in the post-War period of depressed German industrial finance American undertakings, with a desire for international monopolist expansion, have been busy trying to get into closer union with such German concerns through economic and credit arrangements. This period has more or less come to an end with the consolidation of German economic development, but of course the relations once begun have been continued, where a community of interest has proved profitable and desirable. However, this movement of foreign companies invading the sphere of German industrial organisation must not be overrated; far more important has been the development of German international industrial connections through the growing activity of German cartels or corporations themselves.

We may distinguish three possibilities of the international federation of German industrial combinations:

(1) German cartels or syndicates may be federated to foreign monopolist associations by mutual agreement. In that case such associations, "internationale Kartelle", may already exist or be

formed *ad hoc*. The earliest international cartel of that kind was the International Railmakers' Association (I.R.M.A.) founded as early as 1884. It embraced at first German, English and Belgian undertakings, which were later on joined by American, French, Italian, Austrian and Spanish firms. Another example of a great many associations of that kind is the Incandescent Lamp Syndicate. In 1926 the manufacturers of British gas mantles entered into an agreement with the German and certain other foreign manufacturers for a period of five years. The German manufacturers were bound by this agreement not to sell gas mantles in the United Kingdom and certain parts of the Empire, whilst the British firms undertook not to sell to the continent of Europe and the U.S.A. Of course such international agreements may cover very different fields of common action. They may simply relate to prices or, what is most commonly agreed, allocate to their members international markets, or they may regulate both prices and distribution, while agreements relating to a restriction of output among members are not quite so frequent. A prominent example of the latter case is represented by the Tin Producers' Association. This Association had a remarkable influence on recent prices, as in 1933 the much discussed rise in prices was only achieved by putting severe pressure on the members of the Association, whose output was restricted to $33\frac{1}{3}$ % of the rated capacity of 1929. Another metal cartel of that kind, in which, in contrast to the tin agreement, German producers as the second largest of the world are greatly interested, is the Zink (spelter) cartel. The production of spelter in Germany and Poland amounted in 1933 to 140,000 long tons out of a world's total of almost 1 million tons. In 1928 the European, American and Australian producers of spelter formed a cartel, but in connection with export-quota and other difficulties its existence has been frequently endangered, though it was renewed in 1934. The cartel fixes a quota basis, on which the respective rate of production is decided. It also fixes fines for excess of the allowed production. This type of international combination represented by cartels fixing prices and limiting and allocating production may be regarded as the most common as well as the most uncomplicated form of international monopolist organisation. As regards the German industry it may be stated without fear of contradiction that there is a long chain of cartels of that sort, in which German industry has its part.

(2) Another type of international industrial combination may result from the fact that dominant concerns in certain groups of industry are expanding their sphere of activity over foreign economic territories by acquiring manufacturing works or setting up new undertakings abroad, with the intention of conquering or of better controlling foreign markets. This means international "trustification", although, as will be seen below, under (3), it does not represent it exclusively. A typical example, in which German industry played an important rôle, was the International Match Trust formed by Iwar Kreuger of Stockholm. The Swedish Match Trust, being the most important concern in that branch of industry in the world, acquired the two biggest German match companies at Kassel and entered into a community of interest with the third largest factory, the "Union" in Augsburg. A special method pursued by this shrewdly managed concern was the exploitation of the financial straits of foreign countries in exchange for fiscal concessions, very similar to the aims of those famous patentees and projectors in the days of Charles I. While in 1926 the union of German interests had become complete through an agreement between the trustificated firms and the twenty-three outsiders still existing, in the form of a cartel bearing the name of Zündholzvertriebsgesellschaft in Berlin and representing a complete monopolist organisation as regards sales, in 1929 the Reich granted a monopoly of matches to that syndicate in return for a loan granted by Mr Kreuger. Here we have the typical international trust emanating from the strong international position of a single national monopolist concern. It may be mentioned that aims of monopolisation similar to those of the Swedish match interests have been going on in England, where the movement has become most conspicuous since the formation of the British Match Corporation in 1927, a Swedish enterprise started with a capital of £6,000,000. According to Liefmann in 1930 the Swedish trust controlled the match market in twelve countries

by not less than 80 %, in seven countries, among them Germany, by 50–80 % and in most other countries by 50 % or less. The German dye industry, which for a long time had a sort of quasi-monopolist position in the world's markets, is another example of industry having monopolist control of the home market and expanding that domination by foreign acquisitions of all kinds. When the I.G. Farben was founded it possessed a good many undertakings in foreign countries and a network of distributing companies abroad, as for instance in the U.S.A. (one of them the General Dyestuff Corporation with factories in Albany and Patterson), in Spain, China, Brazil, Switzerland and England. Important subsidiary companies in the electro-chemical and metallurgical field were the Societa Electroquimica in Barcelona, in chemicals the Durand and Huguenin factories in Basle, in fertilisers the Koliner Kunstdüngerfabrik in Prague and in artificial silk and textiles the Philana A.G. in Basle. Later, in 1928 and 1929, two companies were formed to consolidate the management of the I.G. partnerships abroad, the one being the Internationale Gesellschaft für Chemische Unternehmungen in Basle (I.G. Chemie), a holding company with a share capital of 290 million francs, the other the American I.G. Chemical Corporation in New York, the latter controlling the Agfa-Ansco Corporation, one of the largest firms in the photographical branch and the General Aniline Works which administers the utilisation of the German dye patents in the U.S.A.

(3) A third form of international industrial combination must certainly be regarded as the most modern outcome of the development of giant concerns. It is represented by quasi-monopolist or at any rate dominating concerns, which either by their original or main production or by branches of production, with which they have become affiliated through processes of technical or financial expansion, are seeking a closer union with foreign corporations or concerns of equal importance. The difference from (2) is evident. While the former international industrial combination, though not a cartel, has its nucleus in the monopolist position of a "national" industry, the latter is due to a co-operation or even amalgamations between dominant partners, having the same or a similar strength in their respective

national and also international spheres of business. Where national cartels in such industries play a more important rôle than single amalgamated firms, an international cartel may replace international trustification. Where, however, this is not the case the giant undertakings may find it useful to replace the lack of cartelisation by closer union of their interests or to strengthen existing, but less efficient, cartel agreements by such union. A very typical example is provided by the international relations in the rayon industry. This industry has been for some time a prominent example of concentration in industry. In Germany the leading—and indeed the pioneer—concern was the Vereinigte Glanzstoff Fabriken of Elberfeld, now federated with the Dutch "Aku" concern, and the J. P. Bemberg A.G. In England Courtaulds are also, with their controlled concerns abroad, one of the largest producers in the world. In Italy the principal place is held by the Società Nazionale Industria Applicazioni Viscose (Snia Viscosa), in the U.S.A. by the American Viscose Company and the Dupont de Nemours concern. There have been for some time arrangements for co-ordination between these giant international concerns. An arrangement for co-operation between Messrs Courtauld and the Glanzstoff was made in 1925. Early in 1927 these two companies together with the Italian Snia Viscosa entered into an agreement, which included an interchange of shares and was stated to aim at the elimination of wasteful competition and the promotion of co-operation of a technical and economic kind. Moreover, it must be remembered that before that arrangement the three participants had connections with rayon concerns all over the world. The I.G. Farben (Agfa) had since 1925 taken an interest in the Glanzstoff and Bemberg companies, thereby acquiring a connection with Courtaulds, which again had a controlling interest in the American Viscose Company, while by its control over the German dynamite concern of Köln-Rottweiler Pulverfabriken A.G., the Dynamite A.G. vorm Nobel and the Rhenish-Westphalian Sprengstoff A.G. the I.G. became directly connected with the English and American Nobel concerns, the former being closely allied to the English Celanese interests and the Tubize concerns in France and Belgium, the latter to the second largest rayon concern of the U.S.A., the Dupont group. So in fact the ramifications of the German rayon industry extended over the whole international field of producers, the Glanzstoff having, besides the before-mentioned connections, important arrangements and common interests with Austrian and Czechoslovakian firms. One is entitled to speak of a world-wide interconnection of the artificial silk industry, the primary condition of which has been the concentration of the national rayon industries of the respective countries. In 1928 the output of the above-mentioned group of German, English and Italian producers, with their connections outside their own countries, was estimated to be over 70 % of the world's production of artificial silk. Since then the great "revolutionary" factor concerning rayon has been the astounding progress of Japanese artificial silk interests. Japan, which in 1929 produced 30 million lbs. of rayon, equal to about half the German or English output and to even a larger percentage of the Italian, had increased her production by 1933 to above the level of the English, Italian or German production. It produced in fact as much rayon as France, Holland and Switzerland put together. As there have been no arrangements or affiliations of the former rayon producing countries with their new competitor, the picture of international trustification in this group of industry must have considerably changed as far as concerns the percentage controlled by the international "trust"-group of producers. International arrangements in the rayon industry do not preclude the existence of very effective national syndicates, indeed these are to some extent the necessary instruments in carrying out the international arrangements of the giant concerns. The cartel system with market quotas continues to be a feature of the rayon industries of Europe; Italian, Dutch, French and Belgian exporters are participating in the home sales of rayon in Germany on a quota basis. A very efficient syndicate, called "Kunstseideverkaufsbüro G.m.b.H. (Viskosekunstseidsyndikat)" in Berlin is responsible for the distribution of almost all German as of non-German rayon coming on the German market. The syndicate has strict rules forbidding any direct sales from the rayon companies to customers. Even members of the syndicate are not allowed to sell or buy their produce to or from each other. The foreign members of the syndicate have been obliged to impose on all their sales outside the German Empire the obligation that the material may not be sold to Germany in an unmanufactured state; as regards the German dealers they are obliged to sell exclusively to the finishing works of the industry and not to any other dealers in the trade. These very stringent obligations of a very potent syndicate, however, would hardly be effective without the existence of marked concentration of the industry in Germany as abroad (the Belgian industry also is now almost entirely controlled by one big combine) and the inter-connections of these combines, which in fact form the backbone of all quota arrangements.

We shall now proceed to discuss some of the prominent examples of international cartelisation or trustification, in which German industries have become partners, besides those already mentioned. The reader will easily find out into which of the three distinctive groups of international monopoly organisation each of these world-wide organisational inter-connections may be ranged, although it must certainly be understood that many groups of industries will exhibit partnerships in all three of these forms of international combination.

The most prominent international combination, with which German industry has become federated, is represented by the international agreements in the steel trade. There can be no doubt that it was post-War depression of markets, which led to strong desire on the part of the producers of Western Europe to form a combination in order to avoid a further catastrophic drop in prices. It has been estimated by the Enqueteausschuss that the increase of steel production by the continental producers amounted to not less than 8·3 million tons from 1913 to 1929. While production had been rapidly expanding in the old continental iron and steel producing centres, the demand in foreign markets had become limited by national programmes of production, and the economic effects of the commercial clauses of the Treaty of Versailles had been a further disadvantage to the organisation and structure of the most important steel districts of the continent. All this was the chief spur behind the formation of an international agreement, in which in all probability English producers would have become partners as well, if the English iron and steel trade had shown a concentration of undertakings sufficient to make it "kartellfähig" (fit for cartelisation). The agreement concluded between the iron- and steel-producing companies of Germany, the Saar territory, France, Luxemburg and Belgium (1 October 1926), later joined by the Austro-Hungarian succession states, took the name of Internationale Rohstahlgemeinschaft (I.R.G.) and had its seat in Luxemburg. The agreements of the I.R.G. are intended to grant protection to the home producers by limiting the quantities of steel imported and by controlling the direction of foreign supplies of steel. The rules and formalities of the I.R.G. have been subject to frequent changes and in 1930 to a sort of reorganisation. But the main purpose, represented by the formation of "Gebietsschutzabkommen" (agreements relating to the protection of certain districts of production or distribution), has remained, and the Enqueteausschuss, though alluding to some unfulfilled hopes with regard to a possible international reorganisation of the iron and steel business by the I.R.G., has recognised that as regards the German industry the I.R.G. has realised expectations as to a better control of competition and the support of home cartels in their aims of stabilising prices. The I.R.G. controls raw steel exclusively. As regards finished or half-finished products there are other international cartels, such as the International Railmakers' Association, one of the oldest international cartels, generally called I.R.M.A., and the successor of an earlier syndicate, the European Railmakers' Association (E.R.M.A.). The I.R.M.A., which has also been joined by English and (in 1929) by American makers of rails, provides what is called "ein gegenseitiger Länderschutz", a mutual protection of home markets. There is for instance under the rule of the I.R.M.A. no direct possibility for German railmakers of making deliveries to France, Belgium, England, etc. The orders which can be caught by rail manufacturers for the supply of international markets have to be reported to a central agency in London, which, in accordance with a committee formed for this very purpose, allocates the contracts to that "national" group of producers which according to a specific quota-tabulation is entitled to get it.[1] The commercial side of the transaction, that is the payment for every contract, is left to the different national groups of producers, which get the contract and have to allocate it among their members. Another international cartelisation in the field of heavy steel products is that of tubes. There had been early German tube cartels, but they had been frequently dissolved, till a stronger combination was formed in 1925. Since there were in Czechoslovakia tube works associated with German concerns it was no difficult matter to draw them into the agreement, which thereby became the nucleus of international understanding. French, Belgian and Polish works joined in, and in 1929 the five most important English tube makers, who had been temporarily outside through failing to reach an agreement among themselves, came to terms with their international competitors by single agreements. As the American tube manufacturers also joined the cartel in 1929 its connections became of the same world-wide character as those in the rail manufacture. The organisation of international sales by the firms affiliated to the cartel is similarly arranged to that in the rails industry. Of late there have been grave apprehensions among the members of the international tube syndicate with regard to the progressive development of tube manufactures in Japan. It was about five years ago that the big Japanese tube firms of Mitsui and Mitsubishi began to compete with European firms for contracts in China and Siam, while in 1933 they were even able to export to the U.S.A. It will be seen how this competition will affect the international tube agreements. In October 1933 an agreement was reached by the international syndicate and the Japanese makers with regard to the export and price-fixing of gas-boiler tubes. The international tube syndicate, now consisting of all the important continental

---

[1] It may be noted in this respect that the development of exports by different countries had greatly changed since 1913. Exports of steel rails from principal exporting countries were as follows:

Thousand tons

|  | From United Kingdom | From Belgium | From France | From Germany | From U.S.A. | Total |
|---|---|---|---|---|---|---|
| 1910–13 (average) | 438·2 | 165·8 | 63·1 | 506·8 | 407·8 | 1581·7 |
| 1926 | 164·3 | 213·2 | 317·1 | 340·2 | 187·6 | 1222·4 |

syndicates and the British, American and Canadian manufacturers, was prolonged until 31 March 1935. Other syndicates relating to heavy steel products are the International Hoop Iron Syndicate, between German, French, Belgian and Luxemburg iron and steel industries, formed in May 1933, and the Wire Rod Syndicate, having the same countries as members and its clearing bureau in Liége.

The above-mentioned international syndicates in the heavy lines of the industry were regarded as a means of getting the iron and steel industries of the world into that contact, though decentralised, which the International Raw Steel Syndicate had not been able to realise. Yet a new International raw Steel Syndicate (the first one was sometimes termed in English the "International Ingot Steel Syndicate") between France, Belgium, Luxemburg and Germany was brought about, after many conflicts and difficulties among the partners. The original Internationale Rohstahlgemeinschaft, formed in 1926, had practically expired in 1932, without having succeeded in bringing about all the expected international advantages. It seemed indeed as if a deadlock in this sector of international industrial agreements would ensue. But at last, in June 1933, a new agreement was entered into, when the Internationale Rohstahl-Export Gemeinschaft, the I.R.E.G., was formed. The chief difference between the old and the new international cartel is that the latter deals only with the exports of its members, while a control of output would only come into consideration under quite exceptional conditions. The quotas of the members are regulated by a rather complicated sliding scale tabulation. The signing of the agreement was made conditional upon the formation of selling organisations for a number of rolled goods. In fact two-year agreements for the formation of six selling offices within the I.R.E.G. were concluded; the German quotas relating to these products are as follows:

| Semis | 23 % | Thick plate | 46 % |
|-------|------|-------------|------|
| Girders | 27 % | Medium plate | 28 % |
| Bar iron | 29 % | Universal iron | 52 % |

Penalties for exceeding the quotas allocated in the selling offices are 15 gold shillings per ton for semis, 20 gold shillings per ton for girders and bar iron, and 25 gold shillings per ton for all other products. If the total quota under the I.R.E.G. is exceeded by less than 5 % an additional fee of 3 R.M. per ton becomes due which rises to 5 R.M. per ton if the quota is exceeded by between 5–10 % and to 10 R.M., if the quota is exceeded by more than 10 %. Prices are to be fixed by the selling organisations, the activity, however, of which will be limited to a registration of the transactions, which will be carried out by the national syndicates. So in fact the German heavy steel industry of to-day has been internationally cartelised by two kinds of arrangements: by the I.R.E.G., which represents the frame combine with regard to a group of products, and by international cartels formed for certain lines of production, both organisations regulating the export quotas. German industrial circles have welcomed the fact that the new Raw Steel Syndicate does not try to regulate production, leaving this to the national spheres of interest. It may be in fact under present economic conditions the best way, to leave the limitation of production to the national syndicates instead of aiming at an international combination regulating the output of all countries concerned. Of course, the new plan will necessitate the existence of strong cartels within the sphere of national industries. In this respect it may be mentioned that both in Belgium and in France cartelisation in the steel industry has been progressing of late (in Belgium notably by the "Comptoir Sidérurgique Belge", Cosibel), thereby facilitating the work of the I.R.E.G. and stabilising its development. Besides their participation in this network of international steel agreements German producers have tried to remedy existing deficiencies by single arrangements with Germany's competitors. Thus in 1934 an agreement was reached with Poland regulating the question of certain imports and the scrap problem up to 1937, while with English makers of ship-building material an agreement was reached which was to expire in June 1934.

In the chemical groups of industry the question of international cartelisation has been of a somewhat minor importance, so long as the big German concerns were in the main interested in the selling of aniline dyes and other chemical and pharmaceutical products, in which they had a dominant position in the inter-

THE INTERNATIONAL SPHERE 97

national markets. This changed when the chemical industries by the new processes of production already mentioned became necessarily entangled with other producers in the world. Liefmann calls attention to the connections by which the I.G. Farben has been linked up with the two principal oil concerns of the world, the Standard Oil and the Royal Dutch Shell group, as being of "great interest and probably of the highest importance for the future". The agreement reached related to a partnership or at least some common action as to the exploitation of the German inventions of coal hydration and the synthetic manufacture of liquid fuels. The I.G. Farben together with the Dutch Shell were participators from the beginning in the formation of the "Bergin Gesellschaften", two in Holland and one with its subsidiary companies in Germany, which were working or financing the methods of liquefaction invented by Dr Bergius. These, as well as the inventions and discoveries made by Prof. Franz Fischer in the same field of research, were of high importance to the U.S.A., who produce about 75 % of the world's petrol production, while consuming about 80 % (the imports reached about 5 million tons in 1931). It is only natural that the Standard Oil Company, while trying to secure for itself some of the new oil properties in different parts of the world, was anxious to associate itself with the exploitation of those chemical processes, which promised to be of great value to the petrol supply of the future.

The great importance of the hydrogenation processes has led to an international understanding, though the final stage of economic production of liquid fuel has not yet been reached. In 1931 an International Hydrogenation Patents Company was founded with the object of a pooling of information and a complete exchange of operating experiences. It remains to be seen how far this agreement will develop into anything like a cartel or syndicate when the commercial utilisation of the new processes has made further progress and exports can be envisaged.

Far more important than in the chemical trade has been the development of international connections in the electric industries. This group of industry shows the most highly developed and the most widespread international affiliations. As the electrical industries do not merely export their produce, but are as much interested in the engineering business abroad, in erecting plant for the supply of electricity, the electrification of railways, the installation of electric tramway lines, etc., it early became necessary to initiate the formation of subsidiary companies abroad or to acquire partnerships in already existing foreign companies. This tendency was largely encouraged by the fact that there had been, as already described, a very strong concentration in the German electrical industry, leaving the domination of the industry to the two giant concerns, the A.E.G. and the Siemens-group with their enormous technical and financial resources. We have already alluded to the early connections of the A.E.G. with electrical interests in the U.S.A. (General Electric). But besides these relations, which date back to the very beginning of electrical engineering and manufacturing in Germany (the German Edison Company was the predecessor of the A.E.G.), the most important field of international electrical relations has become that of a wide network of holding companies. The chief of such holding companies in which the German electric industry is prominently interested are:

Die Gesellschaft für elektrische Unternehmungen (now united with the Ludwig Löwe A.G., one of the biggest German engineering works, and since that amalgamation generally referred to as "Gesfürel").

Die Gesellschaft für elektrische Lieferungen with its affiliation to the "Schweizer Gesellschaft für elektrische Lieferungen".

The Companis Hispano Americana de Electricitad (Chade), formerly known as Deutsch-Südamerikanische Elektrizitäts-Gesellschaft, taking care of South-American markets.

The "Société Financielle des Transports et des Entreprises Industrielles" (Sofina).

But the most prominent example of international interconnection in the electric industry is certainly represented by the history and development of the electric lamp manufacture. We have described the consolidation of interests which had been going on in this industry taken as a national unit, and which as in other cases was the very backbone of the ensuing international understandings. It must not be forgotten that electric manufacturing, by the diversity of its products, their specialisation and differentiation, has not presented in general very favourable conditions for cartelisation; the electric lamp manufacture, however, presented a rather exceptional case in this industry, as standardisation was possible at an early date. Electric lamps could be produced as a trade-mark ware at a uniform price. The first international syndicate was formed in 1903 as "Verkaufsstelle Vereinigter Glühlampenfabriken", an association comprising the most prominent European makers of electric lamps. This syndicate was dissolved in 1914. After the War the movement towards international combination was revived. Agreements of different character were reached between the German, Austrian, Hungarian, Swiss and Scandinavian makers. Out of these rose a much more important international cartel, the "Internationale Glühlampen Preis-Vereinigung" (I.G.P.), in 1921. This agreement did not prove very successful, indeed it was dissolved in August 1924 owing to increasing overlapping by smaller outsiders and a non-obedience to its rules in the national as well as in the international sphere. But the big firms in the international trade had long ago come to the conviction that the salvation of their interests was to lie in the elimination of cutthroat competition and an international co-ordination centralised as much as possible. In fact the international cartelisation of electric lamps is the best possible example of the importance of a concentration of commercial units within the cartel if it is to be successful in the long run. A network of agreements between the big concerns of the world was already in existence. Such agreements between the American General Electric and the three largest German concerns dated from the time before the War and were renewed with the Osram concern in 1921 and in 1929. Similar agreements representing "Freundschaftsverträge" (amicable understandings) or collaboration-agreements existed between the American International General Electric, the Dutch Philips concern, the British Thomson-Houston Company, the Compagnie des Lampes in Paris, the English General Electric and others. By these agreements and understandings not only was a common safeguard of patents secured but also a territorial division of interests was arranged, the partners in the agreement submitting to the obligation not to exploit their patents in places accorded to other partners, an obligation especially relating to the working of licences. There were besides already existing agreements between the giant firms with regard to the exploitation of new inventions and the exchange of technical experience. All this facilitated the final formation of a really effective international combine, when mere cartelistic experiments had failed. It was characteristic that the endeavour of the dominant international concerns to come to terms began even before the I.G.P. had collapsed. At last a settlement was reached in December 1924. An agreement called "General Patent and Development Agreement" was signed and a central agency acting as the head of the international cartel was formed in Geneva, the "Phoebus S.A. Compagnie Industrielle pour le Développement de l'Éclairage". This "world-combine", which after 1924 was joined by a number of firms formerly considered as outsiders, was renewed in 1931 for a period of not less than 21 years, up to the 30 June 1955. A means of dissolving the agreement before is not provided, unless an extraordinary general meeting with a majority of votes, laid down by the treaty, takes a decision in that respect. A single member is not allowed to withdraw from the agreement, except under certain circumstances. The cartel comprises not less than 27 parent companies, among them 8 concerns with 36 affiliated companies. The number of separate States which are partners in the cartel is 18. The only States standing outside the agreement are Russia, U.S.A. and Canada, although the two latter are both indirectly connected with the syndicate. Apart from these two countries the manufacture of electric lamps, represented by the international syndicate, is estimated to be 90 % of the world production. As to the formation of this giant and at last efficient international combine, Mr William Meinhardt, head of the German Osram concern, states in his book on the lamp industry:

In contrast to other international agreements it is remarkable as regards the meetings, which preceded the combination, that they were not arranged between the national organisations and that they were not led by the associated manufacturers of the different countries, but that in the first place the big manufacturers in the world met and came to understandings, asking the smaller firms to join when the main points had been cleared up. Success justified this sort of proceeding, but it must be kept in mind, that special circumstances favoured combination in the lamp trade and that cartelisation was facilitated by the dominant position possessed by the leading firms.

The conditions favouring cartelisation in the electric lamp trade are conspicuous in another of the more "modern" industries, the manufacture of linoleum. Like the manufacture of electric lamps linoleum offered easy opportunities for standardisation. Length, width and the general quality of the product were almost the same everywhere and the distinctions related almost exclusively to difference in design. The raw materials used and the methods of manufacture did not differ anywhere, and while these circumstances favoured production on a large scale, the capital outlay for the single unit of production was rather heavy from the beginning. Prof. Hantos asserts that the linoleum industry represents in fact a classic example of the advantages of large-scale production in industry. Small undertakings are hardly able to compete. The big undertakings are able to keep a much greater variety of patterns and designs, an important factor in the sale of linoleum. Thus the "Deutsche Linoleumwerke" alone keeps not fewer than 2000 patterns. Although the big unit, technically and commercially, has been an important factor in the industry from its beginning, industrial combination has been further facilitated by a process of amalgamation and affiliation among the original undertakings. The linoleum industry is another example of cartelisation combined with a tendency towards trustification. Already before the War a price cartel had been formed by the five leading German linoleum manufacturing companies. In 1911 international depression in the industry led to the first combination of European manufacturers (England excepted). This "convention" has gone on existing ever since, although its structure has been frequently subject to changes. Apart from this a strong concentration movement had been going on in the German linoleum industry. The outcome of this was the "Deutsche Linoleum Werke A.G.", which was formed in 1927 with a capital of 30 million R.M., which was increased to 40 million R.M. a year later. Agreements already existing with Swedish, Swiss and Dutch firms led in 1927 to a closer financial association between the German and foreign undertakings. A corporation called "Kontinentale Linoleum Union A.G." was formed in Zürich, which took over one of the controlling companies of the German concern, the Deutsche Linoleum-Unternehmungen A.G., and which also became the owner of the majority of the shares in the Swiss company in Giubiasco and of the Swedish in Göteborg, which again controlled the leading works in Latvia. In 1929 the Zürich corporation took over the Dutch factory Krommenie, while in fact the whole group was controlled by the big German interests. Since then there have been new participations in the French "Société anonyme Rémoise du Linoléum" (Sarlino) in Reims and in the most important factory in Poland. A giant international undertaking of a trust-like character has been the result of all these affiliations, which, considered from the point of view of company structure, show a rather complicated network of interlocked connections. In 1929 the total production of the continental trust was not less than 35 million square yards valued at about 125 million R.M. The German associated works participated in this figure to an extent of 24 million square yards. The production of the Continentale Linoleum in 1929 was estimated to amount to about 25 % of the world production, while the whole German production amounted to about 20 % of it. There is a central agency and six district agencies; the orders to the various factories are not subject to a system of allocations or quotas, but are distributed among the works according to temporary expediency. The international trust in accordance with the national cartels is endeavouring to keep the home markets for the national works. English manufacturers having formed an association too—some smaller firms excepted—there was a possibility of drawing British producers into the continental agreement relating to the prices for exports, and it was stated that even those English firms which had remained outside the agreement respected these price regulations. Arrangements between the big continental firms relating to the pooling of profits and losses will be discussed later.

There are a great number of other international agreements, in which German industry has become a partner, which are much less complicated in their organisational features and functions than those already mentioned, so that we can refrain from discussing them in detail. The Franco-German potash agreement is a syndicate of that kind. It merely represents a "reconstruction" of the state of organisation existing before the War, when Germany had been the sole owner of potash mines on the continent. The Peace Treaty had disrupted this unit of production in handing over the mines of Alsace and Lorraine to France. It was only natural that the community of interest, which had led to a wholesale monopolist organisation of German potash mines, should not be dissolved by the alteration of political frontiers. But competition was going on between the producers of the two districts (France and the German syndicate), especially hurtful to the German interests owing to the subsidies which the French State was bestowing on its potash interests, till in 1926 an agreement was reached in Lugano, which led to a convention in Paris on 29 December 1926. This agreement was concluded between the German syndicate, which we have discussed before, and the Société Commerciale des Potasses d'Alsace, which controls the whole French production, that of the State works and the only private firm existing, the "Mines de St. Thérèse". There were allocations arranged, Germany getting 70 % and France 30 % of the foreign sales of potash. The unification of sales was followed by an agreement for the fixing of prices. The arrangement was made for a period of ten years, expiring on 1 May 1936.

In another branch of the fertiliser industry, the nitrogen production, the problem of regulating international competition was much more difficult to solve. Production of nitrogen fertilisers, which had been greatly pushed forward during the War, had since 1918 resulted in a tremendous overproduction. After protracted negotiations a conference was arranged, in Spring 1930 in Ostend and later in Paris, by the most prominent representatives of the industry, but an agreement was only reached in August of that year in Berlin, whereby an association known as "Convention de l'Industrie de l'Azote" was constituted. The C.I.A. embraces about 80 % of the world production of nitrogen and embraces 98 % of the European production. A general diminution of output having regard to the diminished agricultural demand for artificial manures was agreed to. But any European agreement about nitrogen fertilisers would be incomplete if the Chilean nitrate production were left out. An attempt was long ago made to bring both groups of producers into one line of action, but it was not until July 1932 that a selling agreement was reached by the principal European producers and the Chilean industry. It must, however, be kept in mind that the importance of the Chilean industry as a supplier of fertilisers to the world's agriculture has greatly diminished and did not even improve, when after 1932 international consumption began again to rise. While in 1928–29 the consumption of Chilean nitrate had amounted to 419,000 tons, it dropped in 1932–33 to 129,000 tons, while the consumption of manufactured nitrogen, which was 1,452,000 in 1928–29, rose to 1,624,000 tons in the latter year, an increase of more than 200,000 tons over the figure of 1931–32. According to the *Economist* of 17 February 1934 this development was due to the relatively high cost of saltpetre to the consumer.

Among the most recent developments of international cartels the Tin Plate Agreement may be mentioned, which was concluded in July 1934 between the most prominent producers: Great Britain, U.S.A., Germany and France. The South Wales tin plate manufacture enjoyed before the War a monopolist position, at least in the home market, as American exports had not yet developed to any considerable figure. On the other hand, while external conditions were most favourable here to industrial combination, as a relative immunity from foreign imports could have been exploited by a combined price policy, there was no tin-plate cartel in Great Britain before the War. I have explained this peculiar fact in my book on English cartels and trusts, as being due (in contrast to American conditions) to the special structure of the English tin-plate industry, leaving technical and commercial opportunities to smaller and "pure" undertakings besides the great combined works.[1] After the War several attempts were made to form a combine, among them the formation of the South Wales Tinplate Corporation which claimed through its members a control of about 60 % of the output of tin plates, but international agreements, having as their object the regulation of prices on export markets, encountered serious difficulties, till at last the above-mentioned pact was concluded.

While we have been discussing the most important international agreements and affiliations, in which German industries have become partners, we have not paid any attention to the "geographical" integration, which might be an important factor in the formation of international industrial combinations. No doubt the most important of the existing international combines must be regarded as displaying a world-wide activity. This is the case where big concerns, having a quasi-monopolist hold on their home markets, have become interlocked by mutual agreements or financial union, as also where certain national combines possess by themselves an international preponderance, as the Standard Oil, Coats or the German potash syndicate.

On the other hand and as regards European conditions, the post-War period, by the alteration of political frontiers, which had meant an economic integration, has certainly stimulated some sort of inter-state understanding between producers of territories formerly geographically united. Prof. Hantos, who has devoted a special study to these cartels, writes:

Central Europe is the classical ground of international cartels. While in other parts of the world cartels have been formed as an emergency measure by the pressure of industrial depression, there is still another, not less important, cause of their creation in the new Central Europe: the structural changes which the once united economic territories have undergone. In post-war Central Europe international cartels owe their existence to a large extent to the endeavour of the manufacturers to correct political facts with regard to their economic effects. The Central-European cartels are designed

[1] Cp. also Fitzgerald, p. 46: "It is true that there is practically no foreign competition in the home market, but there are about 55 separate enterprises, and several of these are highly efficient". An analysis of the circumstances responsible for this diversity of conditions will be found in my book, 2nd ed. 1927, pp. 211–12.

to bring into a closer union the productive and selling activities of economic territories now disrupted by tariff barriers.

While we cannot agree with the contention of Prof. Hantos that industrial combination in other parts of the world is mainly due to "economic depression", he is certainly right, when he describes Central-European cartels and syndicates as being largely the outcome of post-War political decisions which did not have due regard for the economic exigencies of the former frontiers. The cartels and syndicates in question, which can be justly styled as "Central-European", relate to agreements between manufacturers or their associations in various States, especially Germany, Austria, Czechoslovakia, Poland, but according to Prof. Hantos they may also include Jugoslavia, Rumania and other Balkan States. Among these cartels there are agreements, in which most producers in the Central-European States have become partners. Thus the Central-European group of iron works (Alpine Montan-Rima-Czechoslovakian works) joined the Rohstahlgemeinschaft of the Western-European States in 1927; there are agreements between the Austrian, Hungarian and Czechoslovakian steel-plate works, which again have made an agreement with German producers not to invade their respective territories; and there is a Central-European group of cartelised producers within the international wire-rod syndicate. There is a Central-European syndicate for the production of ferrosilicum, of which German, Austrian and Jugoslavian producers are members. In July 1929 a Central-European glass and porcelain syndicate was formed, of which, besides many other Central-European States, Germany became a partner. An association fixing certain selling arrangements, the allocation of by-products and the purchase of raw material was formed in the glue industry between producers of Germany, Austria, Hungary, Poland, Czechoslovakia and Rumania under the somewhat academic name of "Vereinigung zum Studium und zur Vervollkommnung der Knochenleim-Industrie" (association to propagate the study and the progress of the manufacture of gelatine from bones). Besides these cartels embracing most of the Central-European industries of one branch, there are a great number of others between two countries only, as for instance the gas-coke or the cement agreement and many important arrangements in the iron and steel, the electrical and the chemical groups of industry between Germany and Austria. The same relates to a good many arrangements between German and Czechoslovakian producers. While these arrangements are in general formed for the purpose of protecting the home market by a mutual agreement about competition or even excluding competition by "Gebietsschutzabkommen" (agreements to safeguard territorial sales), there are others, which relate to competition in non-Central-European markets, while the industries concluding the agreements are mainly situated in Central Europe. There are for instance arrangements in the paper trade (Rotationspapier-Abkommen), by which German manufacturers have renounced their liberty of selling to the Balkan States, where markets are left to Austrian and Czechoslovakian exporters. There is also a convention regulating the sale of felt hats to the Balkan markets, in which Germany, Austria and Czechoslovakia are partners besides other European manufacturers. There can be no doubt that affinities of economic geography such as those existing within the Central-European States, especially those of the Austro-Hungarian succession States, may facilitate cartelisation, especially where industrial combination of some sort or other had been developed before the peace treaties.

### CHAPTER VIII

## SOME CONCLUSIONS REGARDING ALL
## GROUPS OF INDUSTRY

STUDENTS of the development of cartels and trusts in different groups of industry will be struck by the great variety and diversity of conditions which the various industries present to industrial combination. This does not by any means apply only to the form of organisation, which is in many ways directly or indirectly connected with these differences and which, as we have already seen, covers a great number of different types, from loose associations to mighty cartels and syndicates, from special agreements to wholesale monopolist organisations, from amalgamations and vertical or horizontal combinations of firms to the formation of giant concerns and final trusts, from the mere industrial combination of one group of industry to the ambiguous monopolist concentration of various branches and heterogeneous lines of production. However different these forms of organisation may be, in their common aim at some sort of monopolist domination they may be taken as one, and in fact their diversity may be regarded as more or less "structural". Far more complicated, and one may say, disturbing, seems the question, as to which of the great number and variety of circumstances, which we have been able to trace as being responsible for industrial combination, was the essential condition for the formation and duration of cartels and trusts in general. Let us remember that among the many industrial quasi-monopolies, whose history and present position we have described in the foregoing chapters, there has been very little uniformity in the main conditions, which may be considered as the basis of their monopolistic domination. Cartels and trusts are by no means "Kinder der Not", emergency expedients, enacted under the pressure of severe and repressive competition, as Prof. Hantos still wants us to believe. We have seen that in the chemical industry of Germany, "depression" could hardly be talked of as a factor seriously menacing that group of industry, that on the contrary there has been hardly any industry in the world showing so much prosperity and stable progress as this one, and yet it has become one of the most complete exponents of trustification. This certainly does not do away with the fact that increasing competition and depression has in many industries and in many ways stimulated the desire of manufacturers to combine, in order to avoid individual losses by common agreement. But the sole consideration that desire alone cannot "make" industrial combination, where the material conditions of monopolisation are lacking, shows that it would be very short-sighted to attribute to depression the main cause of cartelisation. The same applies to the question of the influence of tariffs on German industrial combination. Examples such as that of coal or potash can amply show that tariffs are by no means solely responsible for the existence of industrial monopolies, as there may be trades which need no tariff at all to enjoy immunity from foreign competition. On the other hand, there are plenty of German trades in which, in spite of tariffs, it has been very difficult to form cartels or amalgamations of a dominant character. This for instance was the case in the German textile industries, which show very few signs of genuine cartelisation and trustification although tariff protection has not been lacking. Some years ago, Prof. Kurt Wiedenfeld of Leipzig gave the following explanation in a report to a committee of the World Economic Conference:

The German textile industries represent a field of industry, which is characterised by the most divergent varieties in the forms of organisation. Mixed works and a looser kind of concern exist in both the cotton and woollen industries, but they are by no means the rule and have not yet attained any conspicuous preponderance. In the manufacture of the finer grades of woven goods and cloths the works, limiting their activity to one single branch of trade, are still predominant. This is still more the case in other lines of the textile manufactures, except in the jute industry, which, owing to the coarseness of its manufactures, has been much more liable to the development of mixed undertakings. It has been a characteristic of the textile industries that they are permeated by a great number of cartels, but these consist essentially of loose price conventions and agreements about certain conditions of selling which are of secondary importance;

only in a few cases have these agreements become of a more stringent character. In earlier days the textile cartels had the nickname of "mock-cartels", as they left to their partners a great deal of liberty to evade the agreed rules, when market conditions became a stimulus to overlapping.

Conditions in this "protected" industry were just as little favourable to industrial combination as was the case in English free-trade spinning and weaving. It was, therefore, very wisely said by the Committee on Industry and Trade that industrial combination in Germany "has received such encouragement as may be derived from the existence of a tariff". On the other hand there can be no doubt, that in certain groups of industry the existence of a tariff (though not comparable in its height with that of the U.S.A.) has been an important factor in inducing manufacturers to take common action in order to reap the full advantages of it. This is especially remarkable in the history of the iron and steel industries. But there are plenty of others, in which the tariff problem has been of little or no importance. The desire to avoid severe depression resulting from overcompetition and to take full advantage of protective State measures is no doubt a very strong incentive to industrial combination. Yet it must be remembered that the more or less pronounced willingness to combine merely represents a subjective element in the whole problem. Wolfers has rightly called it the "subjektive Kartellfähigkeit", that is to say, that part of the conditions responsible for the formation of combination which are vested in the personal attitude of manufacturers towards combination. No doubt this attitude does not depend exclusively upon certain facts, which may attract the profit-making instincts of manufacturers and satisfy them that a rise in prices or a check to their further drop may be best effected by mutual agreement. There are other circumstances besides these "motives", which constitute subjective "Kartellfähigkeit". These circumstances may be accidental and they may also differ from country to country. The War period, which brought about big schemes for relief measures as regards the supply of raw materials and manufactured goods, has certainly brought the manufacturers of single branches of industry into closer contact, as the semi-public corporations

(Kriegsrohstoffgesellschaften and others) formed at that time were in many cases a starting-point for private industrial co-operation. In many cases of industrial combination the most difficult step was to "bring the people together" and to destroy by some preliminary negotiations their individual suspicion. Dr Hans Schaeffer, a former director of the Ministry of Economic Affairs, states expressly in his treatise on German "Cartels and Concerns" that from the first days of the War the leaders of cartels were considered as the persons best qualified to deal with the listing and distribution of existing goods of all kinds and that the new emergency organisation thus created was soon expanded into branches of industry which had not as yet known any sort of cartelisation and which were now brought into touch with a system of mutual understanding. Again, there can be no doubt that German manufacturers are by their very nature in some sort of sympathy with a system of mutual consent. It was H. v. Beckerath who was anxious to point out that there has always been latent in the German manufacturer the co-operative (guild) spirit and also his military education leading to a certain willingness to subordinate himself, which has in many cases facilitated the formation of industrial combination.

But "subjective" Kartellfähigkeit would be quite powerless, if the "objective" circumstances favouring monopolist organisation were lacking. This does not mean that one should underrate the psychological influence in the matter of industrial combination. There might in fact be cases where the necessary conditions for monopolisation existed, whereas the manufacturers were unwilling to make use of them. There were times, when English coal commanded a monopolist position in many overseas markets, yet a British coal cartel with the object of taking advantage of the possibility of raising the price by common action, though considered by men like Sir George Elliot and others, was never formed, one of the causes being the insuperable reluctance of the mine owners to combine on a broad national scale. While it would be impossible to start or at any rate to keep up an industrial combination by a mere sentiment of the people interested in the particular industry that it was desirable to have some sort of monopolist organisation, where material conditions of quasi-monopoly were non-existent,[1] it is quite as certain on the other hand that these conditions, given their practical value to the manufacturers, will greatly depend upon the existence of an attitude of mind favourable or unfavourable to the principle of industrial combination.

But what then are these material conditions? In reviewing industrial combination in the various most important branches of German industry we have discovered so many circumstances to which monopolist combination may be attributable, that at first it would seem hardly possible to get at a single root of the causes of industrial combination. We have seen that a good many, and perhaps sometimes the most prominent, German cartels and syndicates were connected with and based upon the mono-polisation of raw material, such as those in the coal, iron ore and potash industries. Yet Dr Vogelstein's theory, propounded long ago, that the essential cause of industrial quasi-monopolies was based upon domination over production, which could not be augmented at decreasing or equal costs, has been long dismissed as providing no definitive explanation of the problem, as indeed there are plenty of monopolistic organisations which show that a monopoly of the supply of raw material is by no means a necessary condition for a monopoly in the finishing branches. Our own description of industrial combination in dye-stuffs or electric manufacturing or rayon or electric lamps prove the hope-lessness of a theory which was plausible in times when the cartels chiefly discussed were those in the coal and iron industries.

There are other, what may be called "partial" explanations of the forces leading to industrial combination. Curiously enough the progress of time and experiments in combination, while augmenting these explanations, have not brought to light any tendency towards "concentration", but have rather increased their number and diversity. We have found out that patents had a good deal to do with modern monopoly organisation, almost reminding one of the times of James I and Charles I, when the granting of patents of monopoly to courtiers and projectors was

[1] In fact the psychological attitude may lead to an overrating of the possibilities of cartelisation. The "mode" of industrial cartelisation will then lead to the formation of rather inefficient combines, cp. Schaeffer, p. 330.

one of the conditions leading to monopolies. We have also seen how agreements entered into with regard to the common utilisation of patents and to the exchange of experiences resulting from patented inventions of recent years have—as for instance in the case of liquefaction or electric lamps—facilitated and strengthened industrial combination in the international sphere. But there can be no doubt that the overwhelming number of patents issued, especially in the finishing and highly differentiated lines of industry, has in no way been an essential factor in the growth of monopolisation. In fact the history of modern industries, based or partly based on special patented processes and methods, dates much farther back than that of cartels and trusts. The same holds true with regard to the so-called "old" and "new" industries. One may easily say that industrial combination has been strongest in the so-called "new" industries. We may quote as examples the chemical industries, electricity, rayon, electric manufacturing, and linoleum, which have shown from their very beginning a tendency towards concentration as compared with the already existing manufactures which were differentiated, and scattered into a much greater diversity of many relatively small units. This also applies to English industrial development, where the example of the big oil companies may be added to that of the industries already mentioned. While it cannot be denied that it is the "new" and "newest" industries which have shown a singular "Kartell-fähigkeit", vested in their special technical exigencies, it does not matter very greatly with regard to the general explanation of the monopolist tendency in modern industry whether certain conditions of cartelisation or trustification have been "born" with the industries themselves or whether, as in many other cases, they have developed by a slow but successful process of integration and amalgamation.

The difficulty of finding an explanation of the development of industrial combination is applicable to all of its phenomena and prototypes and is thereby entitled to be considered as being of general and final value; but it is also encountered, in examining special phases or sides of this development. Thus one has been trying to draw certain general conclusions from the fact that industrial combination has been much more prominent in the raw material and semi-finishing branches of industry than in those of high-grade finished goods. It is true that up to the most recent times it was extremely difficult to achieve an effective combination among manufacturers of such produce. It is for instance rather significant that in the highly cartelised German iron and steel industry the branches connected with all sorts of wire manufacturing have not been able to follow in the footsteps of the Rohstahlgemeinschaft or the pig-iron syndicates. Indeed a compulsory organisation had to be ordered in the autumn of 1933, embracing the lines of highly finished wire manufacturers, and forcing all those outside the existing cartel to join an organisation called the "Vereinigung der freien Drahtwerke und Drahtstiftwerke" in Lüdenscheid. But an agreement between the two existing bodies could not even then be effected and disagreement continued. The same difficulties were encountered with regard to cigarette making. The whole historic development of industrial organisation testifies to the much greater difficulties encountered in effecting combination among the much more numerous and differentiated competitors in the finishing trades and high-grade productions than in those lines of production which supply goods of a more or less uniform and simple quality, as is the case in the preliminary stages of production. A good many writers formerly laid stress on that point, such as Kleinwächter, Schönlank, Liefmann, Pohle and also Dr Schacht in a treatise on the subject (cp. Wolfers, p. 49, see literary appendix). But this structural tendency of industrial combination, though certainly of some importance, can by no means be regarded as generally applicable. We have plenty of examples showing the difficulties of combination in the most primitive branches of industry, as for instance in English coal mining, or in the later development of German potash cartels. We have on the other hand the English experiences in the textile group of industries. Here we find industrial combination in the "finishing" and "high-grade quality" trades, such as fine cotton spinning, sewing cotton, calico printing, bleaching and dyeing, while there is none in the spinning and weaving branches in spite of the many earnest endeavours in that direction (Manchester Cotton

Corporation). As regards fine cotton spinning in England, Fitzgerald expressly alluded to the fact that this branch is "in the most exclusive section at least" dominated by a single combine. This is the very reverse of the theory that there is no room for cartelisation or trustification in the high-grade quality productions. Yet one may argue that this contention still holds true, where in the finishing lines of production concentration into bigger units with more uniform production has been possible, as in fact was the case in the English instances already quoted. But even this explanation is of no general validity. H. v. Beckerath, in a study of the German silk manufacture, was able to prove as early as in 1911 that many peculiarities of the finishing lines of production which hitherto had been considered as checking industrial combination might under given circumstances be very advantageous to it. The specialisation and great diversity in the silk weaving industry forces the users of these goods to accept the exclusive buying clauses of the syndicate, because in fact outsiders are not in a position to supply even a part of the desired goods. It is worth while quoting the words of Dr Schaeffer, who wrote in 1928:

It was in those very branches of production where in contrast with some others there was no uniformity of production, and no uniform products, but on the contrary highly differentiated goods, where there were no big units of production, but a great number of small units, that it was possible by cleverly coordinating through a uniform sales agency the undertakings which were complementary in their manufacture, to qualify for cartelisation branches of production which up to that time had not been considered fit for it. I am thinking of the silk and velvet industries, in which it was possible to create what may be called a "combined association" of many differentiated undertakings, the immunity of which in regard to outside competition consisted in its intrinsic diversity, as new competition could not arise by the creation of a new undertaking, but only by the formation of a similar combination of as wide and differentiated a character.

We are far from underrating the fact that industrial combination is more likely to succeed in the primitive stages of production and its half-finished branches, where uniformity of production and the circumstances connected with it technically and commercially favour combination or amalgamation. But it will be seen from the foregoing examples than any analysis relying exclusively on this distinction would be no less "partial" and uncomprehensive a solution than the other explanations we have mentioned with regard to the conditions leading to monopoly organisation in modern industry.

What then is the explanation of the development and rapid growth of industrial combination? Even the very best modern writers on the subject, like Dr Alfred Plummer in his study on *International Combines in Modern Industry* (cp. pp. 54-5), do not attempt to find out anything like a general root to the many different "conditions" they are zealously enumerating and therefore are unable to state the "Gesetzmässigkeit" of the cartel and trust movement in modern economic development. We must reject the idea that "a number" of different circumstances was responsible for it. Eclectic explanation is of no use in this case. We cannot imagine that after a long period of free competition in industries, whose essential capitalist structure did not differ essentially from that of our days—or differed at any rate more in its dimensions than in its basic elements—a series of very different circumstances would have arisen to bring about that new form of organisation which we call industrial combination. In fact, we have been able to state that these very circumstances—for instance certain factors which have influenced the attitude towards combination and have been a stimulus of it, such as the desire to avoid depression or to reap the highest possible benefit from tariffs, or those non-psychological circumstances such as monopolisation of raw material, patents, the special qualifications for combination possessed by the preliminary stages of production; the development of "new" industries with special technical peculiarities—certainly each make some valid contribution to the explanation of the combined phenomena, but that in fact they do not give a clue to its primary root.

The final and definitive explanation of the movement must be sought in the development of concentration in industry. In fact all the numerous components, which we have been able to observe in describing monopoly organisation in different groups of industry, lead back to this. It is, however, necessary to consider the meaning of "concentration" other than in the usual and traditional way. For the purpose in question the use of the word simply to designate a supply of goods by increasing units of production, i.e. an increased unit of undertaking, would be much too narrow. For we want not only to explain the conditions leading to trusts or amalgamations, but also those leading to cartelisation. In fact cartels or syndicates are a concentration as well. Everywhere where a given demand is being satisfied by manufacturers unified into larger or smaller units instead of by a great number of dispersed undertakings, each one separated from the other in its distributive function, the term of concentration may be applicable in a wider sense. This state of conditions is by no means limited to the structure of the unit of the commercial undertaking alone. The term may just as well be applied to local or territorial conditions of concentration. The successful position of the Newcastle Vend was undoubtedly due to the fact that in its days the London and South English markets were forced to buy coal from the northern districts as "sea coal", giving to these districts a position of concentration of supply, which vanished when railway traffic changed the whole structure of the distribution of coal in England. The Ruhr coal or the minette ores of Lorraine enjoyed a similar concentrative position, from a territorial point of view, which of course became a stimulus to monopoly organisation, while extractive industries scattered over a wide and economically differentiated area are not able to offer this incentive. Again, concentration is not necessarily bound to the large unit of production, although this will be the most dominant type of it. We have a concentration in the huge butter manufacturing industry of Denmark. This has not been brought about by increasing the size of farms, on the contrary the co-operative owners of the big dairies are the small farmers united by their associations. The concentrative feature of the industry does not lie in the production of milk, but in that of butter, and it has not been at all necessary to form giant agricultural units to concentrate the industry. The same applies to the German manufacture of gelatine from bone. The small firms manufacturing glue have combined in the assembling of the raw material by collecting it on a co-operative basis. It is said that they have since then been capable of producing gelatine from bone cheaper than their largest competitor, the Scheidemandel concern, which has to buy its material on the market. Thus concentration may be of a very different character indeed, although it must be admitted that the enlargement of the technical unit of production plays the leading rôle.

The question remains, what circumstances are responsible for the fact that it is just during the last fifty years that industrial development has witnessed the growing force of concentration. When Liefmann declares that "the deepest root of cartelisation is that of the large industrial unit", one is tempted to ask, what then is the specific cause of the development of the large unit to such dimensions that it has made industrial combination possible? Was not the large unit in industry developing long before the modern phase of quasi-monopoly organisation and was not the unit of production in relation to the demand, which was so much less than to-day, considered as being "very large" and constantly increasing from 1830 to 1870 or 1880? Why then no concentration? And again, is it not true that cartels and syndicates, most of which have been composed of a rather large number of partners, are formed without any trustification at first, proving that the huge unit, which to-day predominates in so many explanations of monopoly organisation, is not necessarily identical with "concentration"?

What then can be adduced as an explanation embracing all kinds of concentration in modern industrial development? Certainly no other cause than that which has led to every increase in productive units from the beginning of modern capitalism. Technical inventions leading to an enlargement in the size of plant are not made without due regard to economic conditions. And if they are the mere outcome of chance it may happen that for a long time they will not be put into practical use. It was the change in the conditions of distribution, from local to national or even international markets, which led to the necessity of larger units of production or capitalist control over small masters in order to concentrate the sale of their produce, when the handicrafts system of local distribution vanished. The "factory" is not a sudden technical invention but an organisational adaptation of the technical unit of production to the need for selling large and uniform quantities of goods to non-local markets. Exactly the same applies to modern "concentration". Wherever an opportunity arises to supply concentrative markets, instead of spreading the sale of produce over a wide field of scattered demand, there is the primary opportunity for concentration. If it had not been for the supply of the huge and uniform demand of foreign—especially English and German—markets, the Danish dairy factories with their co-operative form of concentration would hardly have come into existence, and the development of beef and canning factories in the U.S.A. points to exactly the same cause. The beef industry of the Middle West with its huge units was founded in contrast to the system of the smaller butchers which supplied the local demands of the big industrial and urban centres in the East in a decentralised way. It was here as elsewhere the revolutionary progress in the means and technique of transport facilities which made it possible to concentrate the production of meat in those areas of the American economic "empire" which, though far distant from the places of consumption, offered the best opportunities for cheap production. In fact every progress in transport by widening the radius of centralised distribution has been active in transferring production to or concentrating it in those places, which, regardless of the cost of transport, allowed the most uniform sort of mass production. This tendency can best be studied in industries which still possess the old as well as the new forms of production and distribution, as for instance in flour milling and paper making. It was when cheap maritime transport made it profitable to transport grain from far distances in large cargoes to concentrated places of consumption that modern flour milling factories were founded, either on the sea coast or, as in Germany, along the big rivers, displacing the old-fashioned smaller inland mills, including even the great number of windmills, which existed in Germany up to fairly recent times. As regards paper making the possibility of drawing large supplies of the raw material—now consisting of wood pulp or cellulose—from distant centres of production, i.e. the concentrative form of the supply of raw material, as contrasted with the decentralised ways of collecting rags in former days, has naturally reacted on the structure and location of the paper industry. A cartel of rag collectors was never heard of. Cartelisation in the paper trade as well as in the manufacture of pulp has been quite common, the last important combination of that kind in Germany being a cartel of soda pulp manufacturers and workers-up. The cartel aimed among other points at a new organisation of the raw material supplies on national lines and a reduction in imports of cellulose especially from Sweden. In the old decentralised state of raw material supply this would not have been possible.

The tendency towards concentration, then, is the perfectly clear result of the progress in transport facilities, the cheapening of freight over long distances by land and by sea and the consequent opportunities for mass transport and mass distribution of goods. In order to exhaust to its utmost these opportunities industry had to concentrate its production, if possible from the assembling of material to the finished article, and to make the organisation of its distribution as uniform as possible, a task including a regulation not only of quantities and qualities but also of prices. This concentration was brought about in many different ways, giving rise to almost as many different explanations, though in fact the root of the whole tendency could have been easily traced back to the one common cause. We have been able to discover in the different groups of German industries cartelised or trustified, or both, almost all the different types and aspects of concentration. We shall now try to enumerate them in a general way. There was:

1. Geographical integration, giving a support to productive concentration. This was the case in the extractive industries. It is quite evident that a natural support of concentrative organisation is given where a supply of raw material in a country is located in a certain well defined economic area and not scattered over many different districts. This is most prominently the case with German coal and potash and with the formerly German minette ores. Such "natural" integration may react on the location of other industries dependent on the raw material, as for instance the concentration of German coal supplies has

certainly assisted the concentrative tendencies of other industries such as of iron and steel[1] or electric power supply.

2. In the international sphere geographical integration is represented mainly in two ways (we except the special case of an industry possessing a patent, the utilisation of which is confined to one country):

(a) A tariff wall separating the one country from others and thereby leading to national integration up to a certain limit. It is quite clear that under free trade quasi-monopolies may flourish in many branches of industry as well as under protection (compare my book on *Monopolies, Cartels and Trusts in England*, 1927), and it is just as possible that, in spite of protection, cartelisation or trustification may be weak, as in the German textile trades, or even non-existent. But where a tariff coincides with other conditions necessary to the formation of industrial combination, especially the possibility of eliminating national competition, a tariff, viewed from the sphere of international competition, must certainly be regarded as an integrative factor in the organisation of national industries. One can justify the attitude of the economists of the eighteenth century who spoke of protection as giving a "monopoly" to home industries, even when this monopoly was not exploited by a ring of those interested in the trade. We have stated before that it has been the successful endeavour of German industries to make use through combination of the integrative conditions afforded by the tariff. In discussing the price policy of cartels in a later chapter we shall have something more to say about it.

(b) A second possibility of industrial integration in the international sphere may exist where national industries enjoy a monopolist or quasi-monopolist position in the international markets. While the tariff may afford the integrative condition as regards the "import" side of the problem, a dominating position of national industries in international markets will act in the same way as regards the "export" side. This domination is rather

---

[1] Quite an interesting parallel to this may be found in the development of the American iron and steel industry, cp. E. D. Maccallum, *The Iron and Steel Industry of the U.S.A.*, 1931, on "Geographical Distribution of the Industry", pp. 34–6.

frequent as regards the supply of internationally consumed raw materials. There are many countries which do possess at least one of such products characterised by monopolist or at least quasi-monopolist features. The control of German (and now German and French) potash over world markets affords a prominent example of it, but there may be mentioned, as a parallel, copper and oil in the U.S.A., nickel in Canada, tin in the Straits, sulphur in Sicily or saltpetre in Chile. Whether these "geographical" conditions of concentration in international supply are practically exploited by the producers through industrial combination remains another question, as certainly this condition may be only one of others necessary to the formation of combines. The case of the English coal trade, ruling many foreign markets between 1850 and 1900 without attempting to exploit the monopolist position by effective mutual understanding, may be cited in that respect. But on the other hand the general movement towards concentration, the root cause of which we have been trying to explain, found, when once it began, a very favourable field of action in those cases of geographical integration afforded by the monopolist location of important international raw materials. In the sphere of finished goods such conditions will only arise where an industry has by special circumstances acquired a dominating position in foreign markets. This, we have seen, has been the case with the German trade in dyes and pharmaceutical materials of a special kind from almost the beginning of the German chemical "Gross-Industrie". Parallels are found in the position of Coats or the whisky distillers in England. Patents of a world-wide importance may play the same rôle with regard to an industry nationally integrated and dominating international markets or also branches of production abroad. The history of the early American and later German patents in electric lamps can be quoted as an illustration to this. Again, national integration within the world-economic production may arise through other circumstances leading to a dominant international position of a national manufacture. The position of the toy-making industry in Germany affords an example of this; before the War German toys made of wood held a monopoly of the foreign markets; this domination was due to the special traditional workmanship in the making of wooden toys exercised by thousands of small families of craftsmen in the Saxon Erzgebirge and in Thuringia (Sonneberg district). Another example is afforded by the tin plate industry of Wales, which enjoyed, for the same reason of having an unparalleled experience in production and a traditionally skilled class of workmen, a dominant position in the world markets, against which continental and American makers fought for a long time in vain. Both industries, however, while illustrating a condition of geographical integration of international importance, have not proved successful as regards industrial combination, as other conditions necessary to make combination successful were missing. In general, conditions of national or international integration in the finishing lines of manufactures will be much rarer than in those of the extractive industries or in the half-finishing groups, since the latter are as a rule connected directly or indirectly with the domination over instruments of production limited geographically and in its extent by natural circumstances which can hardly be overcome (except by replacement through other materials, as in the case of coal and lignite or phosphate and nitrogen), while in the working-up lines a greater ubiquity predominates. This is one of the causes which have facilitated industrial combination in the extractive groups of industry and in those connected with them, in contrast to the finishing branches of manufacture.

(c) A third factor of integration, reserving to industries their respective local or national markets, might ensue from the very nature of the industries themselves. This relates to the so-called sheltered trades, which, however, are more frequent in transport and the small crafts than in big manufactures. Competition from abroad is excluded here by the fact that there are no foreign goods to compete. It is quite impossible to have foreign competition in German books or newspapers. While this, of course, has always been the case the latest movement towards concentration in the newspaper business, represented by the three big Berlin firms, Mosse, Ullstein and Scherl, which have to a great extent invaded the provincial newspaper business, seems likely to show the importance of structural changes of distribution. It was the growing influence of the capital as a news distributing centre and a centre of cultural and political life which concentrated the interest of provincial readers on the Berlin papers, thus creating a market for a vastly greater daily edition than any local press could possibly supply. Indeed the provincial papers characteristic of Germany, and numbering some thousands of independent papers, were to a great extent (the *Frankfurter Zeitung*, the *Kölnische Zeitung*, some papers in Hamburg, etc., were remarkable exceptions) reduced to merely "local" importance, as, of course, will necessarily always happen in a country possessing a relatively great number of small and medium cities with a local press. Moreover, the increasing entanglement of German economic and public life with international life has also helped to widen the mass-market for German centralised newspapers. Another example of industrial integration resulting from the nature of the industry itself is represented by the supply of electricity by power works. This industry has first been integrated locally by "districts" and although to-day, as we have seen, the largest works have greatly increased their radius of distribution the supply will always be reserved (perhaps some border plant excepted) to the national sphere by the very nature of the industry.

Integration, geographical, internal and external, has been one of the conditions underlying all modern industrial concentrative tendencies in some way or other. The means of making this condition practically effective by the manufacturers or industrialists interested in the respective groups of industry has been industrial combination. It is evident that wherever integration of industry becomes conspicuous, inasmuch as it is identical with concentration of industry, it becomes a stimulus to monopolist forms of organisation. It is, of course, quite another question whether the motive as such will suffice to bring about monopoly. In fact the formation of any industrial combination, claiming any permanence, depends on the specific facts allowing for the concentrative exploitation of integration by the producers concerned. This applies to national as well as to international industrial combination. We have been able to show that national concentrative organisation has been the starting point for all international industrial combination. This does not, however, imply that integrated national industries organised into cartels or trusts will in every case associate internationally. There has been no international cartel or trust yet in the manufacture of rayon or its products.

The simplest and most "ideal" form of concentration, qualified to exploit the monopolist domination inherent in integration, would be the existence of one single undertaking, the trust, controlling 100 % of the production in the particular group of industry. The American development of industrial combination was expected to lead that way, but it has never got much further than the formation of more or less dominant "quasi"-monopolies. For cartelisation as well as for trustification a very essential condition will always be the number of existing and the possibility of would-be competitors. Concentrative organisation may find a strong support from the mere existence of this condition, i.e. the paucity of competitors, or else manufacturers or leaders of industry may try to accelerate a tendency of that sort by amalgamation or fusion. In fact, cartelisation should be considered as a means of organising producers concentratively in cases where a relatively great number of competitors nullifies the hope of trustification. Even if trustification in the U.S.A. had not been due to certain legal conditions it is very probable that the trust-form of monopoly organisation would have superseded that of mere associations, as American industry from the 'eighties onwards was rapidly advancing towards large units of production.

The conditions leading to a concentration of the units of production appear to be very numerous and of a rather differentiated character, but it must be repeated over and over again[1]

---

[1] A very interesting statement on this point which is so frequently overlooked was given before the Enqueteausschuss by Mr Petersen (Eisenerzeugende Industrie) from the Verein Deutscher Eisenhüttenleute (Düsseldorf), cp. p. 152, *loc. cit.*: "Market conditions have a very deep influence on rationalisation and the technique of pig iron furnaces. Thus the size of the market in the U.S.A. allows a specialising of single works and therefore the manufacture of similar products in large quantities. This again permits a far-reaching mechanisation, which becomes complete in the works fitted out with conveying appliances...the small countries are in a much less favourable position, especially when they endeavour to supply the home markets by their own production. They will be the least able to employ the conveying system or any cheap mass production".

that they all emanate from the necessity of producing goods in increasing quantities and uniform qualities for markets of growing and, one may add, concentrative capacity of consumption. We have been able to display a good many of these conditions in the different groups of German industry and we have also been able to show that many of such conditions have simultaneously been active in single industries. We shall now enumerate them in a more systematic way.

1. Concentration of units of production in German industry has in many cases been due to more or less technical conditions. Germany was industrialised a good deal later than England, the classic nation of modern industrialism. Units of production have for this very reason—as for instance in the iron industry as regards blast furnaces or in the steel manufacture as regards steel works and rolling mills—been larger from the beginning than in England. This has been frequently emphasised by English writers and official investigations (cp. *Report on Commercial and Industrial Policy after the War*, 1918, Cd. 9035). As regards the iron and steel industry, which is the most conspicuous example in this respect, the Balfour Report on Industry and Trade of 1929 said in a final statement: " British practice in the manufacture of iron and steel tended over a period of years before the War to fall behind continental practice. The problem of keeping up to date was no doubt in some respects more difficult in a country where the iron and steel industry had grown to full stature in an earlier generation than in countries which were establishing the industry for the first time on a large scale, since the latter had not to contemplate the demolition of existing plant and naturally built their own new plant to the most modern designs ". These words may be applied to a good many other of the so-called "old" industries of Germany.

2. The post-War period did not, however, interrupt this development, on the contrary it increased its strength. The work of "reconstruction", which began after the War in German industry, largely backed by foreign credits for dominant German concerns, was guided by a desire for technical improvements which naturally led to bigger units of production. There were other factors moving in the same direction. In Germany, we

were told by the British Commercial Attaché in Berlin, in a report on economic and financial conditions in Germany in 1926, "the stimulus during inflation of mechanising, renovating and re-equipping has become a habit and a complete change has taken place in the ideas governing the application of new and more efficient mechanical equipment". The rationalisation movement, which we shall have to discuss in more detail in a later chapter, became another incentive to the enlarging of technical units. It was to a great extent assisted by the desire to increase export in the fastest way possible by the application of more efficient machinery, while at the same time the shortening of the hours of labour was forcing the producer to install more labour-saving appliances. All this was quite in line with a rapid expansion of the large size of the industrial unit. In fact one may date from 1918 to 1929, when the tide turned, a new era of industrial progress in Germany, which by specific conditions precipitated the tendency towards concentration of units inherent in the big industries.

3. Then there is the technical structure of the "new" industries, which from their beginning have been a field of large units of production. We have been able to show by several examples that Germany has been a keen pioneer in developing industries, whose progress was dependent on costly research work and large and risky outlay of capital. It is a curious fact that industries, not developing directly from existing manufactures, have always been marked by "relatively" large units of production. We may go back to the beginning of modern industrial capitalism to state this, since, for instance, "new" industries were the very playground of monopolist financiers in the seventeenth century in England and again in the later period of the "industrial revolution" the plant of the "new" productions differed in size at the outset from that of the small craftsman. New industries in the capitalist era have always been based on costly technical innovations, making it possible to produce more value per unit than in the traditional sphere of manufacture, in which the tendency towards bigger units, though existing, seemed to be subject to a more evolutionary process. The larger technical unit of pig-iron furnaces

or of spinning mills has slowly developed out of existing generations of very numerous smaller units, while, as we have seen, in the German rayon industry, in electrical manufacturing and engineering, in the production of nitrogen and nitrogen fertilisers, in power supply, liquid fuel or in linoleum, plant controlling from the beginning a relatively large percentage of the national production has been a characteristic feature. This is certainly not accidental. In fact the supply of new goods or services replacing older ones, by their kind as well as by greater cheapness, is generally based on a demand wider and greater than before; which allows and even necessitates the development of a larger size in the unit of production.

4. Besides technical concentration of units we are accustomed to speak of horizontal and vertical combination in industry, which are essentially of an economic and organisational character. Of course it will not be overlooked that both kinds of combination may evolve "technical" changes as well; thus as regards vertical combination we have seen that a combination of blast furnaces and steel works and rolling mills with coking ovens becomes a technical necessity of modern fuel economy, the hot metal from the furnace being converted into steel and then rolled without being allowed to get cold. Vertical combination had become here a direct condition of technical progress. But this seems exceptional. The main advantages of horizontal as well as vertical combination lie primarily in a better economic organisation. The grouping of competing (horizontal) plant or companies into one undertaking diminishes wasteful competition and increases the possibilities of economy in many sectors of producing and distributing costs. As regards horizontal combination a unification and standardisation of production and an organisation of production programmes becomes possible, which will be especially suited to the concentrative demands of large-scale sale. Such advantages of horizontal combination can be well observed, as we have been able to show, in the history of the German manufacture of electric lamps. As regards vertical combination the advantages of "mixed" works are manifold. We must distinguish two motives for the formation of vertically combined undertakings. One is to effect economies by drawing

raw material and half-finished products from one's own companies, thus avoiding the higher prices charged by intermediate stages of production. While there has been as a rule no vertical combination in the German spinning and weaving branches, a huge combination of that kind has existed for a long time in another branch of the textile industry, represented by the Blumenstein concern. This huge undertaking has combined the trade in sacks with the spinning and weaving of jute, through the formation of a horizontal combination in the jute industry (Vereinigte Jute A.G., in Hamburg), and a similar step was taken as regards the manufacture of hemp (Hanfunion A.G., Berlin-Schopfheim). This combination was followed by successful attempts to enter into the business of the users of sacks, the Blumenstein concern acquiring important interests in flour milling works, which had been their customers. A further enlargement of this vertical combination was effected by acquiring share majorities or interests in numerous important companies of the cotton and linen branches and a bank was formed (Bank für Textilindustrie A.G. in Berlin) with a capital of 12 million R.M., which holds the financial control over undertakings federated to the concern numbering as many as 70–75. From this kind of vertical combination, which is mainly due to the desire to increase gains by eliminating the profits of several intermediaries (besides some other "accidental" influences such as the turn-over tax which has acted in Germany as an encouragement to vertical combination, since the latter offered a way of avoiding the sale of goods at each stage of production), we must distinguish, though its effect will be the same, vertical combination due to the necessity of evading monopolist domination either in buying or in selling. In England the latter kind of vertical combination seems to be rare; in fact Fitzgerald expressly states that "the only trusts which have considered it necessary to adopt this form of integration are the alkali, soap and tyre combines". Thus vertical combination in England (especially in the heavy iron and steel industry) was mainly due to considerations of more purely economic organisation and not found "necessary" in order to avoid being strangled by other interests. It is probably from this viewpoint that Fitzgerald underrates the importance of vertical combination, which in his opinion "is not always the cheapest method of obtaining supplies". In the principal instances of vertical combination in Germany, i.e. in the coal, iron ore, lignite and the iron and steel industries, the "necessity" has been very conspicuous. As we have explained before, the monopolisation of raw materials on the one side, with its possible consequence of dangerously increasing the costs of supply to industrial users, and the concentration of the half-finishing and finishing industries on the other, by weakening the position of the sellers of raw material, brought about a movement towards vertical combination from two flanks: the finishing groups being anxious to acquire mines to get greater independence, the mining interests invading the field of iron and steel manufactures to safeguard their previous sales of raw material. That this movement was not confined to Germany—although absent in England —and was therefore not accidental, could be shown by the fact that similar tendencies were active before the formation of the steel trust in the U.S.A.

Geographical integration (local, national, and international) on the one hand, concentration of the size of the industrial unit on the other, effected by technical means and by organisation, must be considered as the two leading forces making industrial combination possible. But it must be added that these conditions are largely interconnected. Horizontal combination in the extractive industries leading to monopoly has directly acted as an incentive to vertical combination in the iron and steel industry, thereby indirectly preparing the way for cartelisation and trustification in that group of industry. The same may be true with regard to fuel supply and electricity. Again, it must be emphasised that cartelisation or amalgamation, once effected, will further accentuate the tendency towards bigger units. Thus, while the increasing size of the unit largely facilitates the formation of effective industrial combination—as decreasing numbers of competitors always mean a facilitating of mutual understanding, and the paucity of undertakings a greater guarantee of its duration—industrial combination, once effected, may strengthen the conditions of its existence by leading to a further reduction of units. This will be the case when cartels or huge amalgamated concerns are willing to follow a policy of active concentration. We have explained how members of the coal cartels from the very beginning were anxious to acquire less efficient mines in order to shut them down and increase their own quota in the syndicate. In the case of big amalgamations the process is still less complicated. It is usually one of the avowed objects of amalgamation to do away with redundant plant; a typical example of this has been the policy of the Stahlverein, the result of which we shall state on a later page. The Enqueteausschuss has called this kind of policy "Negative Rationalisierung" (passive rationalisation), making a distinction between those measures of rationalisation aimed at greater efficiency by technical progress, which might be called "active" rationalisation, and those aimed at greater efficiency by concentrating on the most efficient plant and eliminating weaker works. At any rate, it becomes evident that the process of concentration of industry will in many cases not be terminated by the formation of cartels or trust-like concerns. This also relates to geographical integration, not to concentration of units alone. Thus in 1930 important parts of the Siegerland iron industry became idle, the production quotas having been transferred to more efficient works in the Ruhr district.

This leads us to another aspect of the problem. Cartels and trusts do not appear to be the mere "forms" of industrial combination. They may be active in strengthening as well as weakening the very conditions of organised industrial monopoly. We have observed that in potash and coal mining, cartelisation did not lead to the expected end of monopoly organisation; on the contrary the number of competitors and the stress of competition increased under the shelter of the syndicate. In coal mining, too, cartels did not in the long run succeed in co-ordinating competing interests. In both cases the State had to "protect" the cartel. The lack of success or the instability of monopoly organisation might be due to two facts. There is no doubt that, in most recent times, the movement towards cartelisation, becoming a sort of industrial slogan, has induced industrialists to combine, although in fact the material conditions for combination did not exist. Schaeffer is certainly right in stating that the "penetration of the cartel problem by legal considerations", that is by the opinion that industrial combination might be effected through a clever use of certain legal clauses and arrangements, "has transferred cartelisation to fields of industry, hitherto quite alien to such organisation". He adds that a great number of such cartels were practically ineffective, as those very legal enactments left a good many loopholes for escape. On the other hand the objective conditions, or some of them, which we have been discussing may in fact exist, although cartelisation does not seem to be the proper means of realising an effective state of industrial combination. It is well known that the cartel agreement may, far from attempting to concentrate production in the most efficient undertakings, contain clauses for the protection of plant which would be better destroyed. It was interesting to observe that the difficulties encountered in the English steel industry as regards the formation of a cartel were rather increased by the fact, alluded to by Sir W. Firth in a speech before the London Iron and Steel Exchange on 30 January 1934, that the only prices voluntarily agreed to would have been those that showed a profit to the least efficient plants. If this were the policy of cartels, one would be induced to argue that they were rather slowing down the tendencies towards monopoly than accelerating it, and this paradoxical view will probably be verified in such cases, after such a combination has lingered for a few years. If therefore cartels and syndicates do not intend to follow a policy of rationalisation of undertakings by shutting down redundant plant, the process towards concentration will be carried on by other forces. We have been able to show that amalgamation within the cartel or amalgamations of several undertakings linked together by agreements or by a framework of conventions has become an indisputable tendency of the latest development of industrial combination in Germany. This again has been especially conspicuous in the iron and steel industries, but also in potash mining, in electrical manufacturing, coal and lignite mining and many other groups of industry. Amalgamations or fusions create a concentrative nucleus of interests within the cartel or convention. While cartelisation alone frequently tries to anticipate a development not yet ripe for final organisational solution, by instigating manufacturers to combine, concentration of units of production, horizontal or vertical, may directly or indirectly strengthen the development of concentration in the whole group of industry. In this way it may be argued that the form of industrial combination itself may present another condition assisting the final chance and the stability of quasi-monopoly. The problem of the form of industrial combination on the other hand will not any longer be vested in the alternative "cartel" or "trust", as indeed, as the German example is likely to show, both forms of organisation have become largely interconnected with each other. It may therefore be worth while to consider both forms of organisation in more detail.

## PART III

# THE ORGANISATION OF INDUSTRIAL COMBINATION

### CHAPTER IX

## THE LEGAL ASPECT

ALTHOUGH the "trust-movement" within German carteli-sation, as considered in the foregoing chapters, may be taken as a proof that the "trust"-form of monopoly organisation, as chosen in the U.S.A., is not exclusively due to the structure of American law, and although the predominance of cartels and syndicates in Germany is by no means to be attributed exclusively to the structure of German company law, there can be not the slightest doubt that legal enactments as well as the whole attitude of law towards industrial combination has been largely responsible for certain developments in the forms of its organisation.

In England the doctrine of the English common law that agreements in restraint of trade are void and unenforceable at law has certainly influenced the organisational type of quasi-monopoly, although the courts have shown great reluctance in the application of this principle during the last century; they have tended to recognise the principle of free contract and, generally speaking, to find a contract good, if it appeared in all the circumstances of the case reasonable and if it appeared to be made upon a good or adequate consideration so as to make it a proper and useful contract, even though some of the provisions might be technically in restraint of trade. This development in the practical use of the old English law has led an official English Report (*Factors in Industrial and Commercial Efficiency*, 1927, S. 73) to the conclusion that the state of the law after the beginning of the nineteenth century was not a factor of direct importance in controlling any tendency to combination in industry and trade, although a power of control was embodied in the common law and doubtless would have been exercised had the movement become so widespread as to arouse general apprehension. We cannot quite agree with this view. The question left open seems to be whether, if such latent "power of control" had not existed, the forms as well as the actual development of industrial combination in England would have been the same as they actually were owing to the ever active "danger" of monopolistic agreements being nullified or even prosecuted under the existing legal conditions. Fitzgerald has very aptly hinted at these circumstances in his book, when he says:

It is only in such highly concentrated industries that tacit understandings—or "gentlemen's" agreements, as they are sometimes called—can be really effective. In other industries they have necessarily to give way to formal associations duly constituted and registered, but precarious in that any member can violate his agreement or break away and re-enter into competition whenever he chooses....

And again:

The defect inherent in all associations, even in those which are registered companies, is instability. Their members are united merely by a temporary agreement, and that agreement, being "in restraint of trade", is not enforceable. Consequently, resort is often had to amalgamation, which, however monopolistic, is perfectly legal. The combine may liquidate the associated firms and take over their assets, or—as it is now more usual—acquire their ordinary capital and allow them to retain a separate legal existence.

If this view is taken as correct—and we have no reason to doubt it—the influence of the law against restraint of trade on the "forms", which industrial combination had to choose in England, cannot be contested, even if this influence did not exhibit itself in strong anti-monopolistic measures, because manufacturers were clever enough to preclude such measures by avoiding the "cartel"-form of industrial combination in favour of the amalgamative type of quasi-monopoly. On the other hand, it may well be argued that had these impediments to the formation of associations in restraint of trade not existed, a good many English "cartels" would have been formed before the conditions of amalgamation, resting upon a relative paucity of competitors, were fully realised, just as in Germany the "Kartell" has been in many cases the forerunner of later concentrative movements in industry. At any rate, far from being of no actual importance, English legal conditions as regards monopolies have had a very distinct influence on the form of English industrial combination.

In Germany, on the contrary, quasi-monopolistic combination was never affected by such considerations or apprehensions as regards its legal form. An association of manufacturers could choose whatever legal form it wanted. The German law merely contained two limitations to the lawfulness and enforceability of quasi-monopolistic combination of any sort, either of cartels or of trusts:

1. So-called "Knebelverträge", that is agreements containing certain restrictive clauses, may be against "guten Sitten"—*contra bonos mores*—against good morals, as laid down in the German Civil Code. They may be contested by § 138 of the Bürgerliche Gesetzbuch (B.G.B.).

2. Cartel agreements, which are likely to damage the national economic development or the public interest, can be declared void by the cartel law of 1923.

The above-mentioned paragraph of the B.G.B. has had hardly any influence on the actual powers of the cartel. The German courts have in numerous cases acknowledged the legality of the most stringent cartel agreements. It has become evident that the term of "good morals" is much too vague to be used as a basis or starting point of any cartel policy of the State. Either the law considers all monopolies as *contra bonos mores*, a view which would lead automatically to the dissolution of all industrial combinations of a monopolist character, or else one tries to judge the lawfulness of monopolies by their economic behaviour. This would lead to problems, which by their economic differentiation and complexity, are far outside the sphere of any practical jurisdiction. That being the case it was early recognised that modern industrial organisation of a monopolist type would need sooner or later special legal enactments to deal with its special effects on economic life. But neither the cartel commission, which sat from 14 November 1902 to 21 January 1905, nor the numerous suggestions and proposals made in the Reichstag or by such important bodies as the Deutsche Juristentag or the Verein für Sozialpolitik led to anything like a preliminary shaping of a cartel law. On the contrary, the State by decreeing compulsory cartel organisation in the potash industry by 1910 seemed to be more in favour of than against the principles of industrial combination. The supervision of cartel practice was limited to the mere theoretical collection by official bodies of statistics and facts relating to problems of industrial conditions as revealed by economists or by associations connected with economic research. During the War the dearth of raw materials and semi-manufactures of all kinds necessitated at an early date the formation of corporations entrusted with the collection, supervision and distribution of goods of all kinds (Kriegsrohstoffgesellschaften and others); it was only natural that these bodies should seek the actual support of cartels and syndicates as being the best able to advise and assist the adaptation of industrial production to war emergency measures of all kinds. While in that period the State actually favoured the development of concentrated bodies of manufacturers there was certainly, on the other hand, some apprehension as to the possible price policy of the highly protected monopoly organisations. Sometimes there was a tendency to apply the price-usury acts, which had been found necessary in face of the disturbed equilibrium of demand and supply, to the cartels. But it was only in rare cases that cartels were actually fined for unduly putting up prices. The post-War period showed almost from its beginning—except for some of the first years of the so-called "Übergangswirtschaft", which was partly filled with fruitless plans for socialisation—a desire from many sides and parties to arrive at a comprehensive and decisive cartel law of some sort, a desire increasingly fostered by the price revolution of the inflation period on the one side and by the agitation of friendly societies and co-operative societies, which were opposing exclusive clauses and rebates of cartels and syndicates, on the other. The Government of the Reich seemed reluctant, while the Reichstag was pressing for legislation. It was on the initiative of the new chancellor Stresemann (6 October 1923) that the long discussed enactment of a cartel law became at last a reality.

This act bears the title of "Verordnung gegen Missbrauch wirtschaftlicher Machtsstellungen vom 3. November 1923", "Decree against the abuse of economic power", but is generally spoken of as "das Kartellgesetz" or "die Kartellverordnung". It was amended, though not materially, by a decree of 15 July 1933. Although born in the very last hour of that most disastrous monetary period of inflation, which had greatly added to the demand for legal supervision of industrial combinations, the cartel law of 1923 cannot be regarded as being solely constructed to alleviate the difficulties of price regulation in that period; on the contrary we may agree with Lehnich, when he asserts that this decree has indeed "grasped the most essential general problems of German cartelisation". The main points are the following:

(a) A Kartell Court is established with exclusive and final authority in regard to the matters entrusted to it, and consisting of a judge appointed by the President of the Reich, and four assistant judges.

(b) The decree laid down that every agreement controlling supplies or prices must be in writing.

(c) If any such agreement is detrimental to the public interest the Minister of Economic Affairs may apply to the Kartell Court to have the agreement declared void or may issue an order to the effect that any party to the agreement may terminate it (§ 4). Such offences against public interest are, mainly: if supply or demand are restricted in a manner not economically justifiable, if prices are raised or kept too high, or economic freedom is unreasonably restricted by boycott in buying or selling or by discrimination. In the event of an agreement being declared void, the Minister may require all future agreements to be submitted to him for approval.

If the Kartell Court, on an application from the Minister of Economic Affairs, considers that the public interest is being injured by an exercise of economic power, it may make a general order allowing withdrawal from all contracts included under the condition in question. The Court was further empowered to hear applications from members of cartels for permission to resign from a cartel without giving notice.

The Kartellgesetz, which we have outlined only in its principal features, must be regarded as a turning point in the handling of the matter of quasi-monopoly organisation by the German law. There is no doubt that it gave far-reaching powers to jurisdiction over and State supervision of cartels and syndicates, but it might be concluded from the English example (as in fact German legislation had for the first time approached a condition very similar to that of countries prohibiting unreasonable restraint of trade by law), that one of the main effects of the law consisted in deterring cartels from exercising their power ruthlessly, in order to avoid the interference of the Kartell Court. This "passive" though very important consequence of the decree may be deduced from the fact that the activity of the Court has been relatively small. There has been no sensational cartel "case" reminiscent of the action taken by the U.S.A. Government against certain trusts and leading to the dissolution of cartels of importance. Yet the activity of the Court has manifested itself in many ways. The Kartell Court has dealt with a large number of cases in which members of cartels have sought to resign, and the conditions which must exist before permission is granted may be regarded as to a certain extent defined. Withdrawal has been permitted in cases where it has been shown that the cartel is dominated by and run in the interests of a powerful concern or where a cartel has endangered the existence of smaller members by failing to make an attempt to meet changes in the business situation by altering its terms or conditions of contract. It has also been held that a change in the business situation does not in itself provide an adequate reason for resigning from a cartel. But in general the German Government itself has shown great caution in making use of the powers granted by the decree of 1923. It refrained generally from taking action in the Kartell Court and confined itself to unofficial intervention under the section of the decree which provides that the Minister of Economic Affairs may in suitable cases take proceedings in the first instance before approved courts of arbitration established in connection with trade organisations. Such courts had been established at the Central Associations of Industry, Wholesale and Retail Trade and the Co-operative Societies. The decree, having been prepared at the climax of the inflation period and largely with regard to the price problems of that period, was immediately followed by the stabilisation of the mark and therefore by a period less liable to unsound fluctuations of prices. However, the years following the introduction of the first German cartel law were faced by another difficulty as regards prices, i.e. the adjustment of the general price level to the new standard of money. There can be no doubt that this process was a very slow one and it soon became the general opinion that the level of prices was artificially kept high by industrial combination. In August 1925, the German Government, as part of a scheme for bringing about a reduction of prices, announced its intention of making a more vigorous use of its powers, under the Decree, and in particular of taking proceedings in the Kartell Court against cartels which seemed to have the effect of raising prices or of maintaining them at an unjustified level. The Government stated that it would regard various conditions imposed by cartels as detrimental to the public interest within the meaning of the decree. In the event of the decision of the Kartell Court not being sufficiently favourable to its point of view, the Government announced its intention of even proposing an amendment of the Decree. But while the Kartellgesetz was certainly considered as an efficient instrument for guarding the public and trade against certain abuses of cartels, especially in the sphere of price policy, boycotting clauses and exclusive agreements, it has never been used as a means of attack against industrial combinations as such. Moreover, since the general tendency of prices since 1929 has been downward and the fear of any scarcity of goods and of a restriction of competition has given way to apprehensions of rather too "low" prices and oversupply of goods by too many competitors, the original aims of the Decree seemed to have dropped into the background. This manifested itself, as we shall see later on, in the fact that cartels, far from being considered liable to create economic mischief, were being safeguarded by measures leading to compulsory cartelisation.

The Decree of 1923, which still forms the basis of all German cartel law, has been criticised in some quarters for not having embodied two proposals, which had been frequently put forward when after the War the cartel discussion had reached a new stage. One was the creation of a Cartel Board, as a central body to supervise cartels and to administer the existing cartel legislation, the other the creation of a Cartel Register. Both suggestions have been especially pressed by the former socialist parties. On 1 July 1926 there was even a resolution passed in the Reichstag urging the Government to introduce a bill, at an early date, concerning these two demands (cp. Reichstagsdrucksachen, 1924–26, Nr. 2062). In spite of this resolution the Government was reluctant to approach the subject seriously, being evidently anxious not to forestall the pending findings of the Enqueteausschuss on the subject. The majority of this Commission, however, was not favourable to either of the two proposals. The creation of a special institution connected exclusively with cartel matters seemed to be rather a "concurrence déloyale" to the Ministry of Economic Affairs, while it would have meant a new burden to the financial costs of the administration. On the other hand, stress was laid on the argument that cartel administration or supervision had to be done in concordance with the general and changing lines of economic policy. This, however, was a matter in which the Minister of Economic Affairs was primarily concerned, and it could never be the task of a specialised board, as a Kartellamt would be, a view which was shared by most of the witnesses heard before the Enqueteausschuss. As regards the Cartel Register there was almost the same unanimous consent; while it was stated (cf. a very interesting article on the subject by Dr Oskar Klug, in *Deutsche Wirtschaftszeitung*, 28 May 1931) that theoretically a Register would be a good thing to have, it was generally agreed that it was doubtful whether a really exhaustive and comprehensive record of all associations could be instituted—apart from the question of the very heavy costs incurred—and it was rightly argued that this would not even cover the most important field of individual combines, trusts and concerns. On the other hand it was pointed out that voluntary publicity was in no way contrary to the interests of cartels but that on the contrary

the majority of the witnesses of all groups of industry were in favour of publicity as they agreed that publicity generally represented an effective means of economic policy. In regard to cartel policy this was all the more the case as in the future cartel legislation and supervision would in all probability deal more with associations controlling market conditions than with individual, though quasi-monopolistic, concerns. It was therefore in the interest of cartels to prevent any misuse of their power by supporting publicity, in order to avoid further action by the State.

This attitude of the Committee, coupled with the fact that the Decree of 1923 gives the Minister of Economic Affairs far-reaching powers to require all cartels to furnish particulars of their constitution, membership, prices, etc., and to scrutinise their activities, has induced the Government not to take any further steps towards the much discussed plan of the Register.

As regards the general effects of cartel legislation as laid down by the Decree of 1923 it must be emphasised again that these will not consist primarily in the dissolution of monopolist associations, although, as in the case of the Berlin Asphalt factories, there are cases of that kind. But the main importance of the legislation will consist in the pressure brought on cartels, mainly by § 4 of the Decree, to refrain from abuses in order to avoid legal steps. This also corresponds to the explicit aims of the Decree, as it was stated in its official recommendation that it is not the purpose of the Decree "to abolish cartel organisation, as this would in the long run not favour the freedom of markets, but on the contrary the process of transformation involved by any such drastic action would probably leave the small and medium-sized firms under the domination of the big concerns". It has been sometimes argued that German cartel legislation in no way interfered with industrial combination as represented by powerful trusts and concerns. Thus the English *Report on Factors in Industrial and Commercial Efficiency* expresses the view,

while the Government is thus taking vigorous action with regard to cartels, it is to be noted that the Cartel Decree provided practically no basis for action against trusts. It seems likely that the recent swing of German industry in the direction of the trust form of organisation is not wholly unrelated to the relative freedom of action which the trust enjoys in comparison with the cartel.

We do not believe that this view is quite correct. We have been able to show that the movement of amalgamation within German industry and especially within cartelised industries is far older than recent cartel legislation. If doubtless a desire for greater freedom of action—apart from much more important commercial and technical considerations—has strengthened this tendency it has been certainly not so much the fear of being hampered by cartel legislation as that of being disturbed by the divergent interests of many small and medium-sized firms adhering to the cartel or syndicate. On the other hand the argument overlooks one very important fact. We have seen that all big concerns, also of a trust-like character, are closely linked up with not one, but indeed a great number of different cartels. Whatever the part may be which the dominant firm or the dominant firms may play within the cartels they are associated with, there has been yet no possibility even for the strongest of them to get away from cartelisation. It would be a great error to assume that the "trust movement in German industry" would displace the existence of cartels. On the contrary, the big concerns will show a great anxiety to support cartelisation in order to strengthen the monopolist organisation of industry as a whole, apart from their own dominant position. It can therefore hardly be pretended that cartel legislation has had any practical effect as regards the fostering of trustification in the different groups of German industry, though theoretically it would seem plausible, if cartels and amalgamations had to be considered as two forms of industrial combination excluding each other. This, however, has never been the case in the actual development of German industrial organisation.

It has frequently been overlooked by German writers on the subject that general jurisdiction as mainly practised by the Reichsgericht, the Supreme Court at Leipzig, may lead to the formulation of certain legal rules, which are likely to influence the organisation of cartels. The Reichsgericht is certainly not in a position to create "cartel law". But as the question of cartels is largely mixed up with the problems of company law—especially where the interlocking of companies comes in—any decision of the Reichsgericht may react on the formal conditions favouring or counteracting the formation of cartels or their business rules. Thus it is of interest to note that the Reichsgericht has pointed out in a decision concerning a company in the tar utilisation branch (Gesellschaft für Teerverwertung), that as regards the effect on market conditions it did not matter whether the company possessed any sort of a monopolist or dominant position but that the essential fact was whether it could "influence" market conditions at all (Marktbeeinflussung). Another case seems not less important as regards the jurisdiction of the Reichsgericht: if any association or cartel has made any exclusive agreements—if for instance the said company in the tar utilisation branch was making agreements with its members to deliver all tar to the Association for utilisation and sale—the question arises what would happen if an outside firm, supplying tar to the open market, became fused with another firm belonging to the cartel. Are the exclusive agreements relating to the latter binding for the amalgamated companies or not? The Reichsgericht has decided that they are not. The new company therefore would partly belong to the syndicate, partly not. The Reichsgericht takes the view that such exclusive agreements are meant to be more or less elastic and are therefore terminated whenever a new organisation is created by the way of merger or fusion. We have mentioned these cases not for their importance to the general legal aspect of the cartel problem, but merely to show how deeply decisions of that kind may influence organisational problems connected with industrial combination. Just as in England the Nordenfelt case of 1894 or the Mogul case of 1892 has become of classic importance with regard to the jurisprudence of industrial combination, so in all probability decisions of the Reichsgericht will be largely used in the future as "the" authoritative interpretation of the many points yet left open or only vaguely dealt with by the cartel law. Yet, as regards these functions of the highest and most authoritative German Court there always remains the alternative:

> whether the Court shall be limited to decide on general principles how far in every case brought before it the conditions of fair or unfair economic dealing seem to be violated or not,
>
> or whether it will be possible to create a sort of objective and specified measure of judgment applicable to the actual

development of industrial combination and its problems, as for instance in the question of "fair" prices a comparison of prices with costs schedules.

Here it may be said that as regards the "legal" position in Germany the same point of view holds good as was very aptly put some time ago by Lord Justice Fry in the Mogul case: "To draw a line between fair and unfair competition, between what is reasonable or unreasonable, passes the power of the Courts". But it must not be overlooked that this view is decidedly that of a lawyer, while the difficulty as regards the cartel jurisdiction consists in the fact that this problem is just as eminently surrounded by the necessities of law as by those of economic welfare. With regard to the latter the difficulties of forming a so-called "objective" view are almost insurmountable, as in fact the problem of industrial combination is just as liable to subjective views and political bias as any other question of economic "policy". The German Kartell Court has therefore been endowed with far-reaching powers to make decisions following general economic and social opinions as regards "fair" or "unfair" actions of industrial quasi-monopolies. But here lies indeed the most difficult problem of all cartel jurisdiction. Fritz Koch, writing on English cartel law and comparing in a special paragraph of his book English and German legal conditions, comes to the conclusion:

The fact that the English judge has to decide without the help of trained economists and without any special investigation into the conditions of the specific branch involved, because he is only allowed to use the evidence concerning the economic status of the industrial combination at the date of its agreement, has led to the consequence that this problem, being in general economic and most complicated, is dealt with and a decision is reached by merely taking into consideration the stereotyped aspects of monopoly.

This in fact remains up to our time the most conspicuous difference in the attitude of German and English cartel jurisdiction. The legal bodies destined to decide about the legality of cartel agreements and the legal practice by which they arrive at such decisions differ entirely in both countries. The English ordinary courts, contrary to the German Kartell Court, consider the questions of "reasonableness" and "public policy" not from the economic but from the legal point of view, and have but little regard for any clauses of an agreement which might seem hurtful to national "economic" welfare.[1]

As to the term "national economic welfare", its meaning is partly defined in §§ 4, 8 and 9 of the Decree of 1923. These sections of the law also deal with what has been called "Organisationszwang" and what in fact represents one of the most important topics of cartel jurisdiction. By "Organisationszwang" there must be understood any action on the side of the cartel consisting of coercive measures either as regards its members or outside firms. All three paragraphs are based, in so far as they touch this matter, on the principle of protecting the "general welfare" if it becomes endangered by the restriction of "economic freedom" through cartels. The first of the three paragraphs mentions among other facts boycotting in purchase or sale or discrimination in prices or otherwise. The other paragraphs are more definite, § 8 granting the right of terminating the agreement without giving notice in the case of a stringent reason, § 9 protecting outsiders from unfair coercion through boycotting. A "stringent reason" might be defined as "if the economic freedom of action of the firm wishing to terminate the agreement is restricted in an unjustifiable manner, especially as regards production, sale or price regulation". In § 9 it is stated that neither deposits safeguarding the maintenance of agreements may be used, nor boycotting or other disadvantageous actions be

[1] Prof. Macgregor in his very interesting study, *Enterprise, Purpose and Profit*, published by the Oxford Press in 1934, gives a detailed classification of the different issues of trade practice connected with industrial combination in England. There are practices which are "against good conduct", there is secondly the "intention to create" pernicious monopoly, there are cases where economic enquiry is essential and others "where the problem is whether what is being done goes beyond what anyone ought to expect who goes into competitive business". As regards the practical legal aspect of the problem in England Prof. Macgregor is, however, well aware, although he only wishes to speak as a "layman", that the courts of the country tend to disclaim their competence to deal with "economic results", and this is entirely in accordance with our own view of the subject. But it would be interesting and certainly of great value if the question of the outspoken reluctance of English legal practice with regard to economic issues of this kind could find some scientific and interpretative explanation. And one may add that the economist will have as good a title to be interested in such investigation as the student of English Law.

brought about without special consent of the chairman of the Kartell Court. The meaning and interpretation of § 8 has been the subject of much discussion. On the one side it was recognised that the so-called "Exclusiv-Verträge", exclusive agreements binding the members of a cartel or syndicate to buy exclusively from certain firms or to deal exclusively with members (ausschliesslicher Verbandsverkehr) may lead to very oppressive conditions, which would certainly entail the loss of the last remnant of individual liberty among the members of such agreements. On the other hand it has been argued by many economic writers, such as v. Beckerath and others, that the above-mentioned paragraphs meant rather too much weakening of the power of the cartel, which in fact had to be based on some sort of coercion of its members. The term of "unfair" coercion or of certain "reasons" which may be regarded as "justifying" disruption remains vague and entirely liable to relative interpretation. There can be no doubt that much of this interpretation will depend on the whole attitude of economic policy towards industrial combination, and this attitude will certainly be different in different periods of economic development. It is most significant that the Enqueteausschuss has emphasised more than once (cp. for instance Generalbericht, Part IV, erster Abschnitt, 1930, pp. 16–17) that the Decree of 1923 was not to be considered in any way as opposed to cartels or syndicates, but that it considered the "monopolisation of goods by their proprietors not caused by cartels, but rather by the decay of the value of money (inflation) and the disorganisation of economic conditions", and that its object was principally and essentially to "protect citizens against economic exploitation". How far-reaching exclusive agreements may be, has been illustrated by Liefmann, who quotes the very drastic case of the Deutsche Tuchkonvention. This association in the German cloth trade, together with some cartels in the weaving branch, had arranged in 1921 an agreement relating to exclusive dealing with some associations in the men's clothing manufacture. These latter were asking for the boycotting of no fewer than seventy-two factories in twenty-six different places in the country from the sale of the raw material, because these had bought some material from factories outside of the weavers' cartels at a cheaper rate. While Liefmann urges the Government not to shut its eyes to such tactics and while oppressive coercion might certainly be mitigated under the Decree of 1923 and with the assistance of the Kartell Court and the Reichsgericht, German jurisprudence is not opposed in principle to the system of "exclusive agreements". On the contrary, the Reichsgericht has in a number of cases acknowledged the lawfulness of coercive measures of cartels and syndicates. In other cases German jurisprudence has gone so far as to back the methods of exclusive agreement.

A very prominent case of this kind is to be found in the rayon industry. It is worth while quoting *in extenso* an official announcement of the Kunstseideverkaufsbüro (German Viscose Rayon Syndicate), made in early November 1933, as it throws some light on the practice of exclusive dealing and its legalisation by German courts. It runs as follows:

The German Viscose Rayon Syndicate is distributing the products of the firms, German and foreign, affiliated to it, excluding any individual selling by such firms. It is well known that almost all German and foreign firms, selling rayon on the German market, belong to the Syndicate. The Syndicate has already stated in the spring in several announcements in the press, that it is not allowed to sell outside the Syndicate any artificial silk, which has been manufactured by one of its members. It has emphasised expressly that anyone acquiring such produce outside of the Syndicate is making himself liable to prosecution, because he has acquired this product by taking advantage of another's breach of contract. To disperse all doubts which might still exist the German Viscose Rayon Syndicate emphasises once more that it sells rayon in the German Empire under the express condition, that such rayon shall not be re-distributed in an unmanufactured state, the infringement of this condition being placed under penalty. In so far as rayon goes to dealers these are under the obligation to sell it exclusively to the manufacturers in the following stages of production and by no means to other dealers. In so far therefore as rayon is bought from dealers buyers have to assure themselves, that these sales are authorised by the Sales Bureau. The foreign member firms of the Bureau have entered into an obligation, to insert a condition into all agreements concerning the sale of rayon outside Germany, that this is not to be transported into Germany. The Bureau may claim damages in cases where this obligation has been neglected. The Bureau also watches constantly to see that this obligation is actually kept up. Every buyer therefore, outside the Bureau, who buys rayon from a spinner belonging to the Sales Bureau, must be aware that the above-mentioned obligations have been broken and that the goods originate from a breach of contract. According to the legal ruling of the Reichsgericht such buyers would make themselves liable to damages, if they acquired goods which had been formerly acquired by violation of the agreed obligations.

This case shows that the law has been far from opposing exclusive agreements as such. On the contrary, it has been willing to lend its powers to the backing of such agreements, if it was satisfied that exclusive clauses were not violating the rules of fairness nor being hurtful to the "general economic welfare". In this sense the Decree of 1923 cannot be taken as being "Kartell-feindlich", that is, aiming at a policy directed against cartelisation. The meaning of this law merely consisted in granting a necessary protection to the public against abuses of quasi-monopolies on the one side and in guaranteeing to the individual manufacturer a certain amount of freedom of economic action. But just here, as Lehnich rightly states, the difficulty arises, a difficulty which confronts the Kartell Court as well as the Reichsgericht. It has been frequently emphasised that cartels are not in a position to fulfil their organisational tasks and therefore their possible economic service to the community, if they are not entitled to press effectively upon the divergent interests in their group of industry. This power of the cartel or the would-be cartel may be decidedly weakened by legal measures granting absolute freedom of action to the individual manufacturer, even if he has entered contracts of a binding character; while on the other hand legislation is called upon to protect the individual manufacturer against the abuse of quasi-monopolist power. Here is indeed a Scylla and Charybdis for all cartel law and all cartel jurisdiction. Moreover, this conflict is not restricted to the position of members within a cartel or syndicate, but it may greatly influence the very formation of quasi-monopoly. It is just as difficult to draw the legal limits of monopolist power as regards outsiders not willing to join the cartel or syndicate as to draw definite rules for coercive measures within the combine.

While on the one hand the law may find it proper to protect the freedom of action of independent firms and to oppose any attempt on the side of industrial monopolist organisations to force individual manufacturers to join, general economic conditions and what might be called the disorganised state of trade may make it highly desirable to strengthen by State interference and legal enactments the formation of cartels or similar organisations. It is of interest to quote the following case cited by Liefmann: an association of coal dealers in Pomerania had been refusing to allow some dealers to become members of their association, although these had signed the rules of the East-Elbe Lignite Syndicate. The association defended its action before the Kartell Court by emphasising that the trade was overstocked and an increase in the number of merchant-dealers would lead to a waste of economic costs, the existing dealers being quite sufficient and in the best position to comply with the demand. The Kartell Court, by a decision dated 22 April 1926, though probably recognising the "economic" argument, refrained from permitting the exclusion of the outside firms, arguing that while coercive measures of organisation as such were not against the law, it could not be allowed that measures of that kind could be used against outsiders wishing to join the association. To this Liefmann adds:

Viewed from the economic side this decision would at first seem unsatisfactory, because in fact by the boycotting action of the association an overstocking of the trade and thereby an increase of commercial costs to the public could be prevented. But viewing the matter more closely one might arrive at another conclusion. If once monopolist associations are declared to be legal, the obligation to take in all possible producers who sign the agreed conditions means much more a weakening of such organisations, much more a fostering of free competition than its prevention. For, if the number of partners becomes too large, the association will probably be dissolved, inasmuch as even the producers' cartel is not interested to damage the sale of its products by too heavy general costs of distribution. The obligation to take in willing outsiders is generally more favourable to new competition and especially to technical and economic progress than the creation of a "numerus clausus" would be.

This view, taken logically, seems at first somewhat paradoxical, as in fact, if the argument were right, the cartel movement would appear to strengthen free competition rather than monopoly, and the legal obligation to take everybody in in compliance with the rules would lead to overproduction rather than to restriction, and finally result in a free market. Yet in fact the development in some branches, for instance coal and potash, would, as we have described, have been in that direction, as indeed cartelisation may mean an incentive to would-be producers to start business by taking advantage of the price policy created by the quasi-monopoly as an outsider or by joining the cartel and placing themselves under its protection. In the one as in the other case the development of cartels may indeed lead eventually to renewed overproduction and to a sudden breakdown of quasi-monopolist associations. Where such development has been considered undesirable the State has tried to prevent that *ultima ratio* of competition by having recourse to compulsory cartelisation, and at the same time forbidding new competition. Compulsory cartelisation may be enacted in two ways:

1. The manufacturers of an industry may be called by the State to form some sort of cartel organisation, while it is left to the parties in question to work out a scheme leading to this end. In this case the Government generally makes it clear that in the case of a failure to form an effective cartel or syndicate the formation of a compulsory cartel would be ordered by the Government.

2. A compulsory cartel may be constituted by legislation. In this case no freedom is left to the firms in question to put forward particular schemes, but an existing association will generally be used as the basis of the compulsory cartelisation. It is also possible that the Government may issue an order acknowledging an existing cartel as being the exclusive organisation of the trade, and ordering any outsiders to join it.

The first important step towards compulsory cartelisation was taken, as already mentioned, in the potash industry, by a decree dated 25 May 1910, which, as Passow remarks, cannot strictly be regarded as compulsory cartelisation, since only quotas and prices were fixed by the State, but *de facto* this regulation amounted to compulsion, as the very elements which had endangered the continuance of the quasi-monopoly, quotas and prices, were now regulated by the Government, which thereby eliminated any further possibility of uncontrolled competition.

After the War the most prominent sphere of compulsory organisation was again coal and potash. The very important acts, which led to compulsory cartelisation in both industries, were not merely caused by trade disorganisation and overcompetition, but, in contrast to former attempts to compel the mining interests to combine, to some extent by non-economic reasons. Compulsory cartelisation was in fact meant to be a measure of a socialistic nature, not leading exactly to the "socialisation" of mines, which had been the slogan of socialist parties, but to a sort of administration in the "common interest", that is on a "gemeinwirtschaftliche" basis. This was the idea of the Socialisation Law of 23 March 1919, and of the law regulating coal economy, which was its offspring and was published at the same date but revised and brought to a final shape on 24 August 1919. In this case as in that of potash and other attempts to set up compulsory cartelisation it became pretty clear that organisations of that kind were in need of some control and supervision by the State. Inasmuch as coercive measures are used against all members of a particular branch of industry, and also against would-be competitors, once these measures are sanctioned by law, an enormous power is put into the hands of such monopolies, as in fact the beneficial pressure of competitors and outsiders of the cartel, acting as a deterrent of the misuse of its powers, has been eliminated by the State. State control therefore becomes a necessary and most important complement to compulsory cartelisation. This has been amply recognised in German legislation, and it is well to remember that the organs of control and supervision which we are going to describe are by no means to be considered as a sort of return to paternal bureaucracy, but as a necessary adjustment to compulsory monopoly organisation.

The organisation of the German coal mining industry, according to the compulsory action taken since 1919, has been mainly built up upon the following facts:

1. The proprietors of coal mines in eleven especially named districts had to group themselves into syndicates (cartels). If the association needed for that purpose had not been formed

by a certain date the Minister of Economic Affairs was entitled to form such associations by decree. Following these regulations ten coal cartels have been formed, though not all by the prescribed date: the Rhenish-Westphalian Coal Syndicate (now Ruhrkohle A.G.), the Aachener Steinkohlensyndikat, the Niedersächsische Kohlensyndikat, the Oberschlesische Steinkohlensyndikat, the Niederschlesische Steinkohlensyndikat, the Sächsische Steinkohlensyndikat, the Mitteldeutsche Braunkohlensyndikat, the Ostelbische Braunkohlensyndikat (which we have just mentioned with regard to a suit before the Kartell Court), the Rheinische Braunkohlensyndikat and the Kohlensyndikat für das rechtsrheinische Bayern. (As to the Saar territory no compulsory organisation has yet been enacted, as the administration of that district was not exercised by the Government of the Reich.) Besides these a compulsory cartel has been formed in the gas-coking industry, the owners of gas works producing coke being called upon to form a syndicate. The movement towards co-ordination through compulsory cartelisation has not yet reached its final stage. As there is no "Reichs"-Kohlensyndikat the overlapping of different districts —in so far as they were competing on the same markets—has not been stopped by compulsory group-cartelisation, although, as stated before, it must always be borne in mind that the Rhenish-Westphalian interests (Ruhrkohle A.G.) have a dominant position in German coal mining organisation. A further strengthening of its position showing simultaneously the growing tendency of centralised cartelisation has been effected by the federation of the mines of the Aachener Revier (Aachener Steinkohlensyndikat) to the Ruhrkohle A.G. in Spring 1934. This co-ordination, which was doubtless supported though not enforced by the Government, has done away with wasteful competition and price cutting of both districts in several markets, especially in South-German markets, and was considered as a primary step towards general centralisation of coal mining cartels.

2. The coal syndicates as well as those of gas coke and those German States, which by owning coal mines belong to coal cartels, are obliged to federate themselves into a "Reichskohlenverband", a supreme and centralised association of the

coal trade of the Reich. In the governing body of this central association representatives of miners and of coal consumers must have a seat. The association supervises the organisation, sale and own consumption of coal as decided upon by the syndicates, it has also to give its consent to the general conditions of delivery and fixes and publishes the prices of fuel having regard to the proposal made by the syndicates and to the interests of the consumers.

3. As a supreme body of the whole German coal trade a corporation with the name of "Reichskohlenrat" has been created, a National Coal Council, consisting of not less than sixty members, including representatives of the States, of producers and workers, of gas works, of coal merchants, of consumers and of technical experts. This council is expected to guide the coal mining business according to principles of general economic welfare under the supreme supervision of the Reich. This also includes the regulation of coal exports. The Coal Council has to give its consent to the company-agreements of the Reichskohlenverband and the syndicates. It is entitled to draw up the general lines on which fuel economy is to be conducted, especially with regard to the elimination of redundant plant and also to the protection of consumers. It has to form committees of experts to deal with all questions concerning coal and fuel economy, and also a committee of experts on questions of social policy.

4. The supreme control over coal mining, however, is vested in the Minister of Economic Affairs of the Reich. He is entitled to participate in all meetings and committees of the above-mentioned National Associations, the individual syndicates, and the Coal Council. His influence on price policy, with regard to important questions of organisation, and on the decisions of the before-mentioned bodies is paramount, when the necessity arises for him to interfere.

While in general the practical working of the coal trade organisation, as represented by the above-mentioned bodies, has not met with any relevant public criticism—even the Enqueteausschuss refrained from scrutinising the practical results achieved as regards the different problems in question—criticism has not been lacking on the part of academic writers on the subject. Prof. Passow for instance belongs to those who declare their dissatisfaction with the existing organisation. He points out, that in spite of all the newly created bodies, the preponderance of control is still in the hands of the cartels, which in general refrain from any genuine policy of "common interest", while the admission of workmen's representatives has not been able to change the character of the cartel. While recognising the importance of the fact that prices are no longer fixed arbitrarily by quasi-monopolist organisations Passow is in doubt whether this result could not have been achieved by merely giving the necessary powers to the Minister of Economic Affairs instead of building up a rather "complicated organisation". To this might be answered that it may be regarded as very doubtful whether it would have been and would still be possible to direct the very complex problems and exigencies of branches of industry so widespread and differentiated as those of coal mining and coal distribution for a Ministry not solely connected with them, while in fact it has been by no means and not even primarily questions of price policy alone which made compulsory cartelisation necessary. It would be rather risky to guide all kinds of quasi-monopolist organisations created under compulsory action, and therefore in need of some sort of State supervision, from a Ministry which in the main would be occupied in framing and supervising general conditions of cartel organisation and its policy. There is certainly some need for decentralisation. And the bodies now connected with it can hardly be criticised for not having used their powers for extreme acts of interference, but having rather shown some reluctance with regard to drastic interferences, although such an attitude may have made them seem lacking in the activity expected in some quarters.[1]

The organisation of compulsory cartelisation in the potash industry is very similar to that in coal mining. However, the structure of the organisation is somewhat simpler. There was

---

[1] It is to be noted that with regard to cartel agreements no statute has been compulsorily imposed upon the parties by the Government, but the existing agreements were either compulsorily prolonged or new agreements arranged by the parties.

one single compulsory cartel prescribed by the law regulating
the Potash Trade of 24 April 1919 and the executive order of
19 July 1919. There is no central association as in coal mining.
But a supreme official body, the Potash Council, with various
"Kalistellen"—local branches—corresponds to the national
organisation in the coal trade.

Besides these two prominent examples of compulsory carteli-
sations there have been some other attempts of short duration.
One of these was a compulsory organisation in the sugar manufacture which was enacted in 1922–23 after the lapse of the
cartel which had been organised a year before. The cartel lasted
only one year. In the match trade, which as we have stated was
organised in a monopolistic way through transactions with the
Swedish match concern, a compulsory cartel was constituted
under the name of Deutsche Zündwarenmonopolgesellschaft,
in 1930. This for some time seemed to be the last attempt to
cartelise on a compulsory plan. General experience as well
as the tendencies of economic policy did not seem to have
been in favour of wholesale compulsory cartelisation. The
Report of the Enqueteausschuss on Cartel Policy issued in 1930
did not express a very definite judgment on the subject but
seemed rather to refrain from anything which would look like
recommending further extension of compulsory organisation.
"The majority of witnesses", so it stated, "were inclined to
the view that compulsory cartels, in spite of being under the
special supervision of the State, have neither prevented the
disadvantages of cartelistic association nor brought about all the
advantages expected from voluntary cartelisation." As Passow
points out, even the social sections of the law constituting
National Councils for Coal and Potash have not met with
general satisfaction as the workmen's representatives have hardly
any chance to influence decisions on really essential topics.
In spite of these facts the tendency favouring the extension of
compulsory cartelisation has of late increased. There can be no
doubt that from the manufacturer's point of view cartel legislation as represented by the Cartel Decree of 1923 and the policy
of the Kartell Court meant rather a loosening of cartel organisation—generally spoken of as "Auflockerung". The legal handling

of rebates, of boycotting and exclusive agreements all tended that way, by bestowing on the members of the cartel a hitherto unknown liberty to withdraw from their obligations or to contest their validity. The representatives of German industry, organised to-day in the Reichsstand der Deutschen Industrie, have in general criticised this tendency and among other arguments they have contended that such anti-cartelistic measures were rather strengthening the economic powers of the great concerns, driving them to replace the weakened position of the cartel by increasing concentration. As stated before, we do not quite agree with the view that German cartel legislation of the past has had a decisive influence on trustification, as we consider the tendency towards increasing units as due primarily to economic considerations, but doubtless the argument put forward against the weakening effects of legislation on the enforceability of cartels was very impressive in a time when economic policy became desirous of strengthening the tendency of associative organisation rather than of allowing greater individual freedom. One of the leading figures in German industry and a member of the Committee on Cartels constituted in June 1933 by the Reichsstand der Deutschen Industrie, Generaldirektor Erwin Junghans, explained in a much discussed article in the *Arbeitgeber*, the organ of the industrial Employers' Associations (1 November 1933) the reasons which had led industrialists to urge the Government to enact a law entrusting the Government with a general power to enforce compulsory legislation.

The old law [says Herr Junghans], which was expected to bring about a loosening of market organisation, had the effect in general of strengthening concentration, especially capitalistic concentration. Thus the strong was made even stronger and the weak became weaker. The finishing trade especially suffered under these conditions as in fact every outsider was able to prevent coordination in this section of industry [cp. our former statement about finishing industries being more split up than the foregoing stages of production], and among the finishing industries this applied most to the exporting branches, since nations had begun to bombard each other by the exchange instead of by cannon.

It is interesting to note that the cry for compulsory measures now came from the big men in industry, as this shows that in fact their interest in cartelisation had by no means been displaced by their interest in amalgamation. Yet it was emphasised by Generaldirektor Junghans in his article on "Cartel Policy" (Kartellpolitik), that compulsory powers were not meant in any way to be applied everywhere. On the contrary: "...while we had found it necessary that the Committee should demand compulsory legislation, we were quite aware, that in the case of its being approved by the State, we had to give warning before applying the law, as it is hardly in the interest of manufacturers to be driven to agreements by compulsion".

When in fact the new law was enacted on 15 July 1933 (Gesetz über die Errichtung von Zwangskartellen, Reichsgesetzblatt Nr. 81, 17 July 1933) it gave merely facultative powers to the Minister of Economic Affairs, enabling him to "federate enterprises into syndicates, cartels, conventions or similar agreements or affiliate them to already existing organisations of this kind in order to regulate market conditions, if such combination seems desirable with regard to the exigencies of the enterprises in question" (§ 1). The Minister of Economic Affairs is also entitled to prevent the increase of new competitors (§ 5). If the special conditions of a certain group of industry make it desirable with regard to the demands of the common interest and economic welfare, the Minister may order that during a certain period the formation of new enterprises or an increase in the efficiency or the commercial expansion of existing firms shall for a certain time not take place. In such cases he may also limit the actual amount of production of undertakings.

The new law is the first of its kind empowering the Government to enact compulsory organisation, wherever it seems expedient, while before such enactments had to be framed for individual industries by special law. In the first year of its existence the new law has not been used to any great extent. It seems, indeed, to be the economic policy to regard the law as giving the power to act where voluntary efforts fail. In Spring 1934 the Minister of Economic Affairs ordered all cigarette-making firms to form a cartel. A cigarette cartel was frequently mooted in this industry and it had been declared to be desir-

able by many parties concerned, but owing to the great diversity
of interests in this industry and the many existing firms of small
and medium size, all attempts at cartelisation had hitherto failed.
Under the new order 120 firms were affiliated to the compulsory
organisation, comprising such small manufacturers as those
working without machinery (Handarbeitsbetriebe) as well as the
very big firms of Muratti and Garbaty and the works belonging
to the Reemtsa and Neuerburg concerns. When in the summer of
1934 the German trade balance showed a further tendency to
passivity and the exchange situation became more difficult,
restrictions with regard to the import and distribution of
certain raw materials were enacted, which were accompanied by
a wider application of the Government's power to order compulsory cartelisation. The explicit aim of this step was to prevent
new competition and any reckless increase of production, which
would have led to an undesirable increase in the demand for raw
materials. Compulsory cartelisation has been in force since
20 July for all manufacturers of pneumatic motor-car tyres; then
followed compulsory cartelisation for margarine, for the manufacture of chalk products, for precious stones and for the choco-
late manufacture. Also a further step towards the complete
centralisation of the coal trade was reached by a general agreement between the Central Association of Coal Dealers, compulsorily comprising all wholesale and retail traders, and the
Reichs Coal Association comprising all German coal and lignite
syndicates. This agreement regulating all questions of prices,
rebates and general terms is to be applied by the dealers'
associations also to the few coal mines which are outside the
syndicates, in this way bringing about indirectly some coercive
unification. It will of course depend upon the general trend of
German economic conditions whether the new movement of
compulsory cartelisation will be of a lasting character. The tendency to back cartels in their endeavour to use coercion in
the way of blacklisting, boycotting, etc., lately became more
pronounced, when in September 1934 an amendment of the
cartel law § 9, 1 was ordered empowering the cartel to enact such
measures before the consent of the Kartell Court had been
obtained. As a measure of safety the cartel must make a deposit

in case the Court should at a later date not agree to such action and members be entitled to damages. This very important step was interpreted by the commentators as being the logical result of applying the principles of "leadership" to cartel policy, as it should be impossible for a few opposing members or firms of the trade to combat by their opposition or by lengthy proceedings before a court measures which, from the point of view of unification, might be considered necessary by the leaders of industrial combination.

In looking over the legal enactments surrounding German industrial combination one is led to the conclusion that there has been nothing in the way of "constructive cartel legislation". Indeed Government has been more eager to enact preventive measures than to construct a definite plan by which industrial combination and its policy should be officially guided. There has been a great deal of reluctance as regards any decisive interference with cartels or syndicates and the sphere of amalgamations or trusts has been almost entirely neglected. Legislation, even when leading to compulsory monopolist organisation, has been in the main directed against any possible abuse of monopolist power, but it is hard to discover, among the many decrees and orders or from the action of supervising councils, any clearcut opinion as to whether cartels are "good" or "evil". This the economist can only approve, for judgments of this kind would be as unscientific here as everywhere, but it explains why the whole development of legal enactments as regards German industrial combination has been more or less subjected to the changing attitude of political parties and Government leaders. The political attitude of socialists and trade-union leaders with regard to industrial combination had always been based on the demand for central administration and the taking over of cartel control by an *ad hoc* administrative body instead of leaving it to the judgment of the Kartell Court. In fact this demand was reflected in an emergency order of the Brüning Government of July 1930, when price problems became very urgent in connection with the beginning of the deflation crisis. The decisions as to the validity of cartel agreements and the right to withdraw without notice, in the case of agreements being detrimental to the public interest, were to be vested solely in the Ministry of Economic Affairs and were made independent of the decisions of the Kartell Court. But the favourite plan of the social-democratic party, of creating a special Ministry or Department which would be solely engaged to deal with problems of industrial combination and replace the alleged inertia of the Ministry of Economic Affairs in the matter by the work of specially trained cartel commissioners as well as representatives of the central associations of employers, workmen and friendly societies, a plan laid down in an "Entwurf eines Kartell- und Monopolgesetzes" of December 1930 (cp. Reichstagsdrucksache, Nr. 439, 5 Wahlperiode), was not realised.

While in times of unstable price tendencies and rising apprehensions on the part of consumers the attitude of the Government has rather been in favour of diminishing the power of cartels (1923 and 1929–30) and allowing greater freedom to withdraw from tying agreements, the reverse seems to be the case, whenever industrial combination is to be considered from the viewpoint of industrial co-ordination and co-operation. Then the very object of legislation, as we have seen in the matter of compulsory cartelisation, becomes a further strengthening of monopolist organisation, cartels or syndicates being then viewed rather as the means of preventing further trade disorganisation and undesirable overcompetition. Thus indeed cartel legislation and control seems to be of a highly alternative character. "There is a wide gap between the fighting of those monopolist actions of cartels, which must be considered misuses of their power, and simultaneously a policy of toleration and even support of monopoly organisation by the State", writes Arnold Wolfers, and he infers from this statement that, if it can be shown that controlled monopoly is not much less obnoxious than uncontrolled, a policy of preventing monopolies ought to replace a policy of control. But while this view will hardly find much appreciation under present conditions of economic policy, everyone will agree that up to now no definite policy as regards industrial combination has been followed. The Enqueteausschuss has also hinted at the difficulties of relying on a constructive cartel policy while recognising on the other hand the principles of private enterprise. If one is of the opinion that the State should be entitled to bolster up certain groups of industry by cartelisation in the interest of their own progress while in other instances cartels should be discouraged—an opinion put forward before the Committee—one would arrive at a sort of "concessioning of cartels" (Konzessionierung von Kartell-bildungen). The Committee, being itself unable to form a definite opinion upon the finally desirable form and limitation of State control and cartel legislation, has recourse to a remedy frequently adopted in such doubtful cases, in recommending some sort of "co-operation" between the Government and private interests with regard to certain actions of industrial monopoly organisation, which might be mitigated or limited by the friendly advice of public and administrative bodies invested with authoritative influence. One may, however, argue that to reach such a vague recommendation a commission with so elaborate a programme, sitting for several years and going carefully into the details of almost all important combines, would hardly have seemed necessary, as in fact its proposals do not in any way bridge nor even pretend to bridge the gap so evident when the problem is viewed in its legal aspect.

### CHAPTER X

# THE FORMS OF INDUSTRIAL COMBINATION

As we said before, the forms of monopoly organisation may distinctly influence the power of monopoly itself. Where associative forms of monopoly organisation are discouraged by the law or even made illegal the amalgamative form of monopoly organisation may even become decidedly stronger than any cartel or syndicate would have been. It can hardly be inferred from all that we have been able to say about the legal aspect of the question in Germany that there has been anything like a campaign against monopolist associations. If in the last period of development—since 1923—there have been measures for greater supervision of cartels and a somewhat reluctant tendency to make the withdrawal from tying agreements easier, this has been partly offset by the growing tendency to compulsory cartelisation and by placing cartels under the protection of the State. For it can be hardly doubted that control—as in coal or potash—has meant in many ways protection to the parties seeking monopolist organisation. If the growing tendency to amalgamation, which we have been describing at length, is adduced as the result of legal measures affecting cartelisation, this remains a merely *post hoc propter hoc* contention, so long as it merely relies on "logical" grounds, not taking into consideration that there have been a number of other and much stronger facts supporting trustification within the cartel movement, as, for instance, rationalisation, economic reasons leading to greater concentration of units or undertakings, financial considerations, etc. One might go even a step further and contend that the cartel and syndicate have been in many cases merely the forerunners of trustification.

Political science has in general, and much to the confusion of the problem, regarded both forms of industrial combination as representing more or less antagonistic features. This may be the case where the question of "cartels" versus "trusts" is largely and essentially determined by the state of the law. But in the sphere of free economic organisation it can hardly be argued that trusts are superior to or more efficient than cartels or *vice versa*, or that the one form of organisation seems to be more advisable in the interests of manufacturers than the other. In many cases a trust, faced by numerous outsiders and the growing possibility of new competition, might be regarded as much weaker from the monopolist point of view than a cartel consisting of a few dominating partners. On the other hand, in just as many cases a sort of trustification may appear to be the desirable end where a cartel is composed of a great many partners with divergent interests.

The German development of cartels and syndicates may be taken as an example of the working of the associative form of quasi-monopoly under conditions of law not hampering their progress. The freedom to combine and the protection afforded by law to combination has no doubt not only facilitated the development of the cartel form of quasi-monopoly but even led to the formation of cartels where a trustification would not have had any chance at that stage of industrial concentration. This is shown by the fact that, as we were able to point out, a good many cartels and syndicates were not able to hold their own, their formation being based more on the desire and expectations of the manufacturers than on the material conditions of quasi-monopoly. In such a case the State had to step in with measures of compulsion or a movement leading by and by to greater concentration among manufacturers had to be started to save quasi-monopoly organisation. In such cases it can be hardly argued that trustification had to replace cartelisation. On the contrary, viewing the matter from the general standpoint of monopolist organisation, one would have to say that the attempt to form industrial combination in spite of unfavourable monopoly conditions could only be made when the cartel form of organisation was used. The cartel, so to speak, anticipated the quasi-monopolist tendency not yet ripe for a final organisational solution; it was merely preparing the road towards a more comprehensive form of quasi-monopoly organisation. In other cases trouble of this kind might not arise with regard to the cartel form of organisation. There are cases enough of smooth working of this form of industrial combination, especially in branches of industry where units of production and of undertakings bear some organisational resemblance and are few in number. We have been able to cite examples for such cases too. But even in these, manufacturers or big concerns did not renounce the use of cartels or syndicates or common sales agencies as instruments of common policy. In fact, only in the case of an omnipotent trust dominating the whole of production and its distribution would cartels or syndicates shrink to uselessness.

The organisational structure of cartels or syndicates, being associations formed with the object of eliminating competition by controlling and allocating the production of their members and regulating prices and distribution, does not present problems of special importance to the economist. It is far more from the legal point of view that the study of cartel statutes and forms, as being largely dependent on the attitude of law and public administration, may prove necessary. Thus a specific type of cartel form which has evolved of late has aroused a good deal of discussion among theorists. This is the so-called "Doppel-gesellschaft", "twin"-company. The undertakings interested in cartelisation federate themselves into a "company" or association designated by the civil code (§§ 705–40 of the B.G.B.). The statute contains special arrangements as regards the cartelistic obligations of the partners, including also those of quotas of production. In order to carry out the measures envisaged by the cartel another company is established simultaneously in the form of a limited company or joint-stock company, "Aktiengesell-schaft". The latter is entitled to own the property of the cartel, to be its legal representative and also to be used as sales organisation. But, as we said before, these and other forms of cartelistic company structure have had hardly any decisive influence on the essential economic problems of cartelisation.

It is different in the case of trustification. The different types evolved with regard to amalgamations and fusions have in many ways been responsible for the actual formation of trust-like organisations, as there have been cases enough, where the material conditions of amalgamation were in existence while it was difficult to find the appropriate organisation for making use of them. On the other hand certain forms of amalgamation have been tempting enough to foster a sort of trustification which may not have been justified by the existing conditions of competition. Then a sort of " Überorganisation ", an exaggerated kind of trust-like organisation, may have been the result leading in the long run to a tendency towards the decentralising of what had been carefully brought together. This was to some extent the case with the development of the Vereinigte Stahlwerke, as will be shown on a later page.

Trusts or trust-like organisations, in contrast to cartelisation, may be defined as an amalgamation or combination of undertakings (not of manufacturers) with the object of eliminating competition between these undertakings and gaining control over conditions of production and distribution in the respective groups of industry. This amalgamation in its simplest form may be effected by fusing the companies in question. But another and somewhat more complicated form of union, originally drawn up by an American (S. C. T. Dodd) and greatly practised in the U.S.A., is that of the Holding Company established for the purpose of controlling the undertakings forming the trust or quasi-trust in question, without having recourse to the actual merging of these undertakings into one new corporation. This Trust Company form of industrial combination, represented by the Holding Company, has been developed with great zeal within German industrial combination. The tendency to form big mergers on the Holding Company plan has been greatly fostered by reasons of fiscal expediency, as it is more economical to form a limited company with a small capital, taking over the majority if not the whole of the shares of the companies to be amalgamated, for thus the costly act of creating a new corporation is easily avoided. A typical example of such organisation can be found in the German and international linoleum industry, which we have already described. By such forms of trustification a peculiar condition of organisation arises, which has been rightly called "Verschachtelung", an interlocking of companies. There is no doubt that such interlocking may give to the companies concerned the somewhat dangerous opportunity of hiding their real relations. The defects of these rather complicated forms of organisation with regard to the desired publicity have been experienced in several of the famous "crashes" following the prosperity period of 1924–9 not only in connection with trust-like companies alone but also with big joint-stock companies which became entangled in commercial failures like the "Nord-wolle" of Bremen and others. Even outsiders could remark the difficulties facing the judges in such cases of becoming thoroughly acquainted and conversant with the financial structure of inter-locked companies or directorates, with the tactics of exchanging shares between companies or the interlocked domination of works. A rather complicated structural development has also been experienced by the second greatest German "trust", the Vereinigte Stahlwerke. Here, for many reasons, a simple fusion of the big works seeking amalgamation seemed impossible. Some of the firms interested in the amalgamation were not willing to throw all their property into the merger. Moreover, the new corporation was planned to be established without taking over the existing debts of the old companies. The regulation of these debts was to be left to the old companies themselves. This could only be arranged by the formation of a new company, which was to take over the works of those companies and pay for them in preferred and common shares (Genuss-Scheine). The formation of the new company, representing a capital of 800 millions, was facilitated by the Steuermilderungsgesetz, reducing the tax placed upon the formation of new companies in the case of certain kinds of amalgamation. The shares of the Stahlverein were at first taken over almost entirely by the promoting companies, a smaller part was left to the open market. In this way the promoting companies were still taking the position of holding companies and there was a great deal of interlocking. In the latter part of 1933 a financial reorganisation of the Stahl-verein took place. It had been decided to give back to some of the federated companies their administrative independence, to decentralise in some respects the whole concern and to do away as far as possible with the Holding Company structure. As Dr Vögler, the chairman of the board of directors of the Stahl-verein, expressly pointed out in his speech of 29 November 1933 the system of interlocking, which indeed had become a characteristic feature of the company, had been sharply criticised by the public. Dr Vögler explained in his speech why "eine Entschachtelung", a dis-locking, had been decided upon and why this had not been done at an earlier date. The "roof company", Dachgesellschaft, which had had decisive functions from the time of the formation of the Stahlverein, will in future have only to administer questions of common interest to all of the merged companies. To these belong, besides all financial questions to be handled by the central authority, research work of all kinds, tabulation of costs, statistics and scientific comparisons of the working of the different works. Amongst "practical" matters the supply of iron ore will have to be dealt with from a central administrative place, although special wishes of the leaders of the single ore-using companies will be taken into consideration by the roof company. "But", Dr Vögler explained, "apart from these questions of common interest to all companies of the Stahlverein concerned, which will remain within the domain of the Holding Company, our Works-Companies (Betriebsgesellschaften) will lead an absolutely independent life of their own". In the spring of 1934 the reorganisation, greeted by the press as the "end of concern-holding", was practically carried through, all concerned companies transferring their total properties and assets by fusion to the Vereinigte Stahlwerke A.G., a transaction effected in accordance with § 306 of the B.G.B. (Civil Code) and practically carried through by the exchange and permutation of shares. The interlocking of share capital between the three big concerns, Alt-Gelsenkirchen, Phoenix and van der Zypen, which for their part had promoted the Stahlverein and commonly controlled the majority of its shares, was replaced by a complete merger, while some other important companies which had been under the control of holding companies as well were also to be amalgamated by fusion.

A new type of industrial combination, which has been much discussed as being a strengthening factor in the quasi-monopoly development, is represented by the "concern" (Konzern). Liefmann defines this sort of combination as follows: "A concern is represented by a federation (Zusammenfassung) of firms, which retain their legal independence, but work in common in matters of production, administration, commerce and especially finance. Not all of these four purposes need apply in every case of the formation of a concern". The English *Report on Factors of Commercial and Industrial Efficiency*, 1927, declares on p. 94: "The term Konzerne includes groups bound together in various ways, e.g. by an Interessengemeinschaft (constituted when two or more companies agree to pool their profits and distribute them in certain proportions), by exchange of shares between companies, by interlocking directorates, or by leasing of works by one company to another". All such definitions—which are also shared by v. Beckerath and others—seem to be bound up with too many outside characteristics. On the other hand Oskar Klug, in his able study on the development of Cartels, Trusts and Concerns, states quite rightly that all definitions of concerns excel by a good deal of vagueness. Unfortunately he himself has not been able to carry the matter much further, as by his own admission he has followed in his definition the interpretation of Liefmann and others—while another writer on the subject of "Kartelle und Konzerne", Dr Hans Schaeffer, has not even ventured to give any definition at all.

There can be no doubt that a terminology of concerns offers some difficulty. The reason seems to be clear enough. In fact, the word expresses a form of industrial combination, which may be of a very differing character and therefore "vague" in itself. But all definitions yet known seem to be based far too much on the legal side of this form of association, emphasising that the single companies in question are to retain a greater legal independence than is the custom when trust-like organisations are formed by mergers, fusions or through holding companies. To lay stress on this point may help the lawyer writing on the subject, but it hardly touches the centre of the economic side of the question. The word "Konzerne" has certainly been chosen to express that in an industry or a group of industries certain undertakings have risen to a dominant position not only (although this was in the first stage of the concern development an undoubtedly important factor) by horizontal combination leading to enlarged units of production, but also by invading all sorts of neighbouring fields of production and commercial activity, though sometimes or at first rather distantly related to each other, by mutual arrangements and financial measures, assuring eventually a greater strength of the group of companies in question. This does not necessarily infer any monopolist tendency and certainly concerns must not be taken for trust-like organisations, although most trust-like companies will themselves be "concerns". We may therefore, from the economist's point of view, give the following definition:

Concerns represent a form of industrial combination consisting of an affiliation of undertakings, retaining their legal independence, but economically of equal or similar character, or of undertakings which are mutually interested in production and distribution with the object of strengthening the influence of the so-formed "group" in a single industry or in several industries, which may usefully work together.

A concern in the brewing industry for instance may be the result of a working agreement of numerous breweries or of any agreements of that sort between a big brewery and malting factories; the dominant company may at the same time enter the field of the catering business, by making contracts with inns not to sell any other beer than its own or even acquire restaurants for that purpose, start expensive laboratories and exhaustive schemes for acquiring, improving and utilising new inventions and have its own banking facilities. The result of all this may be that the said company or group of companies may be regarded as a dominant factor in the industry and indeed become a "concern". Such forms of combination will never be identical with "trusts", but they may certainly contain the germs of trustification. If there was some time ago or even still is some talk of the "Farben-Konzern" the term is meant to express all those technical, commercial and financial interests which are in some way or other connected with the great chemical trust, in contrast to other groups or single firms in the branch not representing the same degree of combined strength. But certainly the formation of a concern under normal conditions will always result from certain affinities existing between the firms to be "concerned". When in the period of inflation most heterogeneous undertakings were federated with each other, as for instance the Stinnes group of undertakings comprising the manufacture of coal and steel, shipping interests, hotels and newspapers, such a conglomeration, brought about merely by the desire to escape the effects of a devaluation of money, certainly cannot be regarded as a concern in the proper sense of the word.

A rather interesting example of a "concern" is represented by the so-called "Hugenberg-Konzern". It has been described in full by one of the intimate friends of the able man whose name has been popularly connected with this singular undertaking (cp. Prof. Ludwig Bernhard, *Der Hugenberg-Konzern*, Berlin, 1928). The interests forming the nucleus and one may also say, considering the personal aims and abilities of Hugenberg himself, the pivotal point of this huge concern are to be found in the sphere of public and political propaganda. Hugenberg had recognised at an early date the propagandist links existing between several branches of publicity, which had hitherto not been in any comprehensive degree connected with each other. The fields of his activity, directed to combine the mutual interests of these branches, have been: the metropolitan press, the provincial press, commercial advertising and its propaganda, international news service, films. These five fields of action connected with each other in many ways are each of them controlled by one head company (Haupt-Gesellschaft). In the case of the Berlin press this is the publishing firm of Scherl Ltd., owning such well-known papers as *Der Lokalanzeiger*, *Die Woche*, *Der Tag*, *Sport im Bild*, *Die Gartenlaube*. The provincial Hugenberg press, which is of an outspokenly conservative character, is controlled by the Vera-Verlagsanstalt in Berlin, advertising by the Ala (Auslandsanzeigen), international news service by the Telegraphen-Union, which controls besides its original telegraph service several publishing departments supplying the provincial press with journalistic work of all sorts (Dammert-Verlag), and the Internationaler Nachrichtendienst, while the film business is vested in the Ufa (Universum Film Aktiengesellschaft, Berlin). The latter company is by far the leading German film manufacturing company, possessing extensive studios in Neu-Babelsberg and Tempelhof, the greatest leasing department existing in Germany (Ufa-Verleih)—in fact film "producing" and "leasing" have to be developed into two quite distinct branches of the pictures industry, a vast amount of Ufa-business being done by leasing pictures made by other companies, German or foreign, or by leasing facilities, such as studios, etc., to other makers—and has besides important financial arrangements with American producers (Paramount), which however of late, owing to the depressed state of business and for other reasons, have become somewhat shaken. The Ufa also owns or controls the most important picture theatres all over Germany. Two facts have been responsible for the linking up of the film business with Hugenberg's undertakings: firstly in 1927 the Ufa was endangered by a financial catastrophe; secondly Hugenberg had already been interested through his propagandist activities in the film branch. He had formed in 1920 a company called the "Deulig" (Deutsche Lichtbildgesellschaft), which had been devoted at first to merely propagandist (Kultur) film work, but later expanded its activities to the producing of pictures of the ordinary entertainment type. Of course Hugenberg's motives in entering into this transaction were largely influenced by the fact that by possessing a stronghold in the German newspaper-business he certainly enjoyed a propagandist advantage with regard to the popularising of films.

The central control is vested in an association (Verein), the form of which bears a very unusual character. It is the so-called "Wirtschaftsvereinigung", an association based upon the principle of "common interest" (gemeinnützige Gesellschaft), that is, an association not designed to yield any profit to its members, but to use any accruing profits for the common welfare of the whole concern, either in enlarging its sphere of economic activity or bestowing such profits on matters of social welfare, as indicated in the statutes of the association. The association was formed in 1919, and reshaped in 1921. The property of the association belongs to twelve members, but these are not entitled to ask for a distribution or appropriation of it, just as they are not entitled to draw any profit out of their investment, and even in the case of the liquidation of the association the successor to its property is bound to use it in the same way, that is, for purposes of common interest. Ludwig Bernhard reminds his readers of a certain resemblance between the Hugenberg form of association and certain English plans emanating from the concentration of the newspaper business, and which certainly found their origin in the idea that this branch of business seems to be entitled to some, other than a purely "commercial", domination. The late Lord Northcliffe, owning the majority of the shares in the *Times*, once put forward a plan to transfer his share property to a "National Trust", which would have to be represented by the Trustees of the British Museum and other persons of high standing. There is, according to the writings of F. Harcourt Kitchin, former assistant secretary to the *Times* (cp. *Moberly Bell and his Times*, London, 1925, p. 277), no doubt that Lord Northcliffe was really in earnest in making such a proposal. While the "Wirtschaftsvereinigung" has taken the form of a sort of benevolent society there can be no doubt that this huge undertaking has been managed on strictly business lines. In fact, and in contradiction to the somewhat prejudiced description by Bernhard, the Hugenberg form of industrial combination seems to have more resemblance to a sort of industrial "entail" than to anything like a genuine "gemeinnützige Gesellschaft", or what would be called "Public Concern" in England, if one keeps in mind, as the *Report on Britain's Industrial Future* rightly points out, that "the progression from purely individualistic enterprises to the Public Concern is one of endless gradations and intermediate stages". But it is necessary to remember that whatever the form of a company or association may be, which claims to be "gemeinnützig", that is, working for the "common interest", the running of such a company for any sort of "private profit" should be excluded. Even a so-called "semi-public concern" would not come up to this condition, although it may be considered as one of those "gradations and intermediate stages". It is also doubtful whether the Hugenberg concern can be called a trust. If Bernhard affirms this, he is like many others confining himself to some characteristics of the legal domination of the Hugenberg Association (Wirtschaftsvereinigung), which controls from 75 to 93 % of the federated undertakings, but if we except the Ufa, certainly has no quasi-monopolist position in either the newspaper, the news-service or advertisement branch. But what it must certainly be called is a "concern". If the Hugenberg undertaking had been able or even eager to swallow up the two other leading firms in the German publishing business, the Rudolf Mosse Company and the Ullstein business with its widespread connections, a real trust, in the economic sense, might have arisen. But owing to a great number of circumstances, in the economic, political and financial sphere, this was not attempted by Hugenberg.

Concerns have acquired an important place within the many forms of industrial combination by evolving a "roof" organisation or a framework, connecting the many interlocking and partly diverging interests of a great number of joint-stock or limited companies brought into commercial or technical contact with each other. These "roof" companies are invested with wide administrative powers. Being in general exclusively occupied with organisational and not with controlling tasks, a small capital only is needed for their formation. Examples of this kind, quoted by Liefmann, are the Rhein-Elbe-Schuckert-Union G.m.b.H. with a capital of only 517,000 R.M. One of the greatest brewing and liquor concerns, the Schultheiss-Patzen-hofer-Kahlbaum Ostwerke group, also possesses a "roof" company and so does the Stumm Konzern. These "Dachgesell-schaften" may be distinguished from those types of companies, evolving out of the concern movement, which in fact control the firms so linked up by mutual arrangements or combined interests through the possession of their share capital, or of the majority of it. In contrast to the above-mentioned "roof" companies such companies will have to be called " Kontroll-Gesellschaften ".

As may be already gathered from the foregoing remarks a network of companies co-ordinated with each other and probably headed by Kontroll- or Dachgesellschaften usually surrounds a trust-like combination. There is no doubt that this state of organisation, ending in a conglomeration of interlocked and co-ordinated companies, has had its origin in the tendency to use the joint-stock form of company organisation as a means of promoting huge combines and avoiding the formation of new corporative bodies by fusion. Indeed, taking into consideration German legal and organisational conditions the easiest and most convenient way of creating partnerships in big concerns or would-be combines is to form subsidiary companies, which in German are called "Tochter" (daughter) Gesellschaften, while the term "parent company" would be best translated by "Stammgesellschaften". We have already mentioned the fiscal consideration inducing promoters and financiers to form such companies instead of creating a new one by fusion. Besides, a subsidiary company managing certain interests of a combine is advantageous from the point of view of financial policy, as the parent company by its participation merely shares its gains or losses, but does not bear any responsibility for its debts. Moreover, connections can be easily dissolved, if they are merely vested in such partnerships, and this may be a very tempting factor in the formation of subsidiary companies, in cases where the commercial success of such undertakings, as in that of new branches of production to be affiliated to old established undertakings, seems to be somewhat risky or uncertain. It is characteristic of the popularity of this form of organisation that the Reich itself has chosen it for its undertakings. The "Vereinigte Industrieunternehmungen A.G. ", in Berlin (V.I.A.G.), is indeed the German Government's Holding Company. This company with a share capital of 180 million RM. is the holding concern, by which the Reich controls its property in banking and industrial undertakings. These undertakings comprise the Reichskreditgesellschaft in Berlin, now one of the five big German banks, various important electrical undertakings, which make the Reich the second largest producer of electricity in Germany, the Vereinigte Aluminium Werke, one of the leading producers of aluminium in the world, and a number of other concerns in the lines of shipbuilding, nitrogen production, gun metal and other manufactures. The V.I.A.G. is a holding concern of the Reich. Its subsidiaries are run on strictly commercial lines.

Subsidiary companies may, according to Liefmann's lengthy description, serve a good many purposes. They may (1) merely serve purposes of production, (a) in the supply of raw material, (b) in the finishing branches, (c) in producing goods for distribution by commercial undertakings; (2) they may serve purposes of distribution, being merely organisations for selling and in some cases (glue industry) for buying; (3) they may be concerned with financial tasks, such as the taking over of shares of the concern or trust either as mere partnerships or as a matter of control; (4) they may be used as the very instruments of financial organisation serving as promoters to concerns or trusts; (5) they may just as well be connected with the financing of the buying of goods and the supply of raw material to be bought (Waren-Einkaufs-Finanzierung); and (6) they may be used to finance sales, a function to be distinguished from the "sale of goods" itself (cp. (2)); (7) in some cases subsidiary companies may be formed for the purpose of insurance, either working in harmony with the existing huge insurance companies or being designated to serve the "self-insurance" of the members of the respective industrial concerns.

It is only natural that as a consequence of the diversity of tasks of subsidiary companies, coupled together by partnerships, there is a great deal of interlocking. While theoretically it seems easy to enumerate them according to their different fields of activity, in practical economic development a network of subsidiary companies connected with each other through partnerships of a different kind must in the long run prove a disturbing factor in the organisation of industrial combination. It will certainly be one of the most urgent tasks of concerns and trusts in the near future to get their organisational structure into a clear shape, especially with regard to the co-ordination of subsidiary companies. In fact, Dr Vögler in presenting the new Stahlverein to a wider public on 29 November 1933 was anxious to show that such reconstruction had been attempted. He pointed out that the future structure of the organisation of this trust would rest (1) on Works-companies (Betriebsgesellschaften) comprising the big works from mining and steel making to the finishing stages, such as structural steel, wire, bridge making, etc.; (2) Partnerships "in an organic way connected" with the programmes of the works-companies and to be distinguished as partnerships in mining, in the supply of raw material and in iron and steel making; (3) Companies devoted to selling (a) coal, Kohlenhandelsgesellschaften, (b) iron, Eisenhandelsgesellschaften; and lastly (4) other partnerships, as for instance companies connected with housing and the wholesale supply of goods for workmen and different industrial partnerships partly abroad, such as that of the Alpine Montan Gesellschaft in Austria.

There can be no doubt that the wide acceptance of the system of partnership through the medium of subsidiary companies has been largely due to the special rôle which banking has played in German trust finance. In England amalgamations and fusions have been mainly financed by the respective groups of firms themselves and in the U.S.A. a special type of promoters has arisen in connection with the special demands of trustification. The Macmillan Report of 1931, comparing continental and especially German conditions with English, is quite justified in stating:

In Europe, particularly in Germany, there has been a different relationship between banks and industries, and bankers have been forced to associate themselves more closely with industrial development. This is not because industrialists there were more ready than in England to share the control of their businesses with bankers and financiers or that bankers would not, conditions being otherwise, have willingly adopted the attitude of their English confrères. It arose rather out of necessities of the situation—from the scarcity of capital and of independent investors. Industry started later in these countries than with us. In order to compete with us, it required more help than it could obtain from its own private resources or from the public, whose power of investment was small, and the banks were driven to assist industry to obtain permanent as well as short-dated capital. Accepting these heavy responsibilities, they were obliged to keep in more intimate touch with and maintain a more continuous watch over the industries with which they had allied themselves than were English banks.

To this one may be inclined to reply that it is rather doubtful, whether the "youth" of German industry was responsible for her requiring more capital, but in accordance with the facts explained in former chapters it seems much more plausible that the conditions favouring large-scale production and an early concentration of undertakings existed to a larger extent in Germany than in England, thereby increasing the special needs of company finance in Germany, while at the same time, in contrast to English conditions, the formation of quasi-monopolies was in no way hampered by legal requirements. It must also be taken into consideration that in England the "family" business has survived much longer than in Germany and in many cases a distinct antipathy to the "joint-stock" undertaking and its non-personal features has survived in old-fashioned English business circles, a fact very aptly expressed in Prof. Clapham's famous book on the English "Woollen and Worsted Industries" by the statement that "in all branches of the trade the promoters of a combination have to deal with special obstacles, not the least of which is the strong local feeling and pronounced individualism of the manufacturer". While we have already expressed our view regarding the danger of overrating sociological or psychological motives as being responsible for the existence or non-existence of quasi-monopolies, there can be no doubt that the reluctance of English manufacturers to give up their personal and traditional family connections with the works in favour of a "non-personal" "joint-stock" organisation, has prevented to some extent the co-operation of banking capital with the financial needs of industry. On the other hand there is no proof of the contention that the assistance of German banks to the financing of big works was due to their desire to support these works in their competition with English industry; of course it goes without saying that the financial aid of banks was bound to fortify the competitive position of big industries inside and outside Germany, but it was never given with the special purpose of combating certain foreign competitors. The co-operation of banking with industrial combination in Germany has been in the main the necessary outcome of the early movement towards big units in German industries, due to the special conditions of production and distribution, which had been leading to an earlier concentration than in England, and to the special facilities offered by the German company law. Moreover, it has certainly been assisted by the rise of a good many "new" industries, which from their beginning were in need of big capital (although the history of electrical industries, federated with individual manufacturers such as the Rathenau and Siemens families, may be quoted as an exception). On the whole it can be said that financial assistance by the banks has greatly accelerated the formation of combines in German industry, while on the other hand the conditions favouring the formation of big combines have attracted and necessitated the assistance of banking finance.

The "modus", by which, in general, banks are carrying out their financial assistance to big concerns has been described by Dr Jakob Goldschmidt, who has been regarded for a long time as a champion of this policy. The bank first goes into an exhaustive examination of the economic situation of the undertaking or of the undertakings to be reorganised. If the bank, after examination, decides to found a new company or to organise anything like an industrial combination it draws up a scheme of financing, determines the amount and the type of capital to be issued, and then, in some cases, itself takes a part of the shares into its security portfolio with the intention of issuing them at a later date. In this way the founding bank becomes at the same time the issuing bank, the latter function beginning, however, only with the introduction of the shares to the stock exchange through the intermediary of the bank.

The facilitation of industrial credit-taking by the banks, and in general the assistance given by the big banking concerns to the formation of industrial combines, have certainly evoked the danger of overcapitalisation. One may say that the general advantages of an easy-going credit machinery can turn to disaster when there is a danger that the credit facilities are too lavishly offered or used. In general—and in sharp contrast to the legal conditions in the early history of American trustification—German stock-exchange regulation and company law prevented over-capitalisation to any great extent, the publicity asked for by the "Prospektzwang" (compulsory publication of prospectuses), the "Zulassungsstelle" (stock-exchange regulations concerning the admission and issue of shares), and the law relating to reserve funds having acted as important safeguards against financial abuses of all kinds. Yet, the "boom" years preceding the disastrous year of 1929 had brought about what may be called a sort of "credit" inflation, largely backed by the inflow of American capital into German industry; a great number of companies were formed, the production programmes of which were hardly in harmony with the economic depression which increased after 1929; by the very system of participations and interlocking of holding concerns the existing safeguards against hazardous and unsound financing, especially of companies to be amalgamated with each other, were largely evaded. The consequences were "scandals" such as those mentioned above and throughout almost the whole of industrial business the necessity sprang up of writing down the share capital to a larger or smaller degree and of setting aside large sums for depreciation. There can be no doubt that in the "good" years many competitors had been bought up at prices which indeed meant "overcapitalisation" when prosperity rapidly turned into depression. But it must remain doubtful whether this development, due to special circumstances connected with overrating the "Konjunktur", with special credit facilities and the general policy of increasing exports by leaps and bounds in order to improve the economic condition of the Reich, should be taken as a proof that industrial combination necessarily leads to overcapitalisation.

A form of industrial combination not exactly bearing quasi-monopolist features, but at any rate belonging to those forms of industrial organisation which contain the germ of a further concentration of units, is represented by the much discussed "Interessengemeinschaft". It may be translated by "community of interests", although the term "community" has a somewhat different meaning in English, embracing more the general social character of the matter than the merely associative one as in German. Perhaps the expression "union of interests" would come nearer to the original, but even English official reports—such as that on *Industrial and Commercial Efficiency* of 1927, p. 72—have preferred the verbal translation, while the *Final Report of the Committee on Industry and Trade* of 1931, p. 178, used without special reference to "Interessengemeinschaft" the expression "partial union and agreements", which comes very near the real significance of the German term. The first-mentioned Report calls the I.G. an arrangement, by which "two or more companies agree for a period of years (sometimes as many as fifty) to pool the whole of their profits and divide them up between the companies in pre-arranged proportions ". This is somewhat too narrow and the Report itself by affixing to the term the word "financial" (Financial Community of Interests) and probably limiting its definition to this type of I.G. adds: "the companies retain a separate existence, each with its own management, but they may work closely together by means of joint committees ". In fact, the tasks of the I.G. will in most cases be much wider than those of a merely financial agreement. "The I.G.", so defines Prof. Flechtheim, "represents an agreement, whereby several firms retain their independence as regards the outward ('nach aussen') management of their businesses, while to a certain extent the results are to be pooled." Here again, too little attention is paid to the fact that I.G. agreements may just as well embrace arrangements about the common use of patents, the carrying out of rationalisation, the exchange of research work, etc. Moreover, the I.G. does not represent a loose agreement, but it usually takes the form of a company of the Civil Law (Gesellschaft des Bürgerlichen Rechts, § 732). An I.G. therefore may be defined as "a company for promoting certain mutual interests of several independent undertakings and for concentrating and dividing profits according to a special formula". One of the earliest I.G.s, beginning in 1904, was that of the big dye works which was indeed a merely "financial" community of interests, while the combination of the several existing communities of interests in the chemical trade by the newly formed I.G. in 1916, already widened its scope of common action. The formation of the I.G. Farbenindustrie A.G. in 1925, which was practically the German dye trust, retaining even the term of Interessengemeinschaft in its name, shows how much this type of industrial combination may be considered as the forerunner of genuine trustification. The I.G. Farben still maintains agreements of the I.G. character with the Dynamite A.G., formerly Alfred Nobel and Co. (the gunpowder and dynamite industries were one of the earliest branches to adopt communities of interests, the connections recently finding a parallel in those of Imperial Chemical Industries Ltd. and Nobel Industries), the Deutsche Celluloid Fabrik in Eilenburg, the A. Riebeck'sche Montanwerke in Halle and the Internationale

Gesellschaft für chemische Unternehmungen in Basel, the Interessengemeinschaft guaranteeing to these companies a dividend amounting to 50–100 % of the I.G. Farben dividend. Besides the chemical and gunpowder industries, Interessengemeinschaften have been formed to a great extent in the distilling and brewing group of industry, in the mining and iron and steel group, the Siemens-Rhein-Elbe-Schuckert-Union Ltd. promoted by Hugo Stinnes in 1920 being a conspicuous example, in the beet-sugar industry and others.

Of late the Interessengemeinschaft seems to have lost some of its former popularity as a form of industrial combination. When the Steuermilderungsgesetz of 31 March 1926 was carried through, cheapening the formation of amalgamations, the I.G. was frequently replaced by a clear fusion. Indeed, the I.G. had been frequently considered by the big concerns using this form of agreement as a sort of "trust" surrogate. One of the deficiencies of the Interessengemeinschaft is to be found in cases where its purpose has been the carrying through of big schemes of rationalisation. These, when once effected, cannot be undone, while the I.G. agreement can be dissolved without notice according to the Civil Code, § 723, whenever a stringent reason (triftiger Grund) arises. This right to withdraw cannot be excluded by any agreement nor can it be limited by any special clause. There is no doubt that this possibility greatly overshadows the advantages of the Interessengemeinschaft. For some time, however, the existence of this "deficiency" was hardly felt, as in practice there was little inclination on the part of those who had formed an I.G. to withdraw, and it seemed doubtful what course the courts would take with regard to the question of "stringent reason". Latterly, however, under the pressure of economic depression, things have somewhat changed. In the case of the I.G. between the big brewing concern Schultheiss-Patzenhofer and the distillers Kahlbaum, when the profits of the latter were declining, the brewers asked for a considerable reduction of the Kahlbaum profit quota; otherwise they threatened a withdrawal from the I.G. The same happened in the case of an I.G. between the Humboldt-Deutzer-Gasmotoren I.G. When Humboldt was showing a profit, while Deutz was showing a loss, the former company declined to keep up the pooling arrangement. In both cases an agreement was reached after all, to the disadvantage of the weaker partner. When a dissolution of the I.G. happens under such circumstances, bringing the arrangement to a much earlier end than was originally anticipated, there may be a considerable loss accruing to firms which under the shelter of the I.G. agreement had consented to certain measures of rationalisation, as for instance the closing of less economic plant. In order to prevent such consequences and to alleviate the apprehensions of I.G. partners in that respect numerous expedients have been sought, such as for instance the issue of deferred shares (Genussscheine), which may be retained by the I.G. companies after dissolution, thus enabling them to continue their participation in the profits of their former associates. In some cases the I.G. agreement contains a clause entitling the one company, under certain conditions, to take over the property of the others by paying down a certain sum, or by fusion. But it remains doubtful whether such an arrangement would be in accordance with the legal conditions.

It remains interesting to note that while the I.G. movement has of late been in many cases replaced by trustification, the formation of trusts has, as Flechtheim has pointed out, come about in a somewhat different way than before. While we are generally accustomed to assume that a trust or quasi-monopolist amalgamation is effected by a dominant company or concern "buying out" others, in the case of the I.G. transformed into a trust the new company is far more the outcome of a consent of a number of firms to come into a closer associative connection. In fact, the Interessengemeinschaft prepares the road for trustification, as it is necessarily represented by companies which have already reached a certain "community of interests". The state of concentration of undertakings, which already combine their interests by partial agreements, must certainly be distinguished from the former conditions of trustification presenting one dominant firm with a great number of highly differentiated smaller competitors, to be absorbed either by pressure or persuasion.

The forms of combination found in German industry are, as

we have seen, of a great variety. It is difficult to decide whether the "form" of combination has had a decisive influence on the extent of quasi-monopoly itself. It must be recognised that, in spite of growing tendencies to regulation, the quasi-monopolist movement in Germany has not been obstructed to any considerable extent by legal enactments. Forms of industrial combination could develop freely, and if of late the trustification form of combination has been progressing, using the Interessengemeinschaft or forms of partnership as preliminary stages, it seems much more likely that this evolution has been due to quite natural tendencies to technical and commercial concentration than to any direct or indirect influence of the law or state interference. Moreover, we have emphasised before that the trust movement in German industry should not be regarded as being in contrast to the cartel organisation; indeed the very biggest trusts or trust-like combinations have not discontinued their membership of syndicates or cartels—for instance the I.G. Farben or the Stahlverein—as they are of most decisive importance to the very strength and economic policy of trusts, so long as these are not controlling production and distribution by 100 %.

A controversy as to whether the "cartel" or any form of amalgamative combination—represented by fusion or merger—should be considered as the "stronger" form of industrial combination ought to be regarded as useless talk. The form of industrial combination, if we leave the question of legal or state interference out of consideration, will finally be decided by economic conditions, and not be a matter of organisational wisdom or alternative. In industries where strong concentration and unification of units is progressing for technical, economic or financial reasons, the fusion form of combination will probably evolve quite naturally. In others, where there exists—as especially in the older branches of production—a great diversity of conditions and units which gives way but slowly to concentrative tendencies the cartel or any other form of agreement will be chosen as a sort of experimental form of industrial combination possibly leading itself to a development of amalgamation, or being dissolved after some time as unable to co-ordinate competition.[1] At the same time a cartel between few partners, equally strong in power, might be quite sufficient for the economic or commercial aims of all parties concerned. Indeed there is no pattern amongst the forms of industrial combination which could be regarded as being under all circumstances of the greatest efficiency to the quasi-monopolist. The economic structure of the respective industries and the degree of concentration of units or undertakings achieved remain the determining factor of the forms of industrial combination.

[1] It must be kept in mind, that trustification by fusion does not mean a definitive break of the trust with the system of partnerships. It is generally found that even when the fusion of the main undertakings has been accomplished there remains a wide field for holdings or participations. This can be seen from the publication of the Report of the ordinary general meeting of the I.G. Farben for 1933. There were not less than twenty-eight partnerships mentioned, among which were such with companies connected with the manufacture of dyes, chemicals, coal, lignite, celluloid, motor cars (Ford), fertilisers, ammonia, sugar, etc.

## PART IV

# EFFECTS OF INDUSTRIAL COMBINATION

### CHAPTER XI

## CO-ORDINATING COMPETITION

INDUSTRIAL combination of whatever form is based upon the aim of eliminating or at least limiting competition. This is certainly not, as is frequently said, an object of quasi-monopoly. Limitation of competition as such would not be an aim to be pursued, unless it were the means of attaining what is really the essential object of all combination: an increase of profits to the combined companies. This may be effected by different measures, but it will always centre in those two functions of combined undertakings, i.e. diminishing costs or price policy or both. It matters little in principle whether the reduction of costs is attempted by technical rationalisation, or by shutting down redundant works or by limiting competition within the cartel or trust, or again whether price policy is carried out directly by fixing or administering the price level or indirectly by limiting production by quotas or production programmes or by premiums or bounties. But of course the same action may have different results, as the limitation of production may in some cases be regarded as a matter of reducing costs, by closing down or reducing the production of the weaker works, just as much as an indirect means to keep up or increase prices. In fact, the effects of industrial combination are largely interconnected. But in general it will be useful and logically right not to split up the analysis of the effects of quasi-monopolist combination into too many distinct sections, but rather into these two: the first concerning the effects related to the organisational structure, i.e.

effects connected with the formation and maintenance of quasi-monopolist domination, the second relating to the economic aim of increasing profits (*a*) by reducing costs, (*b*) by influencing the price level.

It might seem something of a paradox to talk about the results of industrial combination at a time when that organisation is not yet even effected. Perhaps it would be more logical to describe such actions as those of a would-be combine buying out competitors or amalgamating firms, etc. But in fact such actions and aims of cartels and trusts do not come to an end with their final formation. It will always and perpetually remain the decisive aim of any industrial combination to strengthen its position and to make safe what has been achieved or even to enlarge the basis of its organisation. We have been able to state in a former chapter, that while concentration of the units of production represents preparatory tendencies towards combination, the combination once effected will on its part accelerate this tendency. Thus the attempt to co-ordinate competitive forces will begin by being the starting point of the activities of would-be or rising industrial combination, while, when once the combination has been effected, it will remain an important part of its subsequent results.

In the co-ordination of competition three fields of action may be distinguished:

1. Competition within the industrial combination.
2. Competition outside the combine.
3. Competition in the further manufacturing stages and between wholesale traders.

We have already discussed some of the problems connected with competition 1 and 2 when we had to analyse the legal aspect of quasi-monopolist organisation, especially that of coercive measures of organisation. The main activities and effects of industrial combination, especially cartels, within its own borders will be the regulation of the production of the partners or in the case of trusts the distribution of production over the amalgamated works. This finds expression in the so-called "quota" system, arranging the proportion of production of the different members of syndicates, or in the actual closing down of inefficient or redundant plant.

It may be useful to note, that measures regulating production may be as well enacted by cartels as "sellers" as in their position as buyers. It has happened that a cartel, being harassed by the increasing prices of the raw material which its members were using, decided to diminish production in order to effect a pressure on the price of the raw material. But of course these so-called "Abnehmer"-Kartelle—Prof. Passow has dealt with them exhaustively—are much less frequent than "Anbieter"-Kartelle, that is cartels limiting production in order to influence the price of the produce to be sold. The necessity of using the "quota" system as a means of regulating production has led to results which may in not a few cases be called dangerous defects of the whole system of cartelisation. While on the one hand the buying out of quotas—a regular trade in quotas, "Quoten-handel", may develop—may lead to a necessary and desired concentration of production by those competitors who are best suited to hold on, it may, on the other hand, lead to speculative "buying out" of competitors to get into possession of their quota, and this again may increase overcapitalisation. On the other hand we have in a former chapter—dealing with the potash industry—been able to point out that weaker works were kept up by the hope of being protected by the cartel through being endowed with a quota (however small), while it might have been much more desirable from an economic point of view that they should have disappeared. We have described at length, taking as examples coal and potash, that it becomes rather hard for cartels and syndicates to resist the increase in the number of single producers, wherever an industry, as was the case with potash, promises future gains and offers at the same time the possibility of increased production. In such cases private and voluntary co-ordination of competition will probably fail, and, as we have pointed out, must be replaced by compulsory measures of the State, if any sort of cartelisation is to be maintained. There was a time, when this very development was regarded by theorists as most beneficial to national economy, as it proved that "competition" was in the end stronger than "monopoly" and could not be suppressed. In the light of the actual effects on market conditions, bringing about in many cases a state of cut-throat competition with fatal results for all parties concerned, such development is viewed to-day with more apprehension than approval. It is very significant that the General Report of the Enqueteausschuss contains in its final conclusions on the Monopoly Problem the passage:

The preferential position, enjoyed by trusts, cartels or cartel-like associations or activities on markets, need not necessarily be disadvantageous to the public economic interest nor should it justify restriction. Apart from the fact that there are aims of cartelisation which may be entitled to support or which do not concern economic policy, the monopoly position as such should not be a reason for State interference. Economic theorists also agree that the exploitation of a dominant position—by keeping up prices above the level of free competition—may have under certain circumstances beneficial effects.

One may compare this with some of the English views as sketched out recently in the very interesting study of Prof. D. H. Macgregor on *Enterprise, Purpose and Profit* (1934, pp. 161 ff.), in which he enumerates some evidence of still existing antipathies against what are called " the ' Black Tigers ' of capitalist combinations ". We have already shown how far differences between the German and the English attitudes of mind may account for the different legal aspect of the problem in the two countries and have its effect on the actual development of quasi-monopoly. But it also follows that any coercive organisation of industrial combination towards its partners may be viewed quite differently, according to which attitude of mind prevails. Viewed from the point of view of "cartelisation as a useful type of modern industrial organisation " the word "coercion " will be likely to be replaced by that of co-ordination, and any struggle of cartel partners trying to rid themselves of the tying clauses of quasi-monopolist organisation will be regarded much more as a lack of subordination than as a demonstration of still existing individualistic feelings. It is from this viewpoint that we must understand the following passage in Liefmann's book:

There have always been a number of entrepreneurs, who, while enjoying the benefits of cartels, were not willing to make the necessary sacrifices. Sometimes one may be able to remain outside the cartel and to cut its prices, thereby getting hold of big orders. But of course this will only last a short time. If outside competition grows too strong, the cartel must dissolve. But it also happens that members of the cartel are trying secretly to gain private advantages and bigger sales by disloyal means or genuine breach of the agreements.

It seems necessary on the part of the cartel to protect itself against such "weaker characters". This must lead to a very stringent and drastic co-ordination of interests and an effective supervision by the cartel. We have mentioned the stringent rules of the German rayon syndicate, the Kunstseideverkaufs-büro, restricting any independent sales on the part of its members and claiming heavy damages in the case of any breach of the respective clauses of its agreement from its partners as well as from those who may have bought rayon from anyone not belonging to the syndicate. Inasmuch as coercion leading to strict cartel discipline may seem important or even essential to industrial combination the submission of the single manufacturer to a network of unshakeable rules may act as a deterrent of any further individual enterprise. Sheltered and ruled by syndicates many entrepreneurs may lose that ardent personal interest in their works which has proved so great a benefit of individual activity. It may even lead, as Liefmann contends, though this cannot be proved by any prominent examples, to a greater inclination on the part of individual manufacturers to transform their business into an "impersonal" joint-stock company. On the other hand, coercive measures of organisation, called by Wolfers "der interne Organisationszwang", inside the cartel or syndicate may differ greatly with the degree of strength of the quasi-monopoly. Wolfers is probably right when he remarks that it is hardly to be wondered at that the inside coercive organisa-tion of cartels seems to be particularly strong where cartels have little to offer to their partners, where therefore the monopolist power of combination is not great. In these very cartels com-plaints about misuses of coercive measures will be frequent. The preponderance of the big partners of the cartel may manifest itself by such measures. Where the stronger partners are little interested in raising prices to a great extent, coercive organisation may prove a weapon against the weaker members who are urging drastic raising of the price level. This shows how far the co-ordination of competition may be linked up with cartelistic price policy.

The next important task of industrial combination with regard to its competitive position lies in its attitude towards outsiders. While "innerer Organisationszwang" only affects cartels and syndicates, since trusts and amalgamations are not in need of it, but are mostly formed to replace coercive measures by absolute unity, action against outsiders lies in the sphere of both forms of industrial combination. Generally speaking there are two methods of fighting outsiders to be distinguished. The one is direct and simple. It consists in the undercutting of prices with the object of weakening the position of outsiders until their surrender to the combination that is forcing them to join the quasi-monopolist association or to sell their works to the combine. Of course there are other forms of such fighting. The potash syndicate for instance had formed in the 'nineties what was called "Schutzbohrgemeinschaft", an association organised as a protective measure against new borings. Wherever anybody began experimental boring for potash the association itself started boring in the actual neighbourhood of the newcomer, in order to get earlier possession of the mineral.

The other means of combating outside competition is indirect and certainly more complicated. Cartels or trusts try by all sorts of tactics to make outside business uncomfortable. It is a well-known fact that many quasi-monopolies have based their position not, or not exclusively, on the domination of the primary branch of their production, but on that of monopolisable stages of production, connected with their own product, or on facilities of transport or distribution. We remember how the monopolisation of German coal fields and iron ore mines was used as a means of creating quasi-monopoly in iron and steel manufacture, which otherwise would have offered no other opportunities for industrial combination than that of gradually evolving larger units of production. To quote another example, the Standard Oil Company has not created its monopoly by monopolising oil fields or oil wells, but by getting domination over the pipe-line systems and thereby combating outsiders and would-be competitors. The English tobacco trust was, as is generally known, much strengthened in its position by taking over the large distributing firms of A. I. Jones and Son and Salmon and Gluckstein, which gave it possession of a great and important number of retail shops. The last-named firm alone had 170. In the same way the huge German film corporation, the "Ufa", owes much of its dominant position to the possession of actually the best situated and most luxuriously equipped cinema theatres in Berlin and in the German provinces. Another concern of this industry, the "Emelka", once the second largest producer in Germany, tried to gain similar advantages over competitors by acquiring or erecting the largest theatres in the southern parts of Germany, especially in Bavaria. While in fact it would seem difficult to monopolise film making, since the raw material is not monopolised, a number of studios are always available to outsiders of the great concerns, and actors, even stars, are numerous enough to make competition with the great firms possible, the possession of the most popular theatres in the most frequented parts of towns will certainly give an advantage to the big concern or trust over smaller outside competitors.

Another indirect way of undermining the activities of outsiders is represented by attempts to monopolise the wholesale traders of the particular branch. If a cartel or trust succeeds in binding wholesale traders not to buy from any other firm than the cartel, syndicate or trust, it will make life very difficult for outside competition. This is effected, as we have seen before, by exclusive agreements of different kinds. Here also the organisation of the viscose syndicate, which we have described at length, may be quoted as an example. The stringent rules binding dealers in rayon, federated by agreement to the sales bureau, to trade exclusively in the produce of the syndicate (Viscose Kunstseide Syndikat) and not to sell it to any other dealers, represent a sort of monopolisation of the wholesale trade, which will make outside competition for rayon producers rather awkward. Boycotting clauses, black-listing or selling at higher prices to those dealers not willing to join the exclusive agreement, on the one side, loyalty rebates and bonuses to those who have proved loyal, on the other, will work in the same direction. In July 1934 an interesting agreement was reached by the manufacturers of radio sets and loud-speakers. The factories concluding this agreement have set up an elaborate code of rules, by which the radio trade will be dominated. The agreement dating for at first one year is called the "Wirufa"-Jahr. As the parties to the agreement have consented to sell only to traders or bodies qualified by the Wirufa conditions to the trade a very stringent monopoly is set up. By the control of the wholesale trade the radio manufacturers have indeed acquired a position making any development of fresh competition from outsiders almost impossible and at any rate very precarious.

This form of combating outside competition will become particularly effective where it is practised between two or more associations, as in the case of coking syndicates binding themselves to deliver their produce exclusively to members of pig iron syndicates, or of the association of envelope-machine producers agreeing to sell exclusively to the association of envelope makers, or in that of the soap cartel obliging the syndicate supplying oils, fats and soda for the manufacture of soap not to sell to anyone else (examples taken from Liefmann). In all these cases, although the agreement may have been suggested by the manufacturers of the finishing lines, yet from the point of view of the associated manufacturers in the primary stage, such as the coking plants, the paper-machine makers or the sellers of fats and oils, such arrangements mean a sort of monopolisation of the seller by the buyer, thereby diminishing the chances of sale to outside suppliers. As a matter of fact it matters little whether the association of "buyers" is a body of producers in the following stage or an association of wholesale dealers. There is no doubt (compare also Schaeffer, p. 329) that of late the monopolist connection between manufacturers' industrial combinations and wholesale traders' associations has become very general; in various cases such agreements have been propagated by the representatives of wholesale trade associations themselves, in order to prevent some factories in the branch from supplying directly to the retailers or consumers.

This has brought us near the third group of effects relating to the co-ordination of competition by cartels or trusts, that is co-ordinating competition as regards finishers and wholesale traders buying cartelised or trustificated products. We have seen that co-ordination of both by agreements, if possible by agreements with their respective associations, will offer a weapon to fight outsiders or to force them to join the combination. But this does not relate to the attitude of industrial combinations towards finishers and traders themselves. It is all very well for cartels and trusts to enter into combination with those buying their products in order to combat outsiders in their own line of production—but the question remains, how to draw the buyers into this combination and what to do, if difficulties arise in that respect. In the beginning finishers and other buyers of quasi-monopolised products or raw materials are certainly outspoken adversaries of the respective cartels or trusts. They are the people, who, besides the last consumer, are the most endangered by monopolist price policy. For them there are two expedients for escaping the most harmful effects of combination. The one consists in entering by themselves the field of production dominated by cartels or trust-like concerns. We have mentioned the successful attempts of finishers in the iron and steel industry to acquire mining interests and to free themselves from the grip of "mixed" works and combinations. Yet, there are, even in branches where this process has been going on among finishers, numbers of undertakings not able or willing to get into vertical combination, even when they may have joined a cartelistic association. The position of these "pure" works will always remain difficult, when their costs of production are compared with those of the mixed undertakings—except in cases where the latter are suffering under the weight of overcapitalisation and therefore are in a disadvantageous position as regards costs of production. But such cases will be exceptional, the rule being that pure works, especially in the finishing lines, have to encounter the effects of cartels or trusts as regards what may be called the "intrinsic" price policy of combines. While the pure works, even those adhering to a cartel or syndicate, must pay the cartel price for their raw material or half-finished supplies, to the big mixed undertakings such prices may be purely "nominal", as in fact they are their own suppliers. While for mixed concerns it may not matter what price they have to charge their subsidiaries for raw material or half-finished goods, as the loss of the one may merely represent gain to the other, the case is the reverse with pure works and their interest is directly opposite to that of the vertically combined undertakings. In the iron and steel industry this problem has been acute up to most recent times, and the same problems exist in the aluminium and brass industries. Early in 1933 the manufacturers of iron and steel goods asked the Government that the whole question of their relations with the iron and steel producers should be gone into. In due course a Commissioner was appointed by the Government to deal with the matter and the following were some results of his activities: All syndicated works must sell their materials to their own finishing works at prices not below those paid by the free finishing works and no offer should be made or order accepted below cost of production. The syndicated works had to agree to keep separate accounts for their finishing works and to close down those of them which showed considerable losses. The President of the German State Railways was requested to issue an order to his buying departments that the practice adhered to hitherto of accepting the cheapest quotation should cease and that offers made at an economic price should be considered. Among the concerns said to be chiefly affected by these measures are the Vereinigte Stahlwerke and the Hoesch works, who had forced their way into the screw, rivet and drop forging industries, offering goods at prices which lay below the costs of raw material to the independent works.

The actual effects of industrial combination on finishers and half-finishers will be quite different where these have recourse to a second means of resistance. Just as consumers can organise into Friendly Societies or co-operative purchase associations (we may mention the "Grosseinkaufsgesellschaft deutscher Konsumvereine"), and place themselves by such co-operation in a very different position with regard to industrial producers, finishers or half-finishers may attempt to start a "counter"-organisation, "anti-cartels", as they have been—not very happily—styled by some writers; these "Abnehmer"-Kartelle formed to resist monopolist practices in selling by organised "buying" are indeed a very important counterpart to producers' monopolist combinations. Of course, as examples quoted by Passow and Liefmann can show, such cartels may have various other functions besides being directed against the "unfair" practices of other cartels or syndicates. Every cartel or syndicate may be partly a buyers' organisation as well as a sellers'. One of the most important organisations of this kind is the "Arbeitsgemeinschaft der eisenverbrauchenden Industrie", an association formed to protect the interests of iron-using manufacturers. This organisation has been paying special attention to the effects, which the price policy of cartels, in combination with the duties on iron, would have on users of iron and steel, and by its organisational strength it has succeeded in getting producers of iron into an agreement, by which inland producers of finished and half-finished goods are to be protected against any rise in cartel prices in so far as it would affect their competitive efficiency with regard to exports; in other words the agreement represents a protection against the effects of dumping of iron or steel to the disadvantage of the German finishers' position in the world market. The agreement was concluded in 1925 between the Roheisen-Verband, the Pig Iron Syndicate, and the Raw Steel Syndicate, Rohstahlgemeinschaft, on the one side, and the Arbeitsgemeinschaft der Eisen verarbeitenden Industrie (A.V.I.) on the other. It comprises on the part of this association, as was explained before the Enqueteausschuss, activities like bridge engineering, in which the percentage of the costs of the iron consumed to the whole costs is 45 %, down to the making of calculating machines, where the percentage of iron is not more than 1·8. The agreement is called the "Avi"-Abkommen, and it is at any rate, however its effects may be judged, an example of what can be achieved by concerted action on the part of buyers endangered by cartel domination.

The position of trade, and to a certain extent transport, as regards the effects of cartels and trusts is similar. Traders may attempt, in order to evade the monopolist domination of producers' cartels or syndicates, themselves to enter the field of production. This has been the case with iron traders, who during the War were eager to acquire iron works, as for instance the Otto Wolf-Phoenix concern. Liefmann states that during the inflation period clever wholesale traders were quicker than manufacturers to recognise the meaning of depreciated money and to try to invest their money or the money credited to them in manufacturing businesses, which had been or would become their customers'. On the other hand big manufacturers' concerns and cartels have formed wholesale trading associations or departments (Werkshandelsgesellschaften) of their own, as for instance the Rhenish-Westphalian Coal Syndicate, by forming as early as 1903 the so-called Kohlenkontor (Rheinische Kohlenhandels- und Reedergesellschaft G.m.b.H.), which combined river transport and trading.

Of late the Report of the Enqueteausschuss on the iron-producing industry has given a very elaborate, though somewhat complex, picture of a second means used by wholesale dealers to protect themselves against too strong a domination of cartels or trusts, i.e. as in the case of the finishers—the formation of associations, trying to embrace the largest part of the wholesale trade (cp. *loc. cit.* pp. 111, 335 and 361). These associations, quasi-monopolistic in themselves, have generally entered into agreements with the combines. Their members are called "Verbandshändler"; in the iron trade associated wholesale traders are considered to represent the "wholesale trade in iron". By agreement with the Stahlverein the whole of the German sales territory has been divided into certain districts allocated to groups of associated dealers. The kind of arrangement of such agreements will naturally depend on the respective strength of either the producers' combination or the associated dealers', but at any rate co-ordination of competition of the wholesale buyers will be the result. In the case of iron and steel the steelmakers seem to be the dominating force. At any rate the Report of the Enqueteausschuss states that in January 1930, "when the sales associations were reorganised, the Stahlwerksverband sketched out new rules relating to the affirmation of the associated traders". In fact, associated traders seem to be in many cases a sort of body privileged by the combines or cartels. The way competition becomes co-ordinated by such agreements is clearly shown in the tube trade. Here there are in existence three organisations of wholesale dealers: the Norddeutsche Röhrengrosshändlervereinigung in Berlin, the Süddeutsche Röhrengrosshändlervereinigung in Frankfurt a./M. and the Rheinisch-Westphälische Röhrengrosshändlervereinigung in Düsseldorf. With these organisations of the wholesale trade in tubes the Stahlwerksverband and its subordinated associations have entered into agreements, by which associated dealers (Verbandshändler) were bound or could be bound not to sell any material to outsiders without permission of the Stahlwerksverband. Moreover, the Stahlwerksverband secured for itself the right of veto in regard to the prices and conditions fixed by the associations of wholesale traders for the further sale of products. For certain products of the tube branch the Stahlwerksverband issued binding rules as regards the prices and conditions of further sales by the dealers. On the other hand the Stahlwerksverband agreed to sell the syndicated products, which could be sold by it directly, to no others but associated dealers.

Although the works trade (Werkshandel) and wholesale dealers' associations (Verbandshandel) have greatly reduced the sphere of the so-called "freier Handel", the independent trader, the Enqueteausschuss has devoted a good deal of work to investigations of what is left of it. In the Minutes of Evidence on the iron industry a whole section is devoted to "freier Handel". But it appears that, at any rate in this industry, which may be considered as typically organised on quasi-monopoly lines, a really "freier Handel" no longer exists. There are of course still "independent traders" in contrast to the associated ones. But the Report states on p. 113, that, although the former are not admitted into the selling organisation of the iron industries, they have become affiliated to it by special agreements with the wholesale dealers' associations. In South Germany, it was stated, all traders, associated or not, are members of the Süddeutsche Eisenzentrale, and thereby obliged to respect fixed prices and conditions and to boycott outside products.

Considering the position of industrial combinations with regard to their own members, with regard to outsiders and would-be competitors and to finishers and the wholesale trade, one is led to the conclusion that the work of combination by no means ends with the formal conclusion of a cartel in the form of a huge amalgamation. The necessity of co-ordinating competition remains. It represents the heaviest, the most complicated and the most important task of existing industrial combinations.

### CHAPTER XII

# DIMINISHING COSTS

THE activity of industrial combination, in so far as it does not consist of action relating to the vigilant safeguarding of its own quasi-monopolist existence and all kinds of organisational work connected with this end, must be mainly and necessarily directed towards an increase of profits of the respective undertakings or amalgamated works. This, as we have said before, can be achieved by reducing costs or by increasing prices or both.

It is well known that from the very beginning of the cartel and trust movement in industry the formation of the new form of industrial monopolies was vindicated by its leaders as well as by many economists as embracing new possibilities of diminishing costs of production and thereby justifying its existence to the public. A very able account of such aims has been given by the English Report on Trusts (1919 and 1924). The Report emphasised the great possibilities of industrial and commercial improvement lying "beyond the confines of free competition" and which "are only (!) to be realised by combination in one or other of its several forms". It then gave a detailed account of what could be effected in the way of economies in the different spheres of such combination, i.e. in buying materials, plant, stores, etc., in making, selling and knowledge. Its conclusions to this effect were certainly largely influenced by taking into account German and American experiences; it is indeed a rather long chain of facts, which may be cited in that respect, as any efficient industrial combination may exert its endeavours to achieve a greater economy in very many directions. This especially applies to a better and steadier supply of material, unification of buying departments and staffs, bulk instead of detail purchase, greater opportunity for comparison and selection, cheaper credit and better discounts, standardisation of materials, standardisation of product, specialisation of product, improvement in plant, use of by-products, equalised distribution of work, quality, transport economics, unification of selling departments and staffs, extension of export trade, collective advertising, lower costs of distribution, fewer middlemen, interchange of data and experiences, standardisation and interchange of costings, collection and dissemination of trade statistics, promotion of scientific and technical research, concerted action and common representation in legal matters, collective promotion of problems, which may be affected by the economic policy of the State, improved opportunities of acquiring patents and of entering into new processes of production at first hand, etc., etc. There is hardly one of these many matters and functions connected with the economic policy of industrial combination of which in the course of this treatise we have not been able to give examples, especially as regards the chemical industry, electrical trades and the steel industry.

Since the end of the War and in the course of the prolonged economic depression the possible effects of industrial combination with regard to better "economy" have been a much discussed topic in connection with which there has been much talk of "rationalisation". It is not the business of this book to deal with "rationalisation", but the author may take the liberty of saying that it seems to him that this "movement" has been in many ways theoretically over-interpreted by economists. One is glad to find that an English economist, Prof. Macgregor of Oxford, while certainly not refraining from treating the matter with great theoretical zeal (cp. his book *Enterprise, Purpose, and Profit*, 1934, Chapters II and v) emphasises—especially with regard to the development in Germany—that rationalisation "had an accidental and temporary meaning". It is certainly far from being a phenomenon of revolutionary economic importance, and again we may quote Prof. Macgregor, when, instead of giving deep-sounding and complicated definitions of it, he simply states that "to rationalise industry is to remove all the duplication and overlap which can be avoided, and introduce as much unity of purpose as is practicable without loss of economy". We can also agree with him, when he affirms that "the

Trust and the Cartel furnished the ideas of rationalisation in a completer degree than otherwise would have obtained, when post-War measures had to be considered".

Indeed, rationalisation, as practised in post-War Germany, was on the one hand nothing else than the application of a technical principle when overproduction and unprofitable prices coupled with certain immobile factors in the costing schedule of production suggested the idea of attempting drastic measures to bring costs down, by the elimination of weaker works, standardisation of production, more efficient application of machinery, etc. On the other hand we may remember here what was explained in a former chapter, that industrial combination may be itself largely supported by rationalisation, inasmuch as it reduces the units of production and the number of undertakings and leads to a greater unification of work which in every circumstance must be favourable to industrial combination. Again cartels and trusts may be regarded as effective instruments in carrying through rationalisation, as in fact collective bodies of manufacturers or amalgamated firms may be better able to carry the costs of expensive technical changes in industry than single manufacturers. Thus industrial combination may as well lead to rationalisation, as rationalisation may strengthen or even create a development of industrial combination.

The Enqueteausschuss has paid much attention to these conditions; the following passages of the general Report of this Committee seem of particular interest, as they reveal the principal conclusions drawn from a great number of witnesses on the subject. The Report states:

The problem of rationalisation was (after 1925) invading the mind of cartels and gave a new and particular impulse to the discussion of the relationship of productivity and profits to industrial combination. This meant that the discussion about cartels, within their own sphere as also in regard to the outer world interested in cartel problems, became drawn into a wider range of thought, which may possibly lead to further important lines of development. A most important factor in this development has been the expansion of Commercial Sciences (Betriebswirtschaftslehre), which directed its attention especially to the penetration of the inner life of works, to a scientific tabulation and valuation of the single costing factors and factors of management, thereby aiming at the attainment of a system of works management based upon scientific principles....

Although the Report does not deny that these new tendencies of economic thought have in many cases found a very fertile ground, where cartels were in existence, and that, wherever rationalisation was leading to a closing of efficient plant, to the transplantation of parts of production by a process of concentration or to a reorganisation of management, the "very mechanism of cartels was immediately concerned", he is of the opinion that "in general" a scientific system of tabulating costs and organising works accordingly has not been attempted by cartels or associations. Moreover, the Report was anxious to state that for sociological reasons cartels were frequently bound not to support a movement of greater centralisation of works or undertakings. It has frequently happened that cartels laid stress on the argument that they were protecting the interests of the smaller and less efficient undertakings against powerful partners, thereby acting more in a spirit of "co-operation" and backing what might be called "gewerblicher Mittelstand" (industrial middle class) than making their aim the utmost possible realisation of economic principles.

This brings us to a much discussed problem. There can be no doubt that the trust form of quasi-monopoly must be regarded to-day as much more in line with the bringing about of measures of rationalisation than the form of cartelisation. There is certainly one very important fact to be kept in mind as regards cartels and rationalisation: the possibility of "buying" out weaker competitors by acquiring their quotas in the cartel. This certainly means "rationalisation", although in the first twenty years of German cartel development it was hardly considered from that point of view. While on the one hand the cartel seems to be destined to protect and keep alive the less efficient it may on the other become an instrument of further concentration. Of course this very much depends upon the whole structure of the group of industry in question, it depends on the progress of concentration already achieved and on the number of single undertakings federated into an association. It may also depend on the "sociological" policy of the cartel as mentioned before.

But taking all that into due consideration one may believe that by such "indirect" measures concentration and thereby a reduction of costs has been accelerated by cartelisation. Of course one has to keep in mind, on the other hand, that the price policy of cartels may have the opposite result. We may remember that in the potash industry fresh competition of a rather "uneconomic" character, if one considers the profitableness of the whole group of industry, was the direct outcome of cartelisation. In view of such different possibilities, which counteract each other, it is not surprising to find that German cartel literature is by no means in agreement on this point. Wolfers, quoting a great number of authors, who have dealt more or less lengthily with this problem—from Brentano and Schaeffle in the 'nineties to Wiedenfeld, Beckerath, Liefmann, Baumgarten-Meszleny, Flechtheim, Reith and others of our days—expressly states that there is hardly any unanimity about this question. The explanation seems to lie much more in the great diversity of conditions of industry than in any lack of academic theory. It also seems possible that a cartel may act on a direct policy of rationalisation as well as by indirect means of concentration by way of reducing costs, as it may happen that by a policy of protection of the less efficient it is counteracting the tendencies of the "survival of the fittest". We have examples enough of the first mentioned possibilities, as for instance cases, in the German glass-bottle manufacture or in the jute industry, where new patents have been secured by the cartel in order to prevent their exclusive exploitation by individual firms, it is reported that in branches of the textile and paper industries cartels have inaugurated studies with the purpose of unifying the accounting systems of their members and of finding an "objective" basis for their price policy. It is of interest to note that plans for collective rationalisation have found their way even into international cartel agreements. This is, as can be seen from Mr William Meinhard's book, the case in the electrical lamp business, where international agreements about the use of patents, the exchange of technical experience and technical standardisation have been concluded. The latter is particularly taken care of by a "standardisation Committee" of the Phoebus (Geneva) S.A., which represents an administrative body for all firms belonging to the international lamp cartel. Mr Meinhard is anxious to refute, as an expert, the argument that an exchange of practical experiences and the common use of patents may relax individual activity. "Just the reverse", so he writes, "is the case. Where scientists remain in mutual touch with each other, there is a constant possibility of suggestions and a certainty that one will not be obliged to sit for years on an invention, only perhaps to learn that another firm has been able to make more progress on it in the meantime. This certainty acts as an incentive and is leading the scientific work in industry from the beginning to untilled fields promising success."

It must also be remembered, as Schaeffer emphasises, that cartels feel themselves in many cases bound to be responsible for a certain standard of quality. In many cases the cartel presses its members for punctual delivery, it may intervene where unsatisfactory goods have been delivered by some of its members and it may induce members producing at high costs to compare their cost of production with more efficient undertakings. All this is in the line of education and rationalisation. Of course there may be quite other cases: when cartels or syndicates merely take the costs of their most inefficient members as a basis for prices, without paying any regard to the question of drastically reducing costs. But according to Schaeffer, "the recognition, that a syndicate should have the effect of improving the status of its works, has been gaining more and more ground and is mostly acknowledged as an object of cartelisation". Even so sceptical a student as Wolfers cannot refrain from stating that while the improvement of the methods of production is regarded by him as merely a "side" activity of cartels, it "has been apparently of late more intensively developed in several places and is attracting an increasing amount of attention".

All this ought to be kept carefully in mind, before one tries to reach any general and rash conclusions that "cartels", in contrast to trusts or amalgamations, are the mere protectors or life preservers of the weak elements in industry. On the other hand, it must be admitted that concentrative bodies of industrial combination, such as trusts or concerns, will be in general in an easier position to carry out schemes of purposeful planning or rationalisation. They are not hampered by any obstacles accruing from a great number and possibly a great diversity of partners. In the many volumes of the Enqueteausschuss, students of the problem of rationalisation will find a great many examples of what has been done by big amalgamated firms in the way of reducing costs through the many before-mentioned means which rationalisation can offer. A very conspicuous case was that of the Vereinigte Stahlwerke.

The process of rationalisation, which has been undergone by this amalgamation, has been described by the chairman of the Board of Directors of the Stahlverein, Dr Vögler, before the Enqueteausschuss on 20 January 1928. Dr Vögler emphasised that the aim of the organisational policy of this trust-like undertaking was to reach a most complete unification and he laid stress on the fact that such all-round rationalisation of its production could hardly be reached within ten years. Then probably it would be possible to speak of what he called "eine absolute Betriebseinheit" (an absolute unification of works). The story of what has been planned and achieved in the Stahlverein seems to be a noteworthy illustration of the giant task awaiting those who wish to construct a clear and indeed "rationalised" body out of an elaborate mass of amalgamations and interconnections grown up in the course of the rather uncontrolled process of trustification. The story of the rationalisation of the Vereinigte Stahlwerke may also prove of importance to those interested in the reorganisation of the English steel industry, for it shows that it is hardly possible to reconstruct the organisation of an industry like this within anything like a given period of a few years. As Dr Vögler explained from first-hand knowledge the foremost task of reorganisation arose at the beginning of the trust, in concentrating production on the original branches of production of the combined works, eliminating so far as possible all those branches which had been occasionally or accidentally federated to some of the amalgamated undertakings, such as engineering or the production of refined steel. A great number of plants of the six promoting concerns of the Stahlverein, "which did not seem to be technically first-rate or which did not fit geographically into the combination", were closed down. We have already referred in other parts of this book to the exhaustive description of rationalisation, which Dr Vögler gave about six years later, in November 1933, before a meeting of shareholders. Dr Vögler laid stress on the fact that the realisation of the rationalisation programme, as projected in its broad outline in the foundation year of the trust 1926, was greatly hampered by the very adverse trade conditions which followed the "sham"-prosperity of 1927–29, culminating in a catastrophic drop of production figures in 1931 and 1932. He also emphasised that the technical reorganisation of the huge undertaking would not have been possible if it were not for "the programme of production of the original promoting works having been in many fields of a similar character". In spite of adverse economic conditions rationalisation in the form of concentrating production on the most efficient plant has been going on. Shafts have been reduced from 48 to 25 since the formation of the trust. In the iron making field there are to-day 66 instead of 145 works. The number of furnaces has been reduced since 1926 from 23 to 9, the Siemens Martin plant from 20 to 8, the hoop iron works from 7 to 3, the number of bar iron and shaped iron works from 17 to 10, the tube works from 8 to 3, the wire finishing works from 9 to 4. It must be confessed that under the régime of mere cartelisation such drastic reductions have never been heard of.

While probably German industrial combination can hardly be criticised for not having made use of the existing possibilities of rationalisation, doubts have arisen with regard to the practical economic advantages derived from it. This has been particularly the case with regard to the purely technical parts of "rationalisa-tion", as enacted by the big firms, such as the installation of new labour-saving machinery, the introduction of the conveyor system, simplification and standardisation so far as it was leading to a greater elimination of manual labour and bigger production per unit of plant. It is of interest to note that doubts of that kind (probably not wholly unrelated to experiences in Germany, and also in the U.S.A.) have found their way into English economic thought, as may be seen from the Final Report of the Balfour Committee on Industry and Trade published in 1929 (cp. pp. 178–9). While this Report lays stress on the fact, that "the more perfect the unification of interest" the more completely certain kinds of economy may be realised, it quotes a passage from a speech made by Sir Josiah Stamp, in which he alludes to "a general tendency in popular discussion to exaggerate the simple economies of straight run standard lines possible through concentration and underestimate the costs of bringing them about". The Report continues: "Such savings are not usually effected without incurring expense, which in some cases may nullify them. Thus a factory is rarely ready to take over the output of another, or to concentrate on making few types of articles only, without considerable changes in layout; and the necessity of providing in some way for the personnel of displaced factories also adds to the cost of transformation".

The problem of the advantages or disadvantages of rationalisation, as it is to be practised by big concerns and cartels, can hardly be solved by such considerations. Indeed the economic and financial results of rationalisation will entirely depend on conditions which by themselves are in no way or may be in no way related to the "principle" of rationalisation. The story of rationalisation in German industry after the War is likely to show that, while for some years rationalisation was regarded as the most promising means of reconstructing industry, a few years later—indeed from 1929 onward—it was discredited as having been disastrous in many ways. The popular slogan of "rationalisation" was soon drowned by an outburst against "overrationalisation" of an almost equal fervour. What had happened was this.

After the War the financial obligations with which German economic life was burdened, led to the desire to increase at all costs the efficiency of plant and the output of production per technical unit and per working man. This tendency, leading to the installation of more efficient and more labour-saving machinery, to the concentration of production upon the most up-to-date plant and in short to the concentration of all energies upon the promotion of the utmost industrial and commercial efficiency, was largely fostered during the inflation period by the "flight from the mark", which made almost any new investment by the manufacturer more tempting than the piling up of money reserves which vanished through the irresistible process of money depreciation; when in 1924 inflation came to an end, the aim of reconstructing industry on more stable lines brought a new impulse towards the elimination of weaker elements from production and further progress of rationalisation. This tendency was not only supported by the industrialists, but also by the representative bodies of labour. We may quote the speech of Herr Leymann, representing German labour before the International Labour Conference in Geneva in 1924, in which he asserted that the reparations to which Germany had obliged herself could only be paid by an increase of industrial production and this again was dependent upon a "higher efficiency of the technical installation of plant". In the Dawes plan too the question of technique was alluded to as one of the factors enabling Germany to fulfil its future obligations.[1] Technical progress bringing about increasing and cheapened production had become the topic of all economic wisdom up to 1929. A semi-official acknowledgment of this doctrine was given by the formation of such bodies as the "Kuratorium für Wirtschaftlichkeit" and other institutions dealing scientifically with all questions of rationalisation and all possible devices leading to greater output and a reduction of costs. In those days manufacturers were frequently attacked for being too reluctant with regard to the introduction of new machinery and processes of rationalisation and it was from the labour side that such criticism could mostly be heard. Particularly in those years, when the reduction in the working hours (eight-hour day) was hotly discussed it was argued from the labour ranks that manufacturers and especially big firms, which were not lacking in capital and credit, could easily compensate any losses incurred by the shortening of the working day by installing more efficient plant or by further rationalisation. In a pamphlet edited in 1926 by the Federation of German Trade Unions, entitled *Present problems of German economic policy*, it was expressly stated that: "Rationalisation is necessary. In accordance with the Memorandum of the National Association we conceive rationalisation, i.e. the appli-

[1] For details of this and the following passages cp. an article written by the author in the *Arbeitgeber* of 1 February 1932, pp. 59–62.

cation of all technical and organisational means, which are likely to increase the productivity of labour and machinery in industry, as the most important condition for improving prosperity". There was another trend of opinion favouring the utmost exertion of the rationalising spirit in industry. Industrial development in the U.S.A., which has frequently been considered in modern German industrial history as an admonition to accelerate technical progress (books like *The Land of the Future* by von Polenz or *The Land of Unlimited Possibilities* by L. M. Goldberger stirred up economic opinion for some time at the beginning of the century), was watched carefully by German economic observers and when the great technical boom in the U.S.A., fostered by unscrupulous credit expansion, was reached between 1925 and 1929, many economic writers exhorted the State and industrialists not to lag behind and to do their utmost to retain competitive strength in face of the new rival in third markets. In a much read pamphlet *Why be poor?* written in 1928, Herr Fritz Tarnow, a then well-known social writer, exclaimed: "We shall have to arrange our plans having regard to the fact that, so far as American competition is concerned, German economic development must not be temporarily, but permanently, enabled to meet it! The speed necessary to attain this end will probably have to be increased at a much greater rate than we are now dreaming of". Besides political and social writers there were a number of academic observers of great standing who were propounding the American "ideal". Thus Prof. W. Müller, in a book entitled *Soziale und technische Wirtschaftsführung in Amerika* (1926), came to the conclusion that "for the next generation it is for the U.S.A. to dictate economic law to the world", and others like Prof. Julius Hirsch and Prof. Moritz Bonn did their best to glorify American rationalisation and technical expansion as the "Wirtschaftswunder", the economic miracle, which was leading not only to an enormous material welfare in the U.S.A. but also to better distribution of the "social product". Thus arose a psychological atmosphere laden with an almost unlimited enthusiasm for technical "progress" and it was only natural that cartels and big concerns were urged to grasp the situation, as in fact they were the very instruments to carry out big and ambitious technical schemes. It may be well to remember that tendencies of this kind were not quite unfamiliar to English industrial development too in those years. In 1926 for instance a very learned book was published by Bertram Austin, M.B.E., M.A., and W. Francis Lloyd, M.A., A.M.I.E.E., to which Sir Walter T. Layton wrote a very persuasive preface. The book was entitled *The Secret of High Wages* and was, though a little more cautiously written, very much in the line of the German opinions just described. Comparing American with English conditions the authors "endeavoured to explain to industrialists and workers alike the reasons for the American economic wonder and have also attempted to show that, although the conditions may be somewhat different, no unsurmountable obstacle presents itself to the attainment of a 'British economic wonder'". On page 105 the authors declared: "Our aim should be to raise wages. This cannot be accomplished unless means are provided for increasing workers' productivity". Although we do not intend in any way to deny that English industry is in many parts in need of schemes and programmes of rationalisation (we have been able to allude in former chapters to special cases), it may safely be stated that it was a piece of luck for British industry that the American example was not so swiftly copied as was here suggested. British conservatism has, without intending it, saved its industry from what would have had most disastrous results on its economic life. When after 1929 the American "wonder" broke down and left the U.S.A. in an almost desperate position of overproduction and overcapitalisation the "secrets" of high wages, of rationalisation and prosperity were discovered to have been no normal device at all and a most dangerous recipe for others; in fact industrial development in the U.S.A. had undergone a development of "inflation" similar to that which European countries like Germany had experienced in the field of monetary conditions.[1] Curiously enough, however, the arguments put forward

---

[1] I have tried to disclose the different forces which led to the American "prosperity" and were responsible for the "great wonder" turning into the "greatest catastrophe", in an article published by the *Weltwirtschaftliches Archiv*, January 1932, pp. 203–32, "Die Wirtschaft der Vereinigten Staaten und die Weltwirtschaftskrisis".

with regard to rationalisation were soon forgotten by those who had been most eager to pronounce them. In fact the very economic and social circles, which had been most enthusiastic about American rationalisation in Germany, began to denounce manufacturers and especially cartels and trusts for having wilfully brought about what was now called "over-rationalisation". A regular literary campaign was started against "technical progress", as may be gathered from Prof. Lederer's writings, a sort of one-sidedness which may be rightly compared with the early "Luddite" agitation in England.

It seems to us that it would be completely wrong to denounce the rationalisation policy of industrial combination by taking these unfortunate experiences as a basis of argument. In fact, circumstances which were in no way related to the regular economics of "rationalisation" were responsible and it would be erroneous to discredit the system, when the conditions necessary for its probation were lacking or disappointing. As with every technical advance economic conditions, i.e. the possibility of disposing profitably of increased production, will be the finally determining factor of any commercial result of rationalisation. German manufacturers in the past have certainly, for many causes and reasons, been driven to overestimate these conditions. But this error, besides being explainable and excusable, does in no way nullify conclusions regarding the undeniable advantages, which schemes of rationalisation may derive from the existence of purposefully guided cartels and trusts.

### CHAPTER XIII

# FIXING PRICES

THERE was a period when the possible functions of industrial combination with regard to the diminution of costs were not taken very seriously. Cartels and other industrial combinations were merely regarded from the point of view of monopoly, and any argument tending to show that their activities might lead to greater efficiency by reducing costs was dismissed as being an attempt to veil the real and fundamental aims of combination, which were to be considered as having their centre in a policy of fixing prices. To-day the possibilities latent in industrial combination with regard to the better organisation of production will no longer be disputed. On the contrary, industrial combination has come to be regarded as one of the principal means of realising organisational progress; this conviction is now so deep rooted that in 1934 the English Government made the further grant of protection to the steel industry dependent on the formation of some sort of combination, while the most recent steps taken by the German Government towards compulsory cartelisation are tending in the same direction. Elimination of uncontrolled competition coupled with schemes for better organisation by the collective reducing of costs seems to have become the acknowledged function of combination. On the other hand discussion on price policy, formerly the main issue of all cartel and trust problems, seems to be rather neglected. The reason for this will probably lie in the fact, that for some time no acute fear has been felt as to the development of arbitrarily increased prices. Between 1929 and 1934 the whole world suffered from deflation in a greater or smaller degree and, while formerly the aims of economic policy were in almost every country directed towards an abatement of prices, and private price agreements were carefully watched or even scrutinised by public administration, to-day a price development leading to a slowly rising level would by no means be regarded as in itself of a dangerous character. Moreover, in Germany cartel and trust organisation of to-day is so closely surrounded by public safeguards of all kinds that a popular fear of an undue and abrupt rise in prices through industrial combination seems to be more or less unjustified. Wolfers reflects the trend of general economic opinion in Germany when he declares: "That cartels aim at a policy which is directed towards an increase of prices or the keeping up of prices at a higher level than would be attainable without cartelisation cannot be denied. This policy is indeed the very justification of private agreements of a cartel-like character...". In face of this, cartels or trusts will be no longer "morally" obliged to prove that they have not raised prices or do not intend to do so. Wherever cartels or other forms of industrial combination are to be recognised as economically harmless or even useful it will be implicitly admitted that the old idea that they ought to be opposed merely because they are monopolistic and able to influence prices will have to disappear. It must also be borne in mind that the influence of industrial combination on prices will not be solely reflected in what may be called price policy. I have endeavoured to show in my book on English industrial monopoly organisation that the mere enlargement of industrial units in a group of industry may act as a deterrent to new would-be competitors thereby leaving to the existing works a margin within which a rise of prices would hardly stimulate new competition. If anybody ventured to-day to erect works equal in size, efficiency and output to those of the I.G. Farben or the Osram works or those of the big electrical concerns, he would depress prices to such an extent that he would make his own works as well as those of the old firms hopelessly unprofitable. This situation leaves automatically to the old monopolists a rather wide margin within which their price policy may be entirely immune from new competition. But of course this situation is limited to industries which have been built up under the development of large units, few in number, and which yet satisfy a great part of the national or international demand.

By acknowledging that the price policy of industrial combinations will be necessarily run in the above-mentioned way and by taking this as an unavoidable consequence of the admission of cartels and trusts into economic organisation one is relieved of the task of "proving" that prices have been raised by the sole action of combination or of criticising official statements by cartels that they have not. Endeavours of that kind have always been more or less futile, as indeed nobody can prove what would have happened to prices if, instead of combinations, free competition had existed. It is not the monopolist influence on prices which to-day remains to be discussed, but rather the extent to which this influence has been used, and how far it was "justified".

To state this does not mean that the problem has become less complex. In fact, there is no possibility of deciding in an "objective" manner what kind of price level, as regulated by industrial combination, must be considered "too high", so long as cartels and trusts refrain from price raising in quite exceptional and "brusque" manner. There has been indeed no attempt in Germany to elucidate by an elaborate investigation of an official or even semi-official character the bearing of industrial combination on prices, and the Enqueteausschuss, while giving a good many sporadic examples of the price policy of cartels within its special monographs, has not come to anything like a definite judgment as to whether prices have been kept "too high" or not. Not even the "Kartellstelle des Reichsverbandes der deutschen Industrie", a body created by the National Federation of German Industries during the inflation period, although it was rather influential in trying to prevent conflicts arising out of cartelistic measures, has attempted to publish definite conclusions on the subject.

In fact, all considerations regarding the price policy of cartels will remain "subjective" and dependent on the viewpoint chosen. Perhaps the most uncomplicated case will be that of cartels being protected and raising prices to the maximum level possible, i.e. world market prices plus duty. We have given an example of this on p. 59. While in the case of unregulated competition this maximum price would hardly be reached, cartels are, at least at certain periods, able and indeed "entitled" by the State to attain it; but, where at the same time production is internationally organised the question arises, how far the inland price is "unduly" raised by an "artificial" raising of the world market price level. The State, in granting protection to an industry, undoubtedly starts from a certain level of prices to which the industry claims to be entitled. While the duty (in general) is a fixed amount, world market prices may vary considerably and even be influenced by the cartels themselves. When in July 1934, by the Tin Plate Agreement between Great Britain, Germany, U.S.A. and France, the price of tin plate was promptly raised from 17s. 3d. per standard to a minimum price of 18s. the question must have become latent as to how far the German cartel would be able and willing to reflect this change in its inland price policy. Therefore, even a price level sanctioned by the State through the grant of tariff duties does not exclude the question of the "fair" price.

The task is not alleviated by a mere comparison of inland and foreign (world market) prices. On the contrary a really competent statistical comparison is hardly attainable. In a memorandum, prepared in 1927 by Buchmann, Mathesius, Dr Petersen and Dr Reichert for the Enqueteausschuss, entitled *Zur Frage des internationalen Eisenpreisausgleichs*, the difficulties of comparing international prices of iron and steel were expressly dealt with. It was laid down by these authors that, apart from purely statistical discrepancies which are difficult to eliminate, it would not be correct to compare German and foreign prices of iron unless an equality of conditions existed as regards the following points: (a) quantities to be delivered, (b) measurement and forms, (c) quality, (d) terms of delivery, (e) conditions of payment, (d) freight and (g) exchange. It must also be remembered that for many products in some countries "c.i.f."-prices are quoted, while in others cartel or syndicate arrangements regulate prices according to a common "freight basis", which necessarily means advantages of delivery to some and disadvantages to other works, besides the concession of "Überpreise" or "extras" in the case of certain qualities, forms or brands. All this forms a considerable drawback, when comparisons are attempted between the prices of cartelised German goods and those of foreign countries.

Then there remains the question of costs and prices. This

opens another field of great difficulty. There is no doubt that costs might be computed to-day with more chance of exactness than twenty years ago, especially in those industries, which have adopted modern and more complete systems of calculation. But even if this were done it is doubtful whether figures of that kind would throw any decisive light on the relation of prices and profits. Inasmuch as the formation of big concerns and of amalgamations of a trust-like character has been carried out by some sort of overcapitalisation, brought about by "high" charges paid for the taking over of less efficient works, the merely "technical" costs, consisting in the cost of material, labour and normal interest and depreciation of capital will not be sufficient to explain the higher price, which may be asked for by industrial combination. In fact, it may happen that a certain price will show some profit to a small independent manufacturer while it will show a loss to a big, technically most efficient, but overcapitalised concern. It is significant that the Report on the iron and steel industry, as presented by the Enqueteausschuss, was not able to arrive at anything like a clear picture of the costs of production. On the contrary, the Report had to confess that "owing to the differentiation of works, the lack of uniformity in the distribution of costs and the varying principles of calculating numerous costing elements the results showed discrepancies up to 100 %". It was also expressly stated that it seemed doubtful whether the costs of closing redundant works should be included in calculating "costs" of production, as the writing off of dead plant, etc. would indeed mean an unbearable burden, if it were to be reflected in costs of production. This may be quite reasonable from the accountant's point of view, but it will hardly make a difference in the discussion of costs and prices, as it will always be argued by the producers that the outlay of rationalisation, however unprofitable it may have proved after 1929, must in some way or other be compensated by prices—and it would indeed be hardly possible to deny that such expenses as are incurred by rationalisation or shutting down inefficient works should not be taken in account to justify a certain level of prices. But, considering all this, the possibility of finding out anything like a *justum pretium* in the iron and steel trade seems to be as good as non-existent. On the other hand, the case might happen that big amalgamated undertakings, far from being burdened with costly financial charges, are enjoying a sort of differential rent when compared with their weaker competitors and cartel partners. This of course will seldom be openly recognised by the leading firms in question. It was rather exceptional that in the summer of 1934, when trying to account for a rather surprising drop in its shares, the greatest German rubber manufacturing company, the Continental Gummi Werke A.G. in Hannover, pointed to the fact "that cartelisation meant a considerable advantage to the big units of production with their relatively low costs of production" (cp. *Deutsche Allgemeine Zeitung*, 19 July 1934). But even such truths, which in fact are rarely to be got at, would have but little influence on price politics, as it could always be argued that for the sake of the conservation of the whole of that industry a level of prices granting profits to the "marginal" producers was considered a necessity.

The experience of the last ten years has shown that it is in times of a general nervous fluctuation of the price level that industrial combination is most likely to get into conflict. While it has been generally acknowledged that price stabilisation must be regarded as one of the main functions of industrial combination (cp. Wolfers, pp. 63–5) it seems to represent the main centre of attack in times of real price revolution. While in the days of wild inflation and in the following first year of stabilisation (1924) the policy of cartels, in trying to avoid the risks of exchange to its members, was sometimes strongly criticised, not least by the "Reichsverband der Deutschen Industrie", this period of transition can hardly be taken as characteristic of the normal price fixing or price stabilising functions of industrial combination. It is rather the period beginning with the fatal year 1929 leading to a prolonged and chronic depression, which might be considered as a sort of test of the limits and fairness of price regulation by industrial combination. From the consumer's point of view it was frequently argued during this period that cartels and amalgamations were keeping prices at an unduly high level. The Yearbook of the National Federation of Trade Unions

(*Allgemeinen Deutschen Gewerkschaftsbundes*) in 1932 alluded to the fact that the index figures relating to "free prices" had been declining since 1926 by the ratio of 100 to 47·9, while "fixed prices" of raw material and semi-manufactured goods had only declined to 84. Of course so rough a comparison of prices applying to the most divergent productions (food, agricultural produce, manufactured goods) can hardly be taken as a measurement of price policy by industrial combination. The unparalleled drop of food prices in the world markets, which of course reacted on protected German food prices as well, could not be expected to have a corresponding effect on German industrial markets. In every country deflation was progressing much faster in certain agricultural products than in those of industry. In England for instance, English wheat went down from 11s. 6¾d. per 112 lbs. on the average of 1927 to 5s. 2⅝d. in April 1931, while Cleveland pig iron Nr. III declined from 73s. 3d. to only 58s. 6d. per 2210 lbs. in Middlesbrough. It seems hardly possible to judge cartelistic activity by price comparison of such a primitive character. On the other hand, even in the face of the lack of exact figures, there could be no doubt that the existence of industrial combination was necessarily checking deflationist tendencies and thereby creating a discrepancy between controlled and competitive prices. Beginning in 1931 the German Government had enacted measures, which were styled a "Preissenkungsaktion" (action to reduce prices) and at first applied to trade-mark goods (Markenartikel). By a special decree, dated 8 December 1931, a reduction of prices was ordered, which was to apply to all goods controlled by cartels and to trade-mark goods. This reduction was to be 10 % on prices current on 30 June 1930. The measure was sharply criticised by representatives of the workmen's (consumers') interest. It was argued that such schematic regulation of prices could hardly do away with existing discrepancies and that special bodies composed of officials and representatives of industry, labour and consumers should be entrusted with decisions relating to cartelistic price policy. It is, however, very doubtful whether such bodies would ever succeed in finding out what the price "fair" to all parties concerned ought to be.

Besides the question of cartelistic price policy in face of commercial depression the problem most discussed for some time was the effect of controlled prices on manufacturers of the following stages of production and on exports. The keeping up of prices of raw material and semi-finished material, even to a relatively small extent, might greatly endanger the possibilities of export to manufacturers in general, as well as especially to those not possessing their own supplies of such material. As the iron and steel industries of Germany had frequently practised methods of dumping and of granting bounties to exports or of differentiating between home and foreign sales, it is just in this industry, so highly cartelised and trustificated, that this problem became of singular importance. The disadvantages arising from a differentiation of this "dual" price level to manufacturers of the following stages has been mitigated by the so-called "Avi" agreement of 1925. The agreement, as already stated, was concluded between the "Arbeitsgemeinschaft der Verbände der Eisen verarbeitenden Industrie" (as the group representing the users of iron and steel) in Düsseldorf and the "Deutsche Rohstahlgemeinschaft", which we have described in a former chapter, as representative of the German steel works and rolling mills. The latter have agreed to deliver iron and steel to finishers, in so far as it is destined to be used for exporting purposes, at world market prices, i.e. considerably cheaper than the German price would be. Since then a home price, "Inlandspreis", calculated by the cartel to relate to a specific "freight basis" (Oberhausen) and the "Avi-Verrechnungs Ausfuhrpreis" must be noticed, the latter being calculated with regard to international price levels. In March 1927 for instance the price of bar iron was 134 R.M. a ton freight basis Oberhausen, while the Avi export price was only 100 R.M. a ton. In July 1932 the inland price for bar iron was 112 R.M., while the special Avi export price amounted to only 62 R.M., the price of the International Ingot Steel Export Federation in L. gold basis being 3 L.

During the last few years the German Government has not been faced by the necessity of interfering by any drastic measures with the price policy of industrial combination. Yet there have been occasional admonitions not to exploit monopolist power in an unjustified manner or to raise prices unduly. The Minister of Economic Affairs for instance strongly urged the leading associations of industry in August 1933 and again even more precisely in November 1933 not to counteract the measures of the Government directed to alleviate economic distress, especially those relating to the schemes of provision of work (Arbeitsbeschaffungsprogramm), by increasing prices. He even ordered the nullifying of certain actions which had been taken by some cartels or syndicates in the direction of an increase of prices and he declared he would take strong measures against such associations, if the former price level was not swiftly restored. While it was agreed that the price level was in many cases much depressed, it was emphasised that the necessary improvement of consumption could at the present moment not be attained if prices were raised. Again, when in Summer 1934, in connection with the difficulties of exchange, a number of compulsory cartels were established and the erection of new works in such cases prohibited, it was expressly stated in official communications of the Ministry of Economic Affairs that provision had been made that no unjustified increase of prices would result from these conditions.

When in Spring 1934 the question of exchange became more embarrassing, the Government, wishing probably to avert apprehensions of a possible rise in prices to be followed by the reduction of certain imports, made several orders to restrict the price policy of cartels and associations. By a decree of 16 May all cartelistic associations were bound not to raise the minimum prices of certain goods or the minimum trade margins (Handelsspannen) without the consent of the price-supervision boards (Preisüberwachungsstellen). This order was extended some months later to industrial goods and services of all kinds. It remains to be seen whether this regulation will be made permanent or be regarded as only an emergency measure.

In fact, there is little prospect of German industrial combination, as it has developed of late, being able to use its price-fixing power in a way which would rouse serious apprehensions on the part of either the consumer, the finisher or official circles. We have seen in another chapter that a number of legal means have been created which represent a safeguard against a policy which would fix prices without taking due regard to the interests of those dependent on a "fair" price level and to the necessities of general economic welfare. Bodies, like the Kartellstelle des Reichsverbandes der Deutschen Industrie, which may have an important influence as arbiters in cases of conflict, have recognised that where costs are not covered by the existing price level and no means of abating them are at hand, an increase of prices will be justified, but it ought to be applied in "small doses". Again, it must be remembered that inasmuch as cartels are coming to be regarded as a sort of "representative", though private, body of industries, a sort of moral responsibility will develop on the part of the "Kartelleiter", that is the leading brain in industrial combination, which will more and more have regard to the exigencies not only of the cartel partners but also of national economic development. As Schaeffer has put it: the important national associations of industries are trying to develop a certain "Kartelsitte", a moral code of cartel policy, which is intended to limit any reckless use of power by single combines.[1] Inasmuch as by the interlocking process of industrial organisation of to-day leaders of one industry have become absorbed in the interests of a great many branches, and inasmuch as such leaders are in general important factors in the central organisations of industries (Spitzenverbände) and likely to be considered as bearing a good deal of public responsibility with regard to the general welfare of national industry, another, psychological, safeguard is arising against a price policy directed merely by the selfish motives of a single monopoly. In this respect the more bureaucratic organisation of German industry has influenced conditions of industrial monopoly in Germany in contrast to the American trusts, which resemble much more the old type of industrial monopolies, which used their powers to the utmost possible limit.

[1] Cp. also the interesting remarks about "the reason for an effective code of trade practice" in Macgregor's essay, *loc. cit.* pp. 54–61.

## SOME RESULTS

The time is past when industrial combination could be regarded as a more or less exceptional condition of industrial organisation. Cartels and trusts can no longer be considered as being mainly devices of industrialists to utilise certain occasional and accidental conditions, or conditions brought about by the "artificial" means of tariff protection, to form monopolies. Industrial combination must be regarded as a form of industrial organisation evolving through and adapted to certain conditions of concentration, technical, geographical, economic, arising in many groups of industry, national or international, and revolutionising the size of the industrial unit or of the industrial undertaking. The main cause of such concentration lies, as we have tried to explain at length, in the fact that the structure of industrial production has in the last fifty years, in connection with the enormous progress of transport facilities, undergone decisive changes. Distribution of industrial goods has in most groups of industry taken a highly concentrative character, whereas in former days it had been decentralised. Local markets were no longer supplied by local manufacturers nor national markets by national suppliers alone. A much larger unit of production supplying a considerable sector of the demand was now becoming profitable, representing in itself a monopolist tendency, as new competitors in face of their prospective efficiency had to make sure of their produce being still sold at prices which would show a profit. Where this bigger unit of production evolving out of a technical adaptation of production to the development of bulk transportation was coincident with certain conditions of geographical concentration, of some natural monopoly, of protective measures or other circumstances favouring concentration —either with regard to inland sales or to the supply of world markets—there existed the conditions for industrial combination. This was the case in the U.S.A., where in many groups of industry concentrative conditions were most prominent, where the necessity of long-distance bulk supply of standardised goods was prevalent from almost the first development in many modern American industries, besides the concentration of natural resources and tariffs favouring monopolist organisation. In Europe conditions differed from this in many respects. The movement towards concentrative distribution was not developing so drastically as in the U.S.A. and the unit of production was not increasing with such rapidity. The country, the industrial structure of which in many respects resembled that of the U.S.A. and was to some extent, before the War as well as later in the rationalisation period, purposely shaped after the American model, was the German Empire. Besides possessing important instances of natural resources, geographically concentrated, and an uninterrupted protection by tariffs, German industry was concentrating its efficiency on "heavy" productions and on goods of cheaper grade highly adapted to bulk and standardised supply. On the other hand, its special and early success in applying scientific research to industry gave it a monopolist position in certain high grade branches of industry. It is therefore not surprising to find that the movement towards concentration and industrial monopoly was developed earlier and more comprehensively than in England. Here centralised natural monopolies were non-existent, industry had been for long accustomed and by increasing international competition more and more forced to aim at a great diversity of highly finished goods, to rely on quality production, which naturally did not necessitate an expansion of bulk sales and thereby of units of production in such a degree as was the case with raw material or heavy goods. Besides, German industry, being in its infancy when the great technical progress of the 'seventies and 'eighties began, was in a much better position to build up big industrial units than English industry, which in almost every case had to overcome old traditions of technique and management in order to remain "up to date". Thus Germany became a much more prominent field of industrial combination than England.

It is not from the merely historical point of view that the material conditions leading to industrial monopoly should be studied. In revealing the concentrative forces prevalent where cartels or trusts are flourishing one is in a position to prove that the psychological attitude is of secondary importance. It is a curious fact that many English economists and politicians, when once industrial combination came to be understood in the broader sense, were apparently of the opinion that the formation of some sort of combination was merely dependent upon the insight and far-sightedness of manufacturers and that where before the "absence" of monopolies (though without reason) was frequently praised as resulting from the genuinely individualistic character of British manufacturers, the latter were now criticised for not being willing to adapt a new form of "collective" organisation. It will not be denied that the German people, through being permeated with admiration for administration and associative organisation, have from the sociological point of view offered better opportunities for industrial combination than the English. In fact, at this very time German cartel organisation comes in many cases very near the conception of a general organisation of industry based upon principles of common action and associative agreement. This may be very alien to English ideas of private enterprise and independence. Yet, such socio-psychological observations should not be allowed to darken the real background of the development of industrial combination. The German example itself, of which we have been trying our best to give a number of prominent examples, shows that certain decisive material conditions must necessarily be present to make cartels or trustification possible and in the long run "successful". They cannot be "made to order", where these conditions are lacking.

The legal conditions surrounding industrial combination will certainly have an influence on their development and perhaps on their strength. German legislation in this respect is of rather modern date and no impediments such as that of the English or American law against restraint of trade had to be encountered or taken into account. While in general no legal interference has been effective in paralysing modern industrial monopolies, as the American example shows, it has been frequently argued that the legal attitude was responsible for the specific form of organisation and that German cartels, in contrast to trustification, are an illustration of it. We have paid due regard to this question. Yet we cannot approve of such a deduction, in so far as German cartel development is concerned. At any rate there is no proof that, wherever a freedom of organising monopoly exists, the cartel is preferred to the trust. What in fact seems to have put the cartel and syndicate in the forefront of German industrial combination, is a purely economic problem. Cartels were the forerunners of industrial amalgamation. Where the conditions of monopolisation are in the stage of development, while the movement towards a crystallisation of undertakings into very big units has not yet reached its final climax, manufacturers may anticipate the coming development by collective agreements of a monopolist character. That this in general means something like a period of transition has been amply proved by the combination movement in German industry, especially in the older industries such as iron and steel, which in that respect we had to contrast with such modern groups as rayon or electricity or chemicals where from the start monopoly organisation was fashioned in a trust-like form. In fact cartels and syndicates seem in no way to be the antipodes of trustification. Amalgamation may develop within the cartel, in fact in many cases be accelerated by it, while, when once in progress, trust-like organisations may find it very useful to retain the advantages of associative combination offered by cartelisation in their relations to the remaining outsiders or new competitors.

There is much in the development of German cartel organisation and in that of huge concerns which may be regarded as due to more or less accidental factors or to developments caused by the very turbulent character of German economic development since the end of the War. Inflation, stabilisation, the overrating of rationalisation, credit schemes of a dangerous kind, the overestimating of the advantages of huge concerns and the financial methods sometimes pursued which led to a complicated interlocking of companies and a rather irrational network of interconnections have blemished in many respects the picture we had to draw of the organisation of industrial combination. The future only can show what remains as the solid foundation of a sometimes too hasty development. The reorganisation of the Stahlverein is an instance of a thoughtful endeavour to attain a clearer and more homogeneous structure of a trust. At any rate it would be wrong to attribute certain defects and deficiencies in the German cartel movement to the system of monopolist combination without paying due regard to a good many exceptional circumstances prevailing from 1918 to 1929.

A study of the results of German industrial combination will certainly dispose of the idea that modern industrial quasi-monopolies are mainly occupied with the aim of raising prices. Even where industrial combination has not yet taken the final form of dominating amalgamations the aim of reducing costs will be almost as strong as that of regulating prices. It is the big concern which will be in the best position to carry through costly inventions and to realise rationalisation, to do away with redundant plant and to simplify production. But, as we have seen, cartel policy of recent times is moving in the same direction. This tendency will in all probability still increase, inasmuch as cartels are more and more considered by their leaders (Kartellleiter) as a sort of organisation called upon to take care of the general interests of the respective industries. Of course there will be always a latent tendency to regard cartelisation as a means of protecting and upholding the weaker elements of competition. But this tendency will be constantly and increasingly counteracted by the further development of concentration within cartels themselves as well as by the widening radius of their organisational tasks. It is perhaps as yet going too far to speak, as has become the fashion in England, about "co-ordination", "co-operation", etc., as being the main issues of cartelisation. Such friendly and suggestive terms seem to originate more from a desire to embellish the picture of quasi-monopoly organisation than in an exact knowledge of their true activities. These are full of conflicts and divergent interests. It seems, when one considers the German experience, much more the force and pressure of economic necessity than that of the gentle spirit of co-operation which is finally leading to unification. We have been able to show that the road towards effective combination is sometimes beset by bitter fights and long struggles between the weaker and the stronger elements, between "pure" and "mixed" works, between those reaping advantages from natural monopolies and those not in a position to do so. Cartels can hardly be expected to result from a mere collective spirit and when they are once formed conflicting interests are not eradicated, although they may be overshadowed by agreement on many points of common economic interest. The development of trust-like amalgamations within the cartel sphere is showing that in many cases cartelisation is not the final solution of industrial combination.

There can be no doubt that the rise of industrial combination will confront the State and its legislation with many new and essential tasks. When cartels and trusts first began it seemed that the State would have to give most of its attention to their possible price policy. In Europe apprehensions of the effect of quasi-monopoly on prices have not been fully realised. As in other countries the German experience of cartels and other forms of industrial combination has shown that, although the aims of fixing and possibly raising prices cannot be denied by quasi-monopolists, there are a good many checks and limits to their actual price "policy". In a time of *laissez faire* the prevalent idea, that everything was to be eventually corrected by the hidden hand of unlimited competition, resulted in a rather general carelessness in regard to the movement of prices. This is no longer the case. The public and consumers are in general much more aware of the "ups" and "downs" of prices than formerly and the economic depression has resulted in a far greater interest being taken in even relatively small variations. The mere existence of industrial combination has resulted in a higher attentiveness to market conditions and a demand for publicity in many respects. Cartels and trusts which overstrained their monopolist position would soon be reprimanded by the public, by trade organisations, organisations of consumers and others and an agitation arising against them under such conditions would certainly cause them grave inconveniences. While we have been trying to show that there exists in fact no "objective" measurement of price policy, there may be at any time a sort of instinctive judgment of "unduly" raised prices. Cartels and trusts will be careful not to arouse public feeling, and inasmuch as they are represented by companies or corporations of a more or less representative character, expected to abstain from measures not conforming with the public interest, they will be limited in their action in quite a different way than was the "private" manufacturer of former days.

This of course will not make constant supervision, if not control, of prices regulated by cartels and trusts, unnecessary. But perhaps it may be inferred from the German experiences that even then the task of the state is less urgent with regard to the price policy of quasi-monopolies than with regard to other of their activities. We have discussed at length the position cartels or trusts may take up with regard to outsiders or would-be competitors, to those dependent on them for their own manufacture, to traders, dealers and middlemen. In discussing exclusive agreements and other features of the monopolist policy we have alluded to the coercive effects of such a position. Here lies a problem of probably much greater importance to State action than that of price supervision, a problem which contains questions of administrative and legal responsibilities which will involve not merely decisions of a more or less occasional character, such as the interference with raised prices, but also decisions on matters of principle. We have seen that in Germany the attitude towards industrial combination has fluctuated from a desire to uphold certain conditions of free competition to the extreme of compulsory cartelisation. Much of this attitude has been and will be dependent on general economic conditions—as for instance in times of depression, overproduction or specific economic difficulties, it might seem opportune to close the ranks of manufacturers, and to assist existing works in their aim of preventing new competition. But apart from these accidental conditions the State will have to decide before long what its attitude towards industrial combination ought to be. Words like "interference" or "non-interference" will hardly touch the root of the problem. In fact, in face of the dominating position which cartels and trusts to-day possess in the organisation of German industry, State action with the object of restoring greater freedom to the single manufacturer might be considered as leading merely to "compulsory competition", which under such circumstances would appear to be as far away from the former "freedom" of trade as compulsory cartelisation. For there can be no doubt that industrial combination represents to-day a development which has grown up in an organic way out of economic conditions not less "natural" than were those of free competition. The best which the State and administration can do will probably consist in their constant endeavour to reconcile the specific aims of this new industrial organisation with the necessities of "general economic welfare". But inasmuch as this very term will always have a relative meaning it will hardly be possible to set up hard and fast rules with regard to such policy.

# A LIST

## OF CARTELS, CONCERNS AND TRUSTS
## DISCUSSED OR MENTIONED

### Coal

Rheinisch-Westphälisches Kohlensyndikat, now Ruhrkohle A.G.
Westphälisches Kokssyndikat.
Brikett-Verkaufsvereinigung.
Oberschlesisches Steinkohlensyndikat.
Ostelbisches Braunkohlensyndikat.
Aachener Steinkohlensyndikat.
Niedersächsisches Kohlensyndikat.
Mitteldeutsches Braunkohlensyndikat.
Kohlensyndikat für das Rechtsrheinische Bayern.
Interessengemeinschaft Oberschlesischer Steinkohlengruben.

### Potash and Fertilisers

Deutsches Kalisyndikat.
Wintershall-Deutsche Kaliindustrie.
Burbach-Salzdetfurth-Konzern.
Convention de l'Industrie de l'Azote (C.I.A.).
I.G. Farben-Industrie A.G. (cp. also Chemicals).
Stickstoff-Syndikat.

### Metals

Zink-Kartell.
Tin Producers' Association.

### Salt

Norddeutsche Salinen Vereinigung G.m.b.H.
Steinsalzsyndikat.

### Cement

Zementbund.
Zement-Kartell.

## Iron, Steel and Engineering

Verein Deutscher Maschinenbauanstalten.
Deutsche Rohstahlgemeinschaft.
Miag-Mühlenbau-Industrie A.G.
Vereinigte Stahlwerke A.G.
Deutsche Maschinen Fabriken A.G. (Demag).
Roheisenverband.
Stahlwerksverband.
Stabeisenverband.
Grobblechverband.
Bandeisenvereinigung.
"A"-Produkten Verband.
Röhrenverband.
European Railmakers' Association (E.R.M.A.).
International Railmakers' Association (I.R.M.A.).
International Rohstahlgemeinschaft (I.R.G.).
International Tube Syndicate.
International Hoop Iron Syndicate.
International Wire Rod Syndicate.
Internationale Rohstahl Exportgemeinschaft (I.R.E.G.).
International Tin Plate Agreement.
Vereinigung der freien Drahtwerke und Drahtstiftfabriken.
Rhein-Elbe-Schuckert-Union.
Stumm-Konzern.
Arbeitsgemeinschaft der Eisen verarbeitenden Industrie (Avi).
Otto Wolf-Phoenix Konzern.
Süddeutsche Eisenzentrale.

## Electricity

Osram-Gesellschaft.
Interessen-Gemeinschaftsvertrag der Glühlampenindustrie.
Allgemeine-Elektrizitäts A.G. (A.E.G.).
Siemens und Halske, Siemens-Schuckert.
Gesellschaft für elektrische Unternehmungen (Gesfürel)-Ludw.
   Loewe A.G.
Rheinisch-Westphälische Elektrizitätsgesellschaft.
Thüringer Gas und Elektrizitätsgesellschaft.
Preussische Elektrizitäts Werke.
Sächsische Werke A.G.
Incandescent Lamp Syndicate.
Verkaufsstelle Vereinigter Glühlampenfabriken.
Internationale Glühlampenvereinigung.
Phoebus, S.A. (Geneva).

## Chemical Industry

Interessengemeinschaft Deutsche Farbenindustrie A.G. (I.G. Farben).
Badische Anilin- und Sodafabriken.
Elberfelder Farbenfabriken.
Höchster Farbwerke.
A.G. für Anilinfabrikation (Agfa).

## Textile Industry

Blumenstein Concern.
Deutsche Tuchkonvention.
"Nordwolle" (Bremen).

## Rayon

Kunstseideverkaufbüro (Viskosekunstseidesyndikat).
Vereinigte Glanzstoff Werke A.G.
I.P. Bemberg.

## Hemp and Jute

Hanf-Union.
Vereinigte Jute Spinnereien und Webereien A.G.

## Linoleum

Deutsche Linoleum Werke A.G.
Continentale Linoleum Union A.G.

## Paper

Rotationspapier-Abkommen.

## Rubber

Continentale Gummiwerke A.G.

## Tar and Asphalt

Gesellschaft für Teerverwertung.
Berliner Asphaltfabriken.
Verkaufvereinigung für Teererzeugnisse.

## Glue

Vereinigung zum Studium und zur Vervollkommung der Knochen-
leimindustrie.
Scheidemandel A.G.

## Matches

Deutsche Zündwarenmonopolgesellschaft.
Zündholzvertriebsgesellschaft.

## Radio

Wirufa-Jahr.

## Press and Film

Universum Film A.G. (Ufa).
Hugenberg-Konzern.
"Emelka."

## Breweries

Schultheiss-Patzenhofer-Kahlbaum-Ostwerke.

# LITERATURE

The author does not intend to give a complete account of what has been written on German cartels and trusts. Besides a great number of books and papers dealing specifically with the problem, there is an enormous amount of material on the subject dispersed in trade papers and in publications not dealing exclusively with the subject but treating it in connection with other or adjacent fields of research such as capitalism, rationalisation, industrial finance, etc. Of the great number of monographs which have been published on particular industries or groups of industry there is hardly one which does not devote some space to the problem and position of industrial combination. Besides this the annual reports of commercial and industrial institutions of all kinds furnish year by year an interesting survey of the subject. We may therefore limit our task here to enumerating those books and works which have been of special advantage to the author, and which contain quotations from a great number of other publications useful to students of the subject.

As for official material of modern date the publications of the "Enqueteausschuss" will be of foremost importance. The lengthy title of these publications, consisting of reports, monographs and minutes of evidence of the most important German Committee on economic matters that has yet existed, is:

> Ausschuss zur Untersuchung der Erzeugungs- und Absatzbedingungen der Deutschen Wirtschaft, Verhandlungen und Berichte (Enqueteausschuss).

This Committee has issued a number of volumes dealing with the specific problems of industrial combination, all printed between 1929 and 1930. A special sub-committee has dealt with "changes in the organisational forms of economic conditions", "Wandlungen in den wirtschaftlichen Organisationsformen". These reports are of particular interest to students of industrial combination. They consist of the following volumes:

> 1. Wandlungen in den Rechtsformen der Einzelunternehmungen und Konzerne (1 vol.).

2. Entwicklungslinien der industriellen und gewerblichen Kartellierung:
   (1) Arbeitsplan, Maschinenbau (1 vol.).
   (2) Bau- und Baustoffindustrie (1 vol.).
   (3) Textilindustrie (2 vols.).
3. Wandlungen in der aktienrechtlichen Gestaltung der Einzelunternehmungen und Konzerne (1 vol.).
4. Kartellpolitik:
   (1) Generalbericht (1 vol.).
   (2) Vernehmungen (1 vol.).

Of these No. 4 (1) and (2), which represent some sort of "final report" with minutes of evidence, have been of special service to this book. Besides this there are not less than 20 volumes dealing with commercial policy in connection with certain branches and groups of industry; there is a good deal of material, especially with regard to cartelistic price policy, to be found in these volumes. This applies still more to the work of another subcommittee which was entrusted with the special task of preparing industrial monographs. The following volumes have been issued, containing, besides other subjects and general topics relating to specific groups of industry, elaborate studies of the development and structure of industrial combination:

1. Die Rohstoffversorgung der deutschen eisenerzeugenden Industrie.
2. Die deutsche Kaliindustrie.
3. Die deutsche Kohlenwirtschaft.
4. Die deutsche Elektrizitätswirtschaft.
5. Die deutsche chemische Industrie.
6. Die deutsche eisenerzeugende Industrie.
7. Der deutsche Wohnungsbau.
8. Die Versorgung der deutschen Wirtschaft mit Nicht-Eisen-Metallen.

Of these volumes Nos. 2, 3, 4, 5 and 6 have been largely used by the author. Another volume, edited by Dr Dernburg, the chairman of the Enqueteausschuss, and his assistants, Dr Hecht and Dr Neu, represents a general report of the whole field covered by the Committee under the title:

Erzeugungs- und Absatzbedingungen der deutschen Wirtschaft.

As regards non-official literature Prof. Robert Liefmann's book,

Robert Liefmann, Kartelle, Konzerne und Trusts. Stuttgart, 1934, 9th ed.,

must be mentioned in the first place. It is generally considered a sort of pioneer work on the subject; indeed it was published in an English translation, *Cartels, Combines and Trusts* by Messrs Methuen in 1933 with a preface by Prof. D. H. Macgregor of Oxford. This book contains an enormous amount of material and facts; it is, however, in the main descriptive and in spite of all his knowledge of the subject the author leaves the student with some feeling of dissatisfaction as regards the fundamental and general economic laws underlying the development of industrial combination. Yet German literature certainly does not lag behind in that respect. This can be gathered from a study of the very able book by

Dr Arnold Wolfers, Das Kartellproblem im Lichte der deutschen Kartellliteratur. Munich, 1931.

This book, which forms vol. 180 of the *Schriften des Vereins für Sozialpolitik*, embodies a very exhaustive survey of German cartel literature, especially that of a theoretical and academic character. The following new publications reviewed by Wolfers may be of particular interest to the readers of this book, in so far as theoretical problems were to be dealt with:

H. v. Beckerath, Der moderne Industrialismus. Jena, 1930.
M. J. Bonn, Das Schicksal des deutschen Kapitalismus. Berlin, 1930.
Josef Dobretsberger, Konkurrenz und Monopol in der gegenwärtigen Wirtschaft. Leipzig and Vienna, 1929.
J. Herle, Neue Beiträge zum Kartellproblem. Berlin, 1929.
O. Klug, Das Wesen der Kartell-Konzern- u. Trustbewegung. 1930.
Liefmann, Internationale Kartelle. Weltwirtschaftliches Archiv. 1927.
H. Mannstaedt, Die monopolistischen Bestrebungen und ihre Bedeutung vor und nach dem Kriege. 1928.
H. Stark, Die Theorie der Kartelle. Berlin, 1930.
S. Tschierschky, Kartellorganisation. Berlin, 1928.
—— Kartellpolitik. Berlin, 1930.

As to the actual development of industrial combination in more recent years the two volumes, *Strukturwandlungen der deutschen Volkswirtschaft*, containing articles the substance of lectures edited by Prof. Bernhard Harms of Kiel (Reimar Hobbing, Berlin) in 1928, supply a good deal of new material and descriptive matter. Attention may be called to the articles by:

Prof. Dr J. Hirsch, Wandlungen im Aufbau der deutschen Industrie.
Dr H. Schaeffer, Kartelle und Konzerne.
Franz Eulenburg, Die deutsche Industrie auf dem Weltmarkte.

The legal aspects of German industrial combination have been dealt with by a good many authors. So far as this book is concerned a small, but rather good study by

Dr Fritz E. Koch, Grundzüge des englischen Kartellrechts. Berlin, 1927,

was very useful, as it draws interesting parallels between the German and English legal treatment of combines. Besides this a treatise by a well-known German legal authority on the subject

Prof. J. Flechtheim, Neue Rechtsformen industrieller Zusammenschlüsse, in Strukturwandlungen (cp. the above remark), 1928,

and

Dr Oswald Lehnich, Kartelle und der Staat. Berlin, 1928,

were particularly useful. The already mentioned "Generalbericht" of the 1st sub-committee of the Enqueteausschuss ("Kartellpolitik") offers a wide range of information on the legal, administrative and judicial side of the present situation, dealing in Part B with the "Practice of the Cartel Policy of the State".

As regards questions of organisation a good many of the above-mentioned works could be used; of most recent publications a treatise by

Prof. Richard Passow, Kartelle. Jena, 1930,

will be of interest, especially as regards the question of compulsory cartels. A book, dealing with questions of monopoly organisation from a mainly theoretical and sociological point of view, is that of

Dr Erich Egner, Der Sinn des Monopols in der gegenwärtigen Wirtschaftsordnung. Leipzig, 1931,

while

Dr W. Hasenack, Unternehmertum und Wirtschaftslähmung. Berlin, 1932,

places considerations of commercial science in the forefront of his study on many problems related to that of industrial combination.

Another book dealing with a theoretical problem bordering on the problem of monopolist organisation in many points—the much discussed "slogan" of Planwirtschaft—is that by an eminent theorist of Berlin University:

Prof. Dr Friedrich v. Gottl-Ottlilienfeld, Der Mythus der Planwirtschaft. Jena, 1932.

All the last-mentioned works will be of more interest from the point of view of academic thought aroused by the latest development of cartels and trusts and their organisation than from that of getting a broader knowledge of their actual structure and activities.

As to the international field of industrial combination, to which we have frequently alluded, two books merit special attention:

C. Lammers, Internationale Industriekartelle. Berlin, 1930, and Prof. Dr Kurt Wiedenfeld, Kartelle und Konzerne. Berlin, 1927.

The last-mentioned study was prepared for a committee of the International Economic Conference. A small volume, which is particularly interesting in connection with cartels in the Central-European zone, is that by a former Hungarian Secretary of State:

Prof. Elèmer Hantos, Mitteleuropäische Kartelle im Dienste des industriellen Zusammenschlusses. Berlin, 1931.

A very able book on international monopolies is that by

Alfred Plummer (University of Oxford), International Combines in Modern Industry. London, 1934.

A good many international cartels and concerns connected with German industrial combination are aptly dealt with in this study. Of monographs on particular industries or groups of industry dealing with problems of industrial combination an elaborate list will be found in Wolfers *loc. cit.* pp. 160-9. For the purpose of this book the following publications were particularly useful in connection with the development of industrial combination in various trades:

Dr Buchmann, Prof. Mathesius, Dr Petersen and Dr Reichert, Zur Frage des internationalen Eisenpreisausgleichs. Berlin, 1927.

William Meinhardt, Entwicklung und Aufbau der Glühlampenindustrie. Berlin, 1932.

Hans J. Schneider, Der Wiederaufbau der Grosseisenindustrie an Rhein und Ruhr. Berlin, n.d.

Prof. Flechtheim and Dr Reichert, Kartelle als Produktionsförderer. Schriften der Kartellstelle des Reichsverbandes der Deutschen Industrie. January, 1928.

Prof. Dr Ludwig Bernhard, Der "Hugenberg-Konzern". Berlin, 1928.

Ausgewählte Kapitel aus der chemischen industriellen Wirtschaftspolitik 1877-1927. Verein zur Wahrung der Interessen der chemischen Industrie. Berlin, 1927.

H. Lüthgen, Das Rheinisch-Westphälische Kohlensyndikat in der Vorkriegs- und Nachkriegszeit und seine Hauptprobleme. Leipzig, 1926.

A. Marcus, Die grossen Chemiekonzerne. Leipzig, 1929.

Wilhelm Grotkopp, Der schwedische Zündholztrust. Braunschweig, 1929.

On many points in the book comparisons with conditions in England have been made. The following publications will prove useful for further research:

Hermann Levy, Monopolies, Cartels and Trusts in British Industry, 2nd ed. London, 1927.

—— Die Grundlagen der Weltwirtschaft. Leipzig, 1931.

Patrick Fitzgerald, Industrial Combination in England. London, 1927.

Harold Macmillan, M.P., Reconstruction. London, 1933.

D. H. Macgregor, Enterprise, Purpose and Profit. Oxford, 1934.

Besides these, parts of the Report on "Factors in Industrial and

Commercial Efficiency" (Committee on Industry and Trade) 1927 and the Macmillan Report on Finance and Industry, Cmd. 3897 could be used with advantage. In comparing German and English industrial conditions and organisation valuable material will be found in the Survey of Metal Industries (Committee on Industry and Trade) 1928, especially as regards coal, iron, steel and electricity (Electric manufacturing industry and electricity supply). A very intelligent Report on economic conditions in Germany by J. W. F. Thelwall (Dept. of Overseas Trade, 1934) may also be consulted with regard to many industries and their organisation.

As regards official or semi-official facts and figures used in this book the following publications may be mentioned:

Statistische Jahrbuch des Deutschen Reiches. Berlin, 1933.
Vierteljahrshefte zur Konjunkturforschung. Sonderheft 19. Die Energiewirtschaft der Welt in Zahlen. Berlin, 1930.
——— Kapitalbildung und Investitionen in der Deutschen Volkswirtschaft 1924 bis 1928. Berlin, 1931.
——— Heft 3. 5 Jahrgang. Berlin, 1930.
——— Sonderheft 31. Die Industriewirtschaft (Dr Wagenführ). Berlin, 1933.
Die Wirtschaftlichen Kräfte der Welt. Herausgegeben von der Dresdner Bank. Berlin, 1930.
Jahrbuch des Allgemeinen Gewerkschaftsbundes. Berlin, 1932.
Wirtschaftsberichte der Commerz- und Privatbank. 1933 to 1 July 1934.
Anlagewerte, Dresdner Bank. 1934.

A number of articles, published by trade papers and reviews, which have been useful in the treatment of various subjects, have been quoted in full in the respective places in the text.

# INDEX

For EU product safety concerns, contact us at Calle de José Abascal, 56–1°, 28003 Madrid, Spain or eugpsr@cambridge.org.

www.ingramcontent.com/pod-product-compliance
Ingram Content Group UK Ltd.
Pitfield, Milton Keynes, MK11 3LW, UK
UKHW010341140625
459647UK00010B/735